Becoming German

Becoming German

The 1709 Palatine Migration to New York

Philip Otterness

Cornell University Press
Ithaca and London

First published 2004 by Cornell University Press
First printing, Cornell paperbacks, 2006

Printed in the United States of America

Library of Congress Cataloging-in-Publication Data

Otterness, Philip.
    Becoming German : the 1709 Palatine migration to New York / Philip Otterness.
        p. cm.
    Includes bibliographical references (p.   ) and index.

    ISBN-13: 978-0-8014-7344-9 (pbk. : alk. paper)
    ISBN-10: 0-8014-7344-6 (pbk. : alk. paper)
    1. Palatine Americans—New York (State)—History—18th century.   2. German Americans—New York (State)—History—18th century.   3. Immigrants—New York (State)—History—18th century.   4. New York (State)—Emigration and immigration—History—18th century.   5. Palatinate (Germany)—Emigration and immigration—History—18th century.   6. Palatine Americans—New York (State)—Ethnic identity.   7. German Americans—New York (State)—Ethnic identity.   8. New York (State)—Ethnic relations.   I. Title.
    F130.P3O88   2004
        974.7'0043102—dc22
                                    2004001488

Cornell University Press strives to use environmentally responsible suppliers and materials to the fullest extent possible in the publishing of its books. Such materials include vegetable-based, low-VOC inks and acid-free papers that are recycled, totally chlorine-free, or partly composed of nonwood fibers. For further information, visit our website at www.cornellpress.cornell.edu.

Paperback printing   10   9   8   7   6   5   4

for Naomi

Contents

Maps and Illustrations

Maps

Illustrations

Acknowledgments

I have been fortunate to write this book with the assistance of many good historians, archivists, librarians, and friends. The book began ten years ago under the guidance of Sydney James, whose patient direction and quiet enthusiasm helped lay the foundation for all that was to come. He was the finest of teachers, and I regret that he did not live to see me finish what he had helped to start. I also owe a great debt to Linda Kerber, who has helped me every step of the way from reading early drafts to advising me on how best to prepare the manuscript for publication. Her wise counsel, careful reading, and pointed questions made the final product a far better work than it would have been otherwise.

Many other historians have provided advice and encouragement along the way. Henry Horwitz, T. H. Breen, and Wayne Bodle all read early drafts. Their careful commentary helped me sharpen my arguments while making me pay closer attention to the broader context of the 1709 emigrants' story. Michael Zuckerman, Alison Olson, Wendell Tripp, and Marianne Wokeck read portions of early drafts and discussed the project with me. They provided many valuable suggestions and much-needed criticism. I am particularly grateful to Eric Fure-Slocum, a historian of twentieth-century America, who was always willing to listen to stories from the eighteenth century and to offer friendly advice and encouragement. I had the good fortune of presenting portions of my work at the McNeil Center for Early American Studies, the Washington, D.C., Seminar in Early American History, and the International Seminar on the History of the Atlantic World at Harvard University. In all three cases, I benefited from the questions and commentary of seminar participants who helped me to refine some arguments and to bury others. I also benefited from the opportunity to try out some of the ideas that are presented in this book in articles published in *New York History* and *Explorations in Early American Culture* (a supplemental issue of *Pennsylvania History*).

Henry Jones, the outstanding genealogist of the New York Palatines, provided immeasurable assistance by lending me his microfilm copies of European records dealing with the 1709 immigrants and by bringing to my attention obscure sources that I would have otherwise overlooked. He was always willing to discuss my research and to share his incredibly detailed knowledge of the thousands of early German-speaking immigrants to New York. His enthusiasm for the project never failed to bolster my spirits during the years of research and writing.

Many other people helped facilitate my work. The staffs at the New York State Archives, the Library of Congress, the Franklin D. Roosevelt Library, the Historical Society of Pennsylvania, the Library Company of Philadelphia, the Lambeth Palace Library, the British Library, and the Public Record Office were always helpful, efficient, and patient. James Folts at the New York State Archives deserves special thanks for uncovering and sharing previously ignored documents dealing with the early German migration to New York. Patrick Jones of the University of North Carolina–Charlotte did a superb job of transforming my sketches into the maps that appear in this volume. Genealogists and descendants of the 1710 German immigrants to New York, especially Frederick Weiser, Ralph Weller, LeGrand Weller, and the late John Dern, have provided me with insights and documents about their ancestors' lives that have helped enliven my description of the migration. I am also grateful to all those who helped turn my manuscript into a book. Karen Bosc did a great deal to improve the manuscript with her meticulous copyediting, and Sheri Englund and Louise E. Robbins of Cornell University Press provided sound advice and encouragement as they shepherded the manuscript efficiently through the many stages from its initial submission to its final form.

This project could not have been completed without the support and financial contributions of several institutions. I am particularly grateful to Warren Wilson College for providing a sabbatical year to finish the book. College President Doug Orr was instrumental in ensuring that the book had maps drawn by a professional cartographer, and the vice president for academic affairs, Virginia McKinley, cheerfully signed off on numerous requests for faculty development funds to carry out research in New York, Britain, and Germany. The college librarians proved that a small college library can help facilitate a research project that draws on sources from around the world. Early on, the University of Iowa provided generous financial support through its Iowa Fellows program, and the University of Iowa Student Assembly helped fund a research trip to New York. A generous fellowship from the National Endowment for the Humanities supported me while I finished research in London and wrote the final manuscript. I am deeply grateful to all of these people and institutions for their support.

Through it all, my family has been a constant source of encouragement. My father-in-law, Allan Norden, a research scientist, was particularly supportive because he knew what an arduous process writing could be. My happiness at finishing this book is dampened by the fact that he did not live to celebrate with me. My parents, James and Adeline Otterness, and my mother-in-law, Catherine Norden, have long encouraged my fascination with the past, even as I left a secure career in the government for the less-certain life of a historian. Nathan and Christopher, my sons, have buoyed my spirits throughout the project. My wife, Naomi, has helped in hundreds of ways. With her facility with languages, she translated French documents, double-checked my German translations, and even wrestled some sense from a few Dutch documents that came our way. She also read early drafts, proofread the final manuscript, and offered many useful ideas on all aspects of the book. She convinced me that the project was worthwhile and ensured that I did not take forever to finish it. She, more than anyone, deserves my heartfelt thanks.

Philip Otterness

Asheville, North Carolina

Quotations and Dates

All quoted material appears as it is in the original text except that super-scripts have been lowered, *ye* has been written as *the*, and *ff* at the beginning of words has been written as *F*. All dates are as they appear in the original sources. British and American dates follow the Old Style calendar. Dates from German, French, and Dutch sources follow the New Style calendar and are designated (NS). Dispatches from British envoys in Europe often bear both Old Style and New Style dates. I have assumed January 1 as the beginning of the year rather than March 25, the date used under the Old Style calendar. Thus, for example, I have written the Old Style date February 14, 1712 (or 1712/13) as February 14, 1713.

Becoming German

Introduction

The poor Palatines. Everyone had them figured out. To the people of London, who saw them flooding into their city in 1709, they were victims of French atrocities and Catholic persecution in the Rhineland. To New York's colonial governor, who wanted to bring these poor people to his colony, they were grateful refugees anxious to repay their debt to the British Crown. And to the German-born pastors who helped succor them along the way, they were misguided and headstrong peasants seeking to escape the lot God had ordained for them. In the middle of it all stood the Palatines, simultaneously fulfilling and confounding all of these half-hearted attempts to make sense of them. Never content to sit idly by, they joined the fray.

Knowing how immigrants see themselves and how they are viewed by others is essential to understanding how immigrant communities are created and how immigrants fit into the broader society that they enter. This book focuses on the migration of thousands of German-speaking people, first to London in 1709 and then on to colonial New York in 1710. As members of the earliest large-scale migration of German-speakers to America, these people were the first substantial group of immigrants to become "German" in America. In the process they not only defined themselves in contrast to the other peoples of British North America but also assumed a shared identity that did not yet exist among the families and friends they left behind in the disparate principalities of the Holy Roman Empire. The process by which the identities of immigrant communities were formed in early America reveals a great deal about both the immigrants themselves and the people with whom they interacted. At the same time, it reveals much about the possibilities of colonial America—paths taken and not taken—and the decisions that helped shape the nature of a multiethnic America.[1]

The so-called Palatine migration of 1709 originated in the western part of the Holy Roman Empire, a region filled with dozens of small German states, of which the Palatinate was but one. During the spring and summer of 1709, thousands of people left their homes, lured by rumors that Britain's Queen Anne would provide them with passage overseas and free land in America. They journeyed down the Rhine River to Rotterdam, and eventually some fifteen thousand of them made their way to London. The British government had just passed a Naturalization Act meant to attract immigrants to the country and was also pursuing a policy of colonial expansion, but it was unaware of the rumors swirling through the Rhineland and certainly had no intention of paying the immigrants' passage to America. For several months the government explored various proposals to settle the immigrants in England and Ireland. As the government pondered what to do with them, the immigrants lived in large refugee camps on the outskirts of London. Although some of the Germans did eventually settle in England and Ireland, many returned home. In the end, the British government finally agreed to send just over three thousand of the immigrants to New York in return for several years' labor producing naval stores—tar and pitch— in the pine forests along the Hudson River. But once the immigrants reached New York, they refused to make naval stores and forced the governor to abandon the project. Although some settled on the Hudson River or moved to New York City and New Jersey, most of the immigrants headed to the sparsely settled regions of the New York frontier. For the next forty years, these German-speaking settlers lived on the far western edge of European settlement in New York, seemingly as much at ease among their Iroquois neighbors to the west as among the British and Dutch colonists to the east.

Anthropologists and historians note that identities are not inherent to groups of immigrants. Instead such identities are constructed.[2] Immigrant groups, in particular, are often forced to adopt, and then adapt to, an identity imposed on them by the more powerful host society the immigrants enter. The 1709 Palatine migration demonstrates that, although many facets of immigrant identity are beyond the control of the people involved, immigrants can play an active role in developing their communal identity. This was especially true in the fluid and unstable society of early America, where the immigrants not only shaped their communal identity but also set the terms under which they would interact with their more powerful British colonial counterparts. Their identity was much more malleable than might be expected—Catholics could call themselves Protestants, Hessians could call themselves Palatines, people who emigrated freely could call themselves refugees. Yet, whether the immigrants' identity had its roots in fiction or fact, it eventually defined who these people were and how they situated themselves in colonial America.

To the extent that historians of German society and culture in early America take up the issue of immigrant identity, they generally focus on how that identity contrasted with a British colonial other. In the process, they usually evaluate the immigrants only after they settled in America and often downplay or ignore the differences among immigrants who came from many principalities, each with different customs, dialects, and forms of government.[3] There was, however, no "Germany" in the eighteenth century, only a loose collection of hundreds of principalities and city-states. And, although the 1709 immigrants were referred to as "Palatines," the majority of the "Palatine" immigrants of 1709 did not come from the Palatinate at all but from dozens of other principalities in the Holy Roman Empire. Some historians argue that these immigrants came from territories marked by frequent in-migrations that left territorial affinities weak, but, as the history of the Balkans demonstrates, people jumbled together for hundreds of years can still maintain a strong sense of difference and cling to identities that bear little relation to modern state boundaries. Just as Scots have had a difficult time becoming Britons, one can assume that Palatines, Badeners, and Hessians might have had a difficult time becoming Germans.[4] The making of a German identity in America was one of immigrants not just defining themselves in contrast to a British other but also first defining themselves in contrast to many *German* others.

Any study of a shared identity among German-speaking immigrants must be as firmly grounded in early modern Europe as in colonial North America. The immigrants' sense of themselves cannot be understood if their varied origins are not recognized. So it is important to determine both where within the Holy Roman Empire the immigrants had lived and the circumstances that had caused them to emigrate. In addition, for the 1709 emigrants, who spent nearly a year in Britain before sailing to New York, it is vital to examine the time they spent in London, where they were first clumped together as one group and took the initial steps toward forming a common identity. In short, the process of identity formation cannot be understood if the transatlantic element of the migration is ignored. What happened along the Rhine, in Holland, and especially in England profoundly influenced the way the 1709 immigrants became "German." This story of early America can be told only in an international context.

Although the Palatine immigrants to New York played a significant role in shaping German society in colonial America, their story is rarely told. The last major study of the migration was Walter Knittle's *Early Eighteenth-Century Palatine Emigration*, published in 1937.[5] Historians of German life in colonial America have instead focused primarily on Pennsylvania. When the papers from a 1983 conference celebrating the tercentenary of German settlement in America were published, the book contained an entire section on the Pennsylvania Germans but did not even list colonial New York in the index.[6] Although Pennsylvania eventually became the most German of the thirteen colonies, Philadelphia did not emerge as the main American port of entry for German immigrants until after 1725. Instead it was in New York that large numbers of Germans first began to envision their New World and attempted to create communities where those visions could be realized.[7]

The 1710 immigrants to New York may have settled farther north than later waves of German-speaking immigrants to British North America, but they shared many characteristics with them. Like the later immigrants, the 1710 immigrants came from the German southwest, often from the Palatinate but also from other territories along the Rhine, Main, and Neckar rivers. They were primarily members of the Lutheran and Reformed churches. Most were farmers or rural artisans. They emigrated from small villages, not cities. They came as families. And they were drawn to America by dreams of prosperity on abundant and inexpensive land free from feudal encumbrance. In these ways, the two groups did not differ greatly from one another. This shared background allowed the 1710 immigrants to New York to play an important role as informants and guides to later waves of German migrants, shaping later immigrants' expectations and attitudes about life in colonial America.[8]

The New York immigrants did, however, differ from later German-speaking immigrants in two important ways that make them apt subjects for the study of the formation of German identity in early America. First, their large numbers ensured that they were closely observed and analyzed. German princes questioned their motives for leaving home. The British discussed them endlessly. Swift complained of their presence during their year in Britain, and Defoe wrote an entire book singing their praises. Their arrival in New York City drew a great deal of attention as the three thousand immigrants threatened to overwhelm a city of fewer than six thousand inhabitants. They were one of the most watched groups of immigrants to enter America, and the volume of writing describing them provides a detailed picture of how they were seen by others and how they developed their own sense of who they were. Second, few migrations during the early modern period left behind so many records rich in the demographic details—age, religion, occupation, marital status, family size—that give character and shape to ordinary peasants who otherwise exist only as shadows on the edge of the historical stage. Crown officials in London carried out elaborate censuses of the immigrants, and colonial administrators maintained exhaustive accounts of each family and the money spent on them. More recently, genealogists have painstakingly tracked down the immigrants' German origins.[9] Taken together, these records provide the data for a finely detailed demographic group portrait of the 1710 immigrants that serves as a baseline for comparison with the varied and changing pictures that the immigrants drew of themselves.

With justification the English referred to the immigrants as the "poor Palatines." Once they reached England, the immigrants had little money and few possessions. Their survival depended on the charity of the British people and the largesse of the government. Dependence meant limited power, and limited power usually means limited possibilities. The immigrants' relations with those who fed and clothed them became crucial to how they experienced the New World and to how they created a place for themselves in that world. From the beginning, the Germans found themselves in a situation in which other people's perception of them became critical to their success. If they wanted to reach America and to successfully establish themselves there, they had to convince the British authorities in London and New York that they would be worthy colonists. The immigrants' religion, language, skills, behavior, and even their history all entered the mix of elements that British officials considered as they evaluated the immigrants as potential colonial subjects.

It was not, however, entirely a one-sided game. Although dependent on British charity and government support in both London and New

York, the Germans soon realized that neither identity nor history is fixed. If Londoners and British officials could label the Germans to suit their prejudices, so, too, could the Germans accept or reject those labels to suit their needs. They could create histories and adopt identities that had little basis in reality but that moved them closer to their goal of free land in America. In the complex interplay between British colonial interests and the Germans' single-minded insistence on land in America, definitions of Palatine and Briton, Catholic and Protestant, refugee and colonist all played important roles.

More important than the labels themselves is what they reveal about the immigrants' dreams of life in America. Just as they would not simply accept the identity that others imposed on them, the German immigrants did not merely accept others' visions of the way life should be in America. The stories they told and the experiences they had along the Rhine, in London, and finally in New York all enhanced the immigrants' sense that they could share in America's bounties under their own terms. New York in the first half of the eighteenth century was a world in flux. British administrators struggled to dominate a colony of diverse inhabitants from Europe and Africa while facing constant external threats to their authority from the Iroquois and the French. Entering this world in 1710, the German immigrants quickly found themselves at odds with the British authorities and attempted to escape their reach by moving to the Schoharie and Mohawk river valleys of New York's backcountry. There they sought ways of living with their Indian neighbors that would ensure the viability of their new communities while fending off further intrusions by the British. Throughout the process, conflicting notions of the immigrants' identity, of their real and imagined pasts, and of their place in colonial New York led to confusion and often to disappointment for both the immigrants and the colonial officials who had to deal with them. Yet, for a brief period, the German immigrants explored America's tantalizing potentials, imagining possibilities for social engagement that the Dutch and English colonizers before them no longer entertained or never perceived. In the end the new Canaan that they attempted to create was never realized, but their experience demonstrates that not all European settlers in British North America played by English rules. The customs and practices of colonial America were many and varied, and at least for a time America could accommodate the poor Palatines' dreams.

CHAPTER 1

"A Particularly Deceptive Spirit"

THE GERMAN SOUTHWEST, 1709

At the time it must have seemed the best solution to their problems. Peter and Margaretha Wagner struggled under a large debt, and their future in Dachsenhausen, a village in Hesse-Darmstadt, looked bleak. Peter was only twenty-one, Margaretha a year older. They had married in March 1708, and two months later their first child had been born. In June 1708 they had to mortgage their land to the village church to pay off a debt. They seemed destined to a lifetime of poverty. Peter's parents were dead, and Margaretha, a shepherd's daughter, could expect little money from her impoverished family. But in 1709 an exciting rumor spread through the German southwest: Britain's Queen Anne had promised free land in America to German settlers. By early spring thousands of people had headed down the Rhine to take advantage of the queen's offer. Not wanting to be left behind, Margaretha and Peter packed their few possessions and joined the throng.[1]

In June 1709 Georg and Anna Catharine Bäst sold two cows, a horse, some farm implements, and their inheritance to Anna's cousin Johann Rumpf. Rumpf paid the couple a small sum and agreed to provide Anna's mother with food and clothing for the rest of her life. He also agreed to transport Georg and Anna from their home in Schönbach sixty-five kilometers west to the Rhine River. Like hundreds of others in the principality of Nassau-Dillenburg, the Bästs had heard promises of prosperity in Carolina and were determined to share in America's wealth.[2]

Some two hundred kilometers southeast of Schönbach in the Württemberg village of Gross Aspach, Johann Conrad Weiser worked as a baker and farmer. Within village society his family had relatively high standing. Close relatives had held the position of *Schultheiss*, the chief administrative office of the village, for many years. Yet life was not easy. The French army plundered the village in 1707, and a harsh winter destroyed Weiser's vineyards in early 1709. In May 1709 Johann's wife, Anna Magdalena, died while pregnant with their fifteenth child. Perhaps she and her husband had already decided to move to America. Or perhaps Johann, an impulsive man, decided after his wife's death to make a new start elsewhere. In any case, he sold his house, vineyards, and fields to his oldest daughter and her husband. Then, on June 24, he and his eight surviving dependent children began their hike to the Neckar River, the first leg of a journey to London and, they hoped, to America.[3]

In the spring and summer of 1709, over fifteen thousand people from the German southwest, unable to resist tales of Queen Anne's generosity and the chance for free land in America, joined the Wagner, Bäst, and Weiser families on their journey to London. The surprised British officials who greeted them in London knew nothing of the stories and assumed the migrants were fleeing French aggression in the Palatinate. Without delving deeper into the migrants' territorial origins, Londoners simply labeled the new arrivals "the poor Palatines."

Over the last three centuries, historians have not done much better. Although historians of the 1709 migration have realized that some emigrants came from territories other than the Palatinate, they have never delineated the group's territorial origins or reflected on how differences in origin might have affected the emigrant community.[4] The tedious work of tracking down the migrants' hometowns was left to genealogists, who, 250 years after the migration, began combing through German church records looking for answers.[5] From the hundreds of individual genealogies they produced, thousands of details have been drawn to create a database of the 1709 migration; that database serves as the demographic foundation of this study (see appendix). The database provides a detailed group portrait of the migrants that can be compared with the Londoner's quick sketch of the poor Palatines. It also reveals, at last, exactly where the 1709 emigrants came from.

When their hometowns are plotted on a map, the first thing that becomes apparent is that most of the so-called Palatines were not Palatines at all. The Palatinate (*Kurpfalz*) consisted of over a dozen noncontiguous regions and was one of many principalities jumbled together in the early eighteenth-century German southwest (see map 1).[6] More than forty territories shared the region with the Palatinate, including Württemberg, Baden, Pfalz-Zweibrücken, the various principalities of Hesse and Nassau, the archbishoprics of Trier and Mainz, and numerous tiny principalities such as Wied and Hanau. Although determining exactly how many emigrants came from each territory is difficult, map 2 shows that at least half of them came from principalities outside the control of the Palatine elector.[7] To understand the immigrants' varied backgrounds, their reasons for leaving home, and the experiences that helped shape their identity, one must begin not just with the Palatinate but with the broader region of the German southwest.

The German Southwest in the Early Eighteenth Century

The majority of the emigrants originated in areas along the Rhine River stretching from Neuwied in the north to Karlsruhe in the south. The whole region was, and remains, one of the richest wine-producing areas of Europe. In addition many orchards dotted the area, and a few fields sported a new crop, tobacco, which had been introduced in the Rhineland in 1654.[8] Fruit, tobacco, and especially wine were commercial products, and the peasants living along the middle Rhine maintained business contacts that extended beyond the region.[9] Such contacts and the easy passage of news along the river ensured that rumors of free land in America spread quickly in the region.

Emigrants also came from regions farther from the Rhine. Some left homes in the Westerwald, a region of rolling, forested hills north of the Lahn River; others moved from the western Palatinate and territories near the French border.[10] They left areas lacking the soil and climate necessary for the kinds of commercial agriculture practiced along the Rhine. In the Westerwald some people supported themselves as iron miners rather than as farmers. The peasants of the western Palatinate and the principality of Pfalz-Zweibrücken relied on raising sheep, spinning, and making various handicrafts to supplement their farm income.[11] Although the people of these regions, lacking good soil and cut off from the commercial activity of a major waterway, were generally not as prosper-

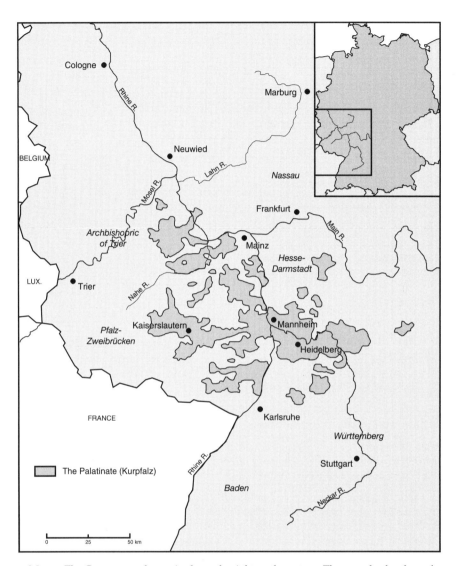

Map 1. The German southwest in the early eighteenth century. The complex borders of the dozens of principalities in the German southwest are almost impossible to depict. This map shows the borders of only one, the Palatinate. The names of other major territories in the region indicate their general location. Many had boundaries as complex as those of the Palatinate. The boundaries of the Palatinate are based on a map by Fritz Trautz in *Die Pfälzische Auswanderung nach Nordamerika im 18. Jahrhundert* (Heidelberg, 1959).

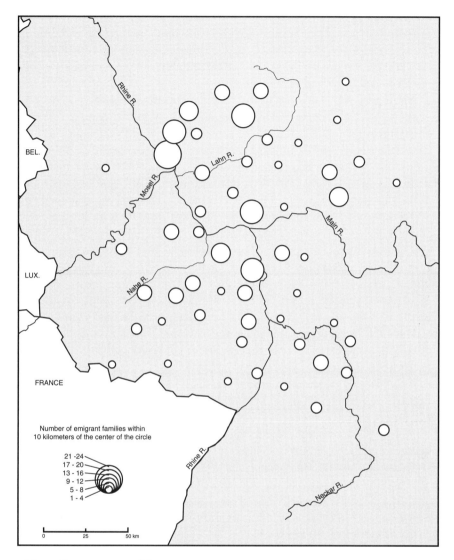

Map 2. German origins of the 1709 emigration. Comparing this map and map 1 illustrates that many of the 1709 emigrants did not come from the Palatinate. The various principalities of Hesse and Nassau east of the Rhine River and north of the Main River provided many emigrants, as did the numerous tiny principalities northeast of the confluence of the Lahn and Rhine rivers.

ous as their neighbors along the Rhine, they were not isolated from the outside world. Visitors and information constantly moved up and down the valleys of the Lahn, Nahe, Dill, Wied, and other small rivers that tied these regions to the Rhine. It took longer, but news of Queen Anne's offer reached the hinterland as well.[12]

Migration was not new to the German southwest. In the hundred years before 1709 the region had suffered constant destruction from war and plague. People moved from village to village within the region to escape advancing armies and disease. Many did not succeed, and the region's princes had to recruit outsiders to repopulate their devastated territories. As a result many of the people whom the British called Palatines would have been more comfortable referring to themselves as French or Swiss or as natives of some other region of the Holy Roman Empire.

During the Thirty Years' War (1618–48) the German states of western and central Europe experienced terrible destruction, losing 30 to 40 percent of their population.[13] The war hit the German southwest particularly hard. The population of the Palatine town of Kaiserslautern fell from 3,200 at the beginning of the seventeenth century to two hundred by 1635. Many towns and villages simply disappeared. The Palatinate as a whole lost 75 to 80 percent of its population.[14] Population losses were generally not as high elsewhere in the German southwest but still often exceeded 50 percent.

The Peace of Westphalia, which ended the Thirty Years' War, did not end the suffering in the Rhineland territories. Twenty years later the plague ravaged the region. In 1667 and 1668 Mannheim lost half its population to the scourge.[15] Later in the century the War of the Palatine Succession (1688–97) brought further misery. French armies overran the German southwest, destroying the area's rich vineyards and laying waste to the chief cities of the region, including Heidelberg, Mannheim, and Worms, as well as dozens of smaller towns. The cathedral city of Speyer, which had a population of more than four thousand in 1670, stood uninhabited for ten years.[16]

Despite the continued destruction during the seventeenth century, the territories of the German southwest slowly recovered. Both the Palatinate and Württemberg regained their pre-Thirty Years' War populations before the mid-eighteenth century.[17] Although fertility rates rose during the period, much of the population gain resulted from immigration from other parts of the Holy Roman Empire as well as from France and Switzerland. Plenty of abandoned farmland stood idle, but cheap land was not enough to bring settlers when abandoned farmland existed

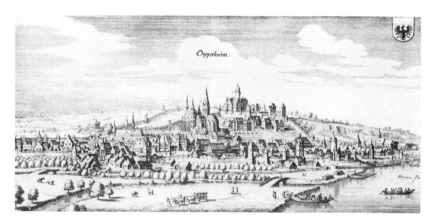

Figure 1. A mid-seventeenth-century view of Oppenheim, a Palatine town on the Rhine River. Several families left Oppenheim in 1709 and eventually settled in New York. They would have sailed down the Rhine in boats similar to those in the illustration. When the emigrants left in 1709, much of the town still lay in ruins from a French attack twenty years earlier. From an engraving by Matthäus Merian in Martin Zeiller, *Topographia Palatinatus Rheni et Vicinarum Regionum* (Frankfurt, 1645).

throughout the empire. Rulers in the German southwest also offered tax concessions and religious toleration to attract new subjects.

In the mid-seventeenth century the Palatine elector, Karl Ludwig, a Calvinist, not only made concessions to members of the two other officially recognized denominations of the Holy Roman Empire—the Catholics and the Lutherans—but also offered religious toleration to Mennonites and Jews. As a result many Lutherans and Catholics and small colonies of religious dissidents moved to the Palatinate from neighboring territories. Large numbers of rural poor and persecuted Mennonites came from Switzerland. In 1656 and 1657 more than one thousand Swiss moved to the Palatinate. In 1671 over six hundred Mennonites arrived from Bern. Portuguese Jews attracted by the elector's concessions settled in Mannheim.[18] By the early eighteenth century, the Palatinate had become one of the most religiously diverse regions of western Europe.

Other principalities followed suit. When Friedrich von Wied established his court at Neuwied, he offered freedom of private worship to draw immigrants to the settlement. Philip Ludwig II, count of Hanau-Münzenberg, made similar concessions to bring settlers to the town of Neu-Hanau.[19] Later, after the War of the Palatine Succession and the revocation of the Edict of Nantes, the German southwest opened its borders to Huguenot refugees. The elector Johann Wilhelm attracted around 2,000 Huguenots to the Palatinate. Another 3,800 settled in Hesse-Kassel, and Württemberg drew about 3,000.[20]

By the beginning of the eighteenth century, people from all over central and western Europe had settled in the German southwest. Villages and towns were inundated with outsiders who spoke different dialects, practiced different religions, and observed different customs. Migration had become a fact of life in early modern Germany; commonly a third or more of the people born in German villages left their homes and settled elsewhere.[21] Few places in the Holy Roman Empire had such a complex mixture of people as the Rhineland territories of the German southwest. A study of four villages in the bishopric of Speyer shows that during the late seventeenth and early eighteenth centuries fewer than half the heads of households had been born in the villages where they resided. In two of the four villages, fewer than a quarter were natives.[22]

The Palatine town of Lambsheim illustrates the phenomenon. Between 1593 and 1780 about 48 percent of the town's citizens were nonnatives.[23] Lambsheim's inhabitants included Huguenots from France, Catholics from Tyrol, Mennonites from Switzerland, and Protestants from Belgium and various German provinces. A few Jewish families also lived in the town. Migrant workers, who came to the town to help bring in the harvest, added to the mixture, as did the destitute *vagabundi* occasionally mentioned in the town's records.[24]

Although the influx of people with diverse religious backgrounds may have added to the religious turmoil in the German southwest, such turmoil had marked the region since the beginning of the Reformation. Many rulers converted to Lutheranism soon after the Reformation, although Catholicism remained a force in some areas, particularly those governed by the archbishop of Mainz and the bishop of Speyer. The principle of *cuius regio, eius religio* established in 1555 by the Peace of Augsburg effectively made a ruler's religion the religion of his subjects. Therefore, as rulers changed so did religion, and the people of the German southwest faced an ever-changing stream of priests and pastors. After the mid-sixteenth century Calvinism spread to the Rhineland, and several rulers joined the Calvinist, or Reformed, Church. Friedrich III of the Palatinate adopted Calvinism in 1562 and made his residence in Heidelberg a center of the Reformed Church. Friedrich's son reintroduced Lutheranism as the state church, but his grandson brought back Calvinism and strengthened the denomination by inviting Calvinist refugees to settle in the Palatinate.[25]

The Peace of Westphalia guaranteed religious freedom for members of the three recognized German churches (Catholic, Lutheran, and Reformed), but religious freedom did not mean the freedom of public worship, only liberty of conscience. The right to public worship continued to be controlled by the territorial ruler.[26] Rulers often denied certain denominations the use of churches and sometimes put limits on private religious gatherings. In many territories one religion continued to predominate. Württemberg and Hesse-Darmstadt remained consistently Lutheran throughout the early modern period.

The Palatinate, however, grew increasingly diverse. After the Thirty Years' War the Palatine electors, whether Lutheran or Reformed, tolerated people of all religions in order to repopulate the region. During the War of the Palatine Succession, French forces occupying the Palatinate reopened Catholic churches, and some non-Catholics faced persecution. The French-controlled area around Germersheim was aggressively Catholicized from 1682 to 1697.[27] In 1685, when the Pfalz-Simmern line of rulers died out and the Pfalz-Neuberg line replaced it, the new Palatine elector was Catholic. Although he granted privileges to the Catholic Church, he apparently did not condone the religious persecution carried out by the French in his territory. Nevertheless, many Protestant rulers within the German Empire were concerned by reports that the elector did not treat his Protestant subjects fairly. In 1694 the Brandenburg elector wrote to his Palatine counterpart, Johann Wilhelm, noting people's comments about "how badly and harshly the Protestants in [the Palatine elector's] lands are oppressed."[28]

Although Johann Wilhelm disputed the charges, he finally issued a *Religionsdeklaration* in 1705, partly to clarify the religious situation in the Palatinate and partly to secure the support of Protestant princes in his new struggle against France in the War of the Spanish Succession. The declaration gave religious freedom to all subjects but divided the churches on a 5:2 ratio between Reformed and Catholic. Lutherans were not allowed churches of their own and fell under Reformed protection.[29] Although religious tension persisted, the Palatinate supported one of the most religiously diverse populations of Europe. In 1727 in the district around Heidelberg, 53 percent of the people were Reformed, 24 percent were Catholic, 22 percent were Lutheran, and slightly over 1 percent were Jewish.[30]

In the last quarter of the seventeenth century the pietist movements in the Lutheran and Reformed churches added to the religious mix in the German southwest. Pietists called for a more inward-looking and emotional faith than the established churches showed in their formal and ritualistic services. Philipp Jacob Spener, a Lutheran pastor in Frankfurt, did much to inspire the movement. The corruption and disorder of seventeenth-century Europe and the resulting spiritual decline of the German people distressed Spener. In *Pia Desidera*, published in 1675, Spener emphasized the priesthood of all believers and encouraged the formation of groups to read and to discuss the Bible. Spener did not intend for the small, private meetings of pietists, known as conventicles, to separate themselves from the Church or the community, and most pietists remained members of the established churches.[31] Nevertheless the creation of pietist conventicles further split the already fractured religious communities of the German southwest.

The university at Halle became the center of German Pietism and enjoyed the support of Prussia's rulers, but Pietism had a mixed reception in the German southwest. The movement was most active in Württemberg. By the 1680s pietist conventicles existed in most major towns in the territory.[32] The conventicles represented a challenge to established Church authority and, because of their exclusiveness, often caused divisions in the towns and villages. In 1678 Hesse banned conventicles, and the government in Württemberg put them under close control in the 1690s.[33] Within the Palatinate the pietist movement was not as strong as in Württemberg, but it remained an important force, especially in the Kraichgau, a region south of Heidelberg, where Swiss immigrants introduced Reformed pietist ideas.[34] Although Pietism caused divisions within communities, at another level it helped bind the German southwest together as pietist loyalties superseded denominational differences and as pietist conventicles in one area established contacts with like-minded souls in other parts of the region.[35]

Whatever their religious beliefs or territorial origins, most people in the German southwest were bound together by their labor on the land. Few cities existed in the region, and most people lived in agricultural villages.[36] In early eighteenth-century Württemberg, more than 70 percent of the population supported itself through agriculture.[37] Most of the rest were rural artisans closely tied to agricultural production.

For many peasants in the German southwest, rural life meant working in vineyards. Viticulture was labor-intensive and risky. Bad weather could quickly destroy an entire crop, and most vintners raised other crops to ensure their survival if the grape harvest failed. But along with the risks, viticulture offered the opportunity for high financial returns from small areas of land. To realize such gains the farmers had to sell their wine, and that activity brought them into contact with a wider market than most peasants knew.[38] Rather than living in isolated communities, they inhabited a world easily penetrated by news and rumors of other places and events.

Inheritance patterns often affected the economic viability of rural communities. Partible inheritance predominated in most areas of the German southwest during the early eighteenth century. Peasants distributed their property equally among all their children. In the seventeenth century, when land was plentiful in the depopulated region, partible inheritance had led to faster population growth. Young people knew they would inherit property and have a decent chance of achieving some economic independence. More people married; they married younger; and they had more children.[39] In some areas of the western Palatinate where the land was poor and could not be divided without threatening its economic viability, partible inheritance began to disappear by the early eighteenth century. But for much of the German southwest the division of land into smaller and smaller parcels would not cause subsistence problems until after 1720.[40]

Nevertheless, as children inherited less and less land, some turned to other occupations to supplement their incomes, and during the eighteenth century the number of artisans in the German southwest began to grow.[41] Although part of the growth can be attributed to increased occupational specialization during the eighteenth century, many rural artisans did not become artisans for life. They learned a handicraft only to support themselves until they could buy or inherit enough land to become full-time farmers. Others worked as craftsmen only part of the time while continuing to work their fields.[42] Although the number of rural artisans increased in the eighteenth century, craftsmen remained close to the land.

Just as inheritance patterns shaped peasant life in the early eighteenth century so too did remnants of the old feudal order. Serfdom was not abolished in the Palatinate until 1803, and, until then, people in the German southwest were categorized as either *Leibeigene* (serfs) or *Leibfreie* (free subjects). Most of the rural population were Leibeigene, but they were no longer bound to the land, nor did the taxes and other obligations they faced differ greatly from those faced by free subjects. In theory their lord had to approve any sale of land, but in practice the lord simply took his percentage of the sale (commonly 1 to 2 percent) and interfered little in the transaction. In some cases the peasants also had to provide a few days of labor each year or pay a fee in lieu of such service. The most onerous taxes that Leibeigene faced were those paid when a peasant died and property was passed on to inheritors. Although not subject to many of the taxes paid by Leibeigene, Leibfreie had to pay similar taxes, and some historians have argued that the status of serf and free subject in the eighteenth-century German southwest differed little.[43] Whether free or unfree, peasants resented outside interference in their lives. Leibeigene in particular realized the claims other held to their labor, and many willingly paid the large fees necessary to release themselves from serfdom.

The costs of manumission were particularly important for potential emigrants. Leibeigene who wished to move from the principality where they resided had first to purchase their freedom. Manumission duties varied from territory to territory. In the Palatinate they amounted to 10 percent of a peasant's net assets. In Pfalz-Zweibrücken men paid 5 percent; women paid 7 percent.[44] Women often had to pay higher manumission duties than men because children inherited the status of serfdom through their mother. Women in effect paid to manumit their future children.

Although most villagers shared the status of Leibeigene, a social hierarchy still existed in the rural villages. Wealth, occupation, and, especially for women, marital status defined that hierarchy. The village pastor, the schoolteacher, and the richer peasants usually dominated village government. Artisans and less wealthy peasants stood below them in the social order. The village poor and those living on the periphery of village society, including day laborers, herders, charcoal burners, widows, and old unmarried women, occupied the lowest levels of the village hierarchy. The chief administrative officer of the village, the *Schultheiss*, served as the link between village government and the representatives of the ruling prince. Peasants in Württemberg elected the village Schultheiss, but in the Palatinate he was appointed by the central government.[45]

Although the Schultheiss needed to be literate, many of the villagers he represented could not read or write. Literacy was just beginning to spread to the German countryside in the early eighteenth century. Villages usually had schools for both boys and girls, but the schools often held classes only in winter, when children had little work to do elsewhere. Children learned to memorize and recite the catechism, but many never learned to read it.[46] Literacy was less important to the work of the farmer than to the work of the Church. Only when Pietism, with its emphasis on daily Bible reading, began to influence school curriculum in the second quarter of the eighteenth century did literacy begin to rise.[47] At the end of the eighteenth century as many as 30 percent of the adult population in the Palatinate remained illiterate.[48]

A political map of the German southwest in the early eighteenth century displays a bewildering maze of territories. Certain traits, such as officially sanctioned religious toleration and the existence of villages filled with migrants from throughout the German-speaking world, differentiated this complex region from the rest of the Holy Roman Empire. Yet despite the distinctiveness of the German southwest, territorial differences remained important. Forms of government differed from principality to principality, as did inheritance and educational practices. A certain measure of religious toleration existed in many areas, but each principality had its own mix of religions and religious practices that dominated spiritual life.[49] Certainly migration into the German southwest was common, but everyday life remained local. The world of most peasants did not extend far beyond their doorsteps. The people of the German southwest never coined a common term to refer to themselves, and those who later moved to America carefully identified themselves in the early church records by the specific principality where they had once lived. The emigrants who left their homes for America in 1709 arrived in London as Palatines, Hessians, Nassauers, and Württembergers. It was left to the British to find a term to identify them all.

Demographic Characteristics of the 1709 Migrants

The mass migration of 1709 was ill-defined and unorganized, but its sheer size—over thirteen thousand people left their homes—ensured that the migrants left their mark in the records of the governments that dealt with them. Using these records and recent genealogical studies of the migrants, it is possible to paint a demographic group portrait of the German exodus.[50]

The 1709 migration was a migration of families. Of the adult migrants, 80 percent were married, and most had children with them. On average each family had 4.7 members.[51] Some couples left behind older children who had married, and many of the younger couples had no children. A few widows and fewer widowers joined the migration, but they were almost always accompanied by their children.[52] Less than 7 percent of the adult emigrants were single men or women, with single men outnumbering single women by about 4 to 1.[53]

For the emigrants who eventually reached New York, the average age of the adult men was thirty-six; of the women, thirty-four.[54] Over a third of the men and almost a quarter of the women were forty or older. With the exception of the very old, the emigrants represented a fairly well-balanced cross section of the adult population. Even some of the very old were undaunted by the thought of emigration. One remarkable emigrant, Johann Martin Matheus, who at age seventy-nine had made a three-year journey from Pfalz-Zweibrücken to Sweden, now undertook a longer and even more arduous journey at age eighty-eight.[55]

Most of the migrants came from rural communities. Only five of the families who eventually settled in New York have been traced to the seven Palatine towns that had populations over two thousand by 1777.[56] Only one emigrant family has been traced to Frankfurt, a city of 27,500 inhabitants in 1700.[57] Given the emigration's rural focus, it is not surprising that the London censuses listed two-thirds of the adult men as "husbandmen and vinedressers." The most common other occupations included carpenter (5.3 percent), weaver (4.7 percent), tailor (3.4 percent), blacksmith (2.9 percent), and mason or stonecutter (2.8 percent). The re-

Figure 2. A mid-seventeenth-century view of Mosbach, a small town on the Neckar River southeast of Heidelberg. At least five families emigrated from Mosbach in 1709 and eventually settled in New York. From an engraving by Matthäus Merian in Martin Zeiller, *Topographia Palatinatus Rheni et Vicinarum Regionum* (Frankfurt, 1645).

maining men worked in over twenty other jobs, most commonly as brewers, coopers, shoemakers, millers, and bakers. Less than one percent were pastors or schoolteachers.[58] The London censuses revealed nothing of the women's skills, but a report to the Board of Trade in 1708 describing another migrant group from the German southwest noted that "the women were versed in and understood" the business of their husbands.[59]

Tying occupation to place of origin reveals that those men described as husbandmen and vintners generally came from the richer farmlands of the Rhine Valley. Their dual description was apt since most vintners did not limit themselves to raising grapes. Many of the men listed as herdsmen or artisans came from the less productive agricultural regions of the Westerwald and western Palatinate.[60]

All three of the officially sanctioned German churches were represented among the migrants. Reformed parishioners were most numerous, making up 39 percent of the group. Lutherans made up 31 percent, and Catholics 29 percent. The remaining 1 percent were Baptists or Mennonites.[61] The migrants' religious background reflected the religious diversity of the German southwest. Mennonites, who faced religious persecution in parts of the region, emigrated in larger numbers than the censuses revealed, but because their migration tended to be supported and organized by coreligionists in Amsterdam or America they made up only a small part of the unorganized masses who left for London in 1709.[62]

The Causes of the Migration

The emigrants' demographic characteristics provide some clues about why the people left their homes. First, the people deciding to leave made a decision that affected an entire family. For the most part the migrants were not young, single persons seeking employment or adventure.[63] Neither did they include large numbers of people over age fifty—a sign that they had left their homes willingly, unlike the Huguenot refugees who had arrived in London in the late 1680s.[64] Because partible inheritance was practiced in most of the German southwest, the emigrant men were not second- or third-born sons without an inheritance seeking a living elsewhere. They were as likely to be first-born sons as later-born.[65] The emigrants traveled as families. Since a couple usually postponed marriage until an economic niche existed for them in the local economy, most of the adult emigrants left established, if no longer economically viable, livelihoods.

In an economy based on agriculture, anything that hurt the harvest, including the weather or marauding armies, could tip the scales against the rural population. In the early eighteenth century both war and bad weather struck the German southwest.

During the War of the Spanish Succession (1701–14) French armies once again overran the German southwest. In 1706 Marshal Villars sent French cavalry forces on raids toward Koblenz and Mainz, and beginning in May 1707 he marched across the German southwest, destroying fields and villages and forcing contributions from towns in his path. He occupied Mannheim and Heidelberg for a short time before withdrawing to France in September.[66] Although the Palatinate felt the brunt of the war's destruction, people in neighboring territories also shouldered the war's burdens, paying higher taxes and quartering troops in their homes. After the many incursions of previous years, peasants probably wondered if peace would ever come to the region.

The harsh winter of 1708–9 added to the people's economic woes. According to the pastor in the Nassau village of Runkel, "Right after the New Year, such a cold wave came that the oldest people here could not remember a worse one. Almost all mills were brought to a standstill, and the lack of bread was great everywhere. Many cattle and humans, even the birds and the wild animals in the woods froze." In Selters the pastor wrote, "From the 6th to the 26th of January there was such a raging cold the likes of which has not occurred in 118 years . . . A great many trees have frozen, the autumn sowing has suffered great damage, and this year there will be no wine at all."[67]

A study of oak tree rings in southern Germany confirms the pastors' reports: the width of the rings fell dramatically from 1708 to 1709.[68] Crops failed in many parts of Germany. The 1709 emigrants left Germany well before the harvest, but already bread prices were rising. Grain prices in Worms hit their highest point for the period 1700–61 in 1709. In Frankfurt and Cologne rye prices more than doubled between 1708 and 1709.[69] The wine harvest, on which the Rhineland depended, was ruined.

Historians generally blame the 1709 migration on the War of the Spanish Succession and the terrible winter of 1708–9.[70] Although both events added to the misery of peasant life in the German southwest, they were not sufficient reasons for the mass exodus of 1709. Most of the destruction from the war had occurred earlier, in 1706 and 1707. In addition, many of the migrants came from parts of the German southwest relatively untouched by the fighting. The connection between the harsh winter and the migration is also difficult to prove. France was hit equally hard by the winter of 1708–9, with some French regions suffering from famine in 1709. Yet France saw no large-scale exodus of its inhabitants. At the same time, parts of the Rhineland that had not been hit by a subsistence crisis contributed heavily to the migration.[71]

Petitions that the emigrants left behind suggest other reasons for the migration. The principalities of the German southwest carefully regulated migration, requiring people to petition the government for permission to leave the territory. Once they received such permission, emigrants had to pay a departure tax and a tax on any property they removed from the territory. In addition Leibeigene had to pay a manumission fee before emigrating.[72] In their petitions, potential emigrants often described their economic condition and typically explained why they wished to leave. The government usually called on the village Schultheiss to confirm the particulars of each petitioner's report. The petitions of sixty-two men from villages throughout the principality of Nassau-Dillenburg survive in the German archives.[73] They provide important clues about who was emigrating and why.

Poverty and hunger fueled the migration. The sixty-two petitioners invariably listed *Armut*—poverty—as the reason they wished to emigrate, defining it as the inability to feed their families. They saw little hope of escaping poverty under the current economic conditions, forcing them, in the words of one petitioner, "to look for [their] bread elsewhere."[74]

For good reason the petitioners tended not to be specific about the causes of their troubles. While seeking manumission they were wise not to blame their plight on the extravagance and economic mismanagement of their rulers. Instead they referred more generally to "these bad times" or "these poor times."[75] Although it would have been easy to do so, they did not blame recent invasions or bad weather. Clearly it was not a sudden subsistence crisis but long-term economic instability that made their lives miserable. As the territorial princes levied higher taxes to support their armies and to finance new palaces built in imitation of Versailles, their poorest subjects found themselves left in despair. Three men spoke of falling into poverty "because of the bad times and turmoil of war met over many years."[76] Many mentioned huge debts that they could not hope to repay, and village officials confirmed that many petitioners were so poor that they could not contribute a penny to their taxes.

Several petitioners were artisans. They, too, complained of poverty. Conrad Asbach, a weaver, said he no longer earned enough to feed his family. The Schultheiss commenting on Asbach's petition reported that too many weavers lived in the area. They had high costs and a poor market for their cloth, and many could not pay back the money they borrowed to buy wool. Daniel Focht, a shoemaker, complained of his inability to advance in his trade.[77] He remained a journeyman earning low wages while working for other masters—a predicament shared by many eighteenth-century journeymen who found few opportunities for advancement and a decent wage.[78]

At the beginning of the eighteenth century the cost of migrating to America was high for the people of the German southwest. In addition to the fees the migrants had to pay before receiving permission to emigrate, they had to raise enough money to pay for the transatlantic voyage. Although most migrants left home with dreams of a brighter economic future, a community's poorest people—the ones who presumably would have benefited most from migrating—could not afford to move to America. After 1720 a system gradually developed that allowed migrants to travel on credit. The redemptioner system relied on relatives or friends in America to "redeem" an immigrant's transportation costs, usually in return for the immigrant's labor over a certain period.[79]

But the redemptioner system was not in place in 1709, and the Nassau-Dillenburg petitions reveal that many of the emigrants of 1709 were very poor—certainly too poor to afford the journey to America. Many also lacked a network of relatives or friends who might have been able to bear some of the costs. The petitioners themselves saw the 1709 migration as one of the poor. Jacob Weijel, a petitioner from the village of Driedorf, stated he wanted to go to Carolina "with other poor people."[80] Village officials confirmed the poverty of the petitioners. The officials repeatedly commented that the petitioners were so poor that they could not pay their debts or taxes and that they could be allowed to emigrate without any loss to the community.[81] On the other hand, village officials were anxious not to lose productive members of their communities. Several times they argued that petitioners had overstated their poverty. In such cases the petitioners did not receive permission to leave.[82]

Just as the poverty of the emigrants distinguished the 1709 migration from most other eighteenth-century migrations from the German southwest, the direction of the migration also set it apart. The 1709 emigration was not the first large-scale migration from the German southwest; people had begun leaving the region in large groups during the late seventeenth century. But most peopled headed east, not west. During the War of the Palatine Succession refugees from Mannheim moved to Magdeburg.[83] After the Habsburg victories against the Turks at Vienna in 1683, the emperor attracted settlers from the German southwest to Hungary and other Habsburg territories in the east. Prussia's rulers also encouraged emigration to their eastern territories. Beginning in 1683 a few people ventured westward across the Atlantic to British North America, but before 1709 the movement from the Holy Roman Empire across the Atlantic had numbered only a few hundred people and had been dominated by religious dissenters.[84] Throughout the eighteenth century, North and South America drew about 125,000 German emigrants, while almost 700,000 Germans emigrated to Prussia and areas to the east.[85]

In many ways, then, the 1709 emigration was unusual. Unlike most German migrations, it headed west instead of east. It included large numbers of impoverished families—people who could not usually afford to migrate together. The emigrants did not leave gradually in small groups, waiting for news from the first arrivals before others prepared to leave. Instead, the migration was sudden, large, and concentrated over only a few months.

The Golden Book

Poverty, like war and bad weather, had always been a part of peasant life in early modern Europe. Certainly, as the emigrants' petitions make clear, poverty played a role in the decision to move, but the migration also stemmed from another key element: propaganda. Promotional literature for Britain's American colonies set loose the sudden flood of immigrants. In 1709 a book penned by Joshua Kocherthal, an obscure Lutheran pastor serving several small parishes south of Heidelberg, spread quickly through the German southwest. The book hinted that Britain's Queen Anne might give free land in America to willing settlers and might provide them with transportation to it.

The timing of the book's publication explains some of its success. People moved west in 1709 partly because nobody from the east was recruiting them. The plague had devastated East Prussia from 1708 to 1710, and, although the loss of life eventually led to efforts to attract more immigrants, the region did not again draw large numbers of peasants from the German southwest until the 1720s.[86] Nor were the Habsburgs busy recruiting immigrants to their eastern territories in 1709. For the moment, calls to America faced little competition from other places.

Books and pamphlets describing Britain's North American colonies, particularly Pennsylvania, had been circulating in the Rhineland since the 1680s. William Penn wrote or commissioned several such pamphlets to promote his colony. In 1700 Daniel Pastorius, who had helped found Germantown, Pennsylvania, in 1683, wrote a book describing the colony and its geography that circulated widely in the German territories.[87] Two years later Daniel Falckner, a pietist with close ties to Halle, wrote a promotional book entitled *Curieuse Nachricht von Pennsylvania* (*Interesting News of Pennsylvania*).[88] Falckner had accompanied a group of pietists who had settled in Pennsylvania in 1694. He returned home in late 1698 or early 1699 and, at the behest of August Hermann Franke, the pietist leader at Halle, wrote the book to describe Pennsylvania, its people, its economy, and the passage overseas. The book consisted of a series of questions written by Franke, who was interested in Pennsylvania as a place of settlement for pietists, and of answers supplied by Falckner. Falckner described Pennsylvania as a fertile land that lacked little except settlers. In response to the question "What is there a deficiency of in America?" Falckner wrote: "The chief deficiency consists in people and craftsmen. The other deficiencies will be easily supplied."[89] Falckner's popular book was combined with Pastorius's book, and the two were reprinted and issued as one volume in 1704.

Although the books and pamphlets by Penn, Pastorius, and Falckner helped spread information about British North America, they were not directly responsible for the 1709 emigration. When a British parliamentary committee investigated the causes of the 1709 emigration, it reported that the emigrants mentioned a "golden book" with a picture of Queen Anne on it and a title page embossed in gold.[90] The book contained glowing reports of Carolina, not Pennsylvania.

The parliamentary report never mentioned the author or title of the golden book, but the migration's timing and a few scraps of evidence that the emigrants left behind point toward Joshua Kocherthal's *Ausführlich und Umständlicher Bericht von der berühmten Landschafft Carolina, in dem Engelländischen America gelegen* (*A Complete and Detailed Report of the Renowned District of Carolina Located in English America*).[91] Unlike most books about the British colonies circulating in the German southwest, Kocherthal's book described Carolina rather than Pennsylvania. Many of the 1709 emigrants' petitions referred specifically to Carolina, even though Pennsylvania had clearly received more advertising in the German southwest before that year. Kocherthal's book seems to have first appeared in 1706, but it went through three new editions in 1709, each more detailed than the one before. The new editions demonstrate the book's popularity and availability in the year of the emigration.[92] It was printed in Frankfurt, near the center of the emigration, and one would-be emigrant even indicated that the English envoy in that city might have helped with its distribution.[93] Finally, a book printed in 1711 and critical of the 1709 emigration specifically set out to repudiate the claims in Kocherthal's book, suggesting that Kocherthal's work had triggered the migration.[94]

Joshua Kocherthal came from Württemberg.[95] He studied for the ministry and in 1696 moved to the Kraichgau, a region south of Heidelberg, where he served three small Lutheran parishes. Eight years later he journeyed to London. Little is known about why he traveled to England or what he hoped to accomplish, but while in London he evidently met with the Carolina proprietors and agreed to write a promotional booklet for distribution in Germany.[96] His *Bericht* was the result.

Kocherthal probably never visited the Carolinas, and his book relied on information commonly found in English promotional tracts.[97] Still, Kocherthal created an effective work, well designed to appeal to a semi-literate audience. He wrote the book in a simple, straightforward style. The chapters were short, the paragraphs numbered, and the main body of the book was less than forty pages long. He created a book to be read aloud, thus ensuring the rapid transmission of its contents beyond those able to read its pages.[98] In fact the emigrants' description of the book in terms of its appearance (as the "golden book" with Queen Anne's picture on the cover) rather than its title indicates that most emigrants saw the book and heard it being read rather than reading it themselves.

In the book, Kocherthal described the land and government of Carolina. He started with a description of the geography and wrote separate chapters on the colony's government, the fertility of the soil, the climate, the security of the region, its commerce, and the other Europeans living there. Kocherthal praised Carolina for its low taxes, the lack of any feudal obligations, and the maintenance of religious freedom—three points that would appeal to German peasants. According to Kocherthal, the colony's fertile soil was well suited for growing tobacco and various fruits, including grapes, apples, and pears—all crops familiar to Rhineland farmers—and the climate was much milder than in Germany. The only disadvantage of the land was that it was so far away and, thus, expensive to get to.

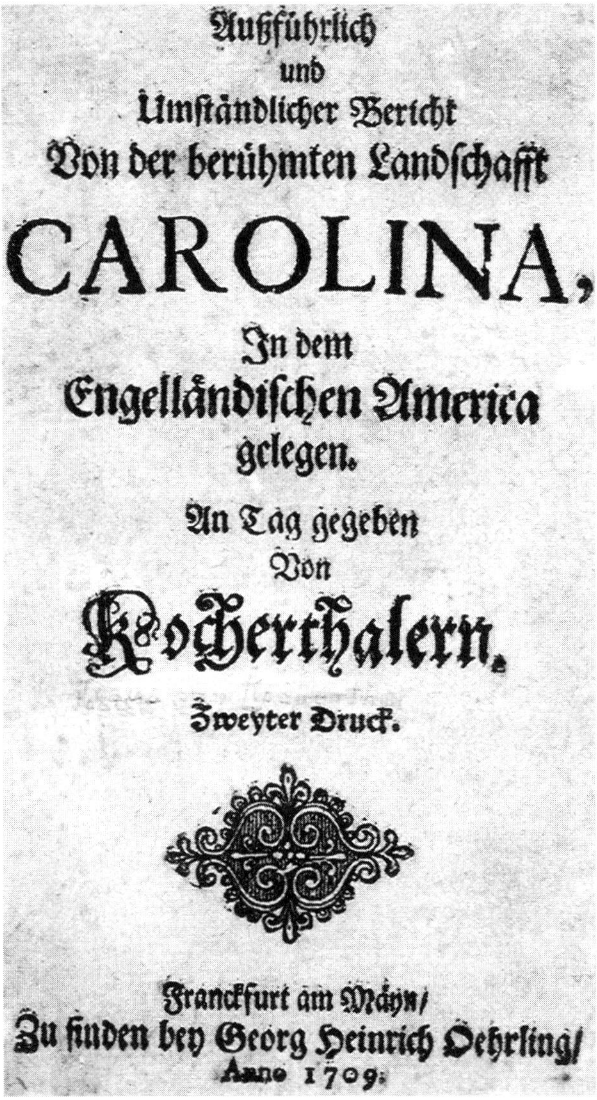

Außführlich
und
Umständlicher Bericht
Von der berühmten Landschafft
CAROLINA,
In dem
Engelländischen America
gelegen.
An Tag gegeben
Von
Kocherthalern.
Zweyter Druck.

Franckfurt am Mayn/
Zu finden bey Georg Heinrich Oehrling/
Anno 1709.

Figure 3. Title page of Joshua Kocherthal's *Ausführlich und Umständlicher Bericht*, 2d ed. (Frankfurt, 1709). This was the so-called golden book that spurred the 1709 German emigration. Courtesy of the Rare Book, Manuscript, and Special Collections Library, Duke University, Durham, North Carolina.

In the final chapter Kocherthal compared Carolina with Pennsylvania, which he acknowledged was better known to German-speaking people because of Pastorius's and Falckner's books. In Kocherthal's estimation Carolina proved more attractive. It did not have the bitterly cold winters of Pennsylvania, so grapes could be grown and cattle did not need barns. Kocherthal admitted that some grains grown in Pennsylvania might be more familiar to Germans and that, unlike Carolina, some Germans already lived in Pennsylvania who could help the immigrants as they settled in the New World. But in Kocherthal's mind, these advantages did not outweigh those of Carolina. Besides, it cost more to live in Pennsylvania, and most of the good land there had already been claimed.

Although the 1706 edition of Kocherthal's *Bericht* did little to mobilize the Germans, Kocherthal himself evidently believed the claims he made. In 1708 he recruited forty-one settlers from the German southwest to travel to the land he had so glowingly described. They traveled first to England, where they sought government aid for their settlement. Posing as refugees from French attacks on Landau in the southern Palatinate, Kocherthal's group managed to secure government support for a small settlement in America. Before the group left England, a few late arrivals joined them, and in October Kocherthal along with some fifty Germans set sail for America. They settled in New York rather than in the Carolinas, but the Crown paid their travel expenses and provided them with a small subsistence.[99]

If the 1706 edition of Kocherthal's *Bericht* sparked little interest among the Germans, the same cannot be said for the third and fourth editions that appeared in 1709.[100] The third edition contained a new appendix, and the fourth edition added another. Both appendixes extolled the life of ease awaiting those who moved to America. One claimed that "in Virginia . . . a man, when he wants to be only fairly hardworking, without even being particularly diligent, can raise 3000 pounds of tobacco and 20 pound barrels of grain in a year."[101] The third and fourth editions also included a map of Carolina that had not been part of earlier editions. It showed the region from the Chesapeake to Florida as a wide-open area filled with numerous rivers. A few gentle animals dotted the landscape, among them a turkey, a heron, and a deer, but the map also included farm animals—a pig, a cow, a goat, a horse—that any German peasant would have found familiar. The only human figures were a few Indians living in peaceful villages well beyond the mountains on the western fringe of the map.

Although these bucolic descriptions must have made Carolina attractive to the *Bericht*'s peasant readers, it was what the book hinted that Queen Anne might do for prospective settlers that really caught their attention. In discussing the costs of moving to Carolina, Kocherthal suggested that if enough people decided to emigrate, the queen might find it worthwhile to cover some of their expenses.[102] The early editions promised no more than this possibility, but the third and fourth editions of Kocherthal's *Bericht* included a letter indicating that the possibility of free passage had become a reality. The letter, written from London in July 1708, related the experience of Kocherthal's band of forty-one pioneers who left the German southwest in the spring of 1708.[103] It described the charity the emigrants received as they traveled along the Rhine and the support that the government gave them in Rotterdam as they waited to sail to England. It praised Queen Anne's generosity toward them after they had arrived in London and remarked on the goodwill of the English. More important, it reported that Queen Anne had given the group free passage to New York and granted them land for a settlement. Furthermore, she had promised to support the new settlers until they had established themselves in America.[104] The letter did not say that the queen would do the same for other emigrants, but its inclusion in the book, printed in larger type than any other section of the book and placed prominently at the end of both the third and fourth editions, implied that the riches the book described could belong to any German peasant. Surely Queen Anne would like even more settlers for her vast American possessions. All they had to do was make the relatively painless and inexpensive journey to London; once they were there, the queen would take care of the rest.

The Weilburg Petitioners

Among the people enticed by visions of a better life in America were nineteen men from Nassau-Weilburg. Soon after petitioning to leave the territory in May 1709, they found themselves called before officials of the prince to explain why they wanted to go. The prince of Nassau-Weilburg was worried about losing his subjects and had instructed court officials to find out why families were leaving. The nineteen men were subjects of the resulting inquiry. Each man had to answer a series of questions that explored his background and the motives behind his petition to leave. A clerk recorded the answers for the scrutiny of the prince.[105]

The clerk's record provides a wonderfully rich account of the reaction of peasant men to the propaganda circulating in the German southwest. It allows one to see how the men interpreted the stories they heard and to catch a rare glimpse of how such propaganda spread through mostly illiterate peasant communities. This document, more than any other, captures the sense of excitement and urgency that Kocherthal's book created.

The clerk's record is not without its problems. The clerk did not write a verbatim transcript. He shortened answers and summarized much of what the petitioners said. As the questioning went on, he summarized even more. The petitioners probably felt nervous about appearing before court officials and had to be cautious in presenting their case. Under the law they needed the prince's permission to move from the territory; not surprisingly they made few direct criticisms of the regime. Despite the constraints on what they said and how their answers were recorded, the responses are a marvelous source for determining who was leaving, why they were leaving, and how the emigration craze spread through a community.

In many ways the nineteen men were typical of the adult male segment of the emigration as a whole. All nineteen were married. Their average age was thirty-five, and on average they had three children. Thirteen had been born in the principality; the other six had moved there from surrounding territories. Nassau-Weilburg was a predominantly Lutheran principality, and fifteen of the respondents were Lutheran. Of the remainder, one was Catholic and three Reformed. From their responses, it appears that at least eleven were farmers. One man reported he was a "poor shepherd." Two were apparently carpenters, and one was a blacksmith. One referred to his "craft" without specifying what it was, and three men left no information on their occupations.

Nassau-Weilburg had not seen great devastation in the early eighteenth century from warring armies, and the religious disputes of the last two centuries no longer caused serious problems in the region. All outward signs indicated that Count Johann Ernst of Nassau-Weilburg presided over a peaceful and prosperous territory. He lived in a large castle overlooking the town of Weilburg with views across the surrounding countryside. For the last decade, enough money had somehow flowed into his treasury that he could undertake the transformation of his castle into a magnificent baroque palace. As it had for many other rulers, Versailles served as his model.

When asked why they were leaving, none of the petitioners blamed warfare for their troubles. Nor did any mention religion. They did not, however, share in the prosperity that made the construction of new palaces possible. Instead, they must have felt the irksome presence of the count's palace as they explained why they had decided to leave the territory. Almost all nineteen petitioners gave the same reason: poverty. Johann Klein did not know how he could sustain his wife and himself in "the current bad times." Johann Hezel, the poor shepherd, reported he could no longer feed his six children. One farmer mentioned how the harsh winter had destroyed his fruit crops and how he had no hope for a harvest in the current year. Valentin Römsbott, a blacksmith, could no longer afford bread. Georg Gäberling, a carpenter, complained that "even if he labored day and night at his carpentry work he would not earn enough to feed himself."[106] Only one of the men seemed without worries. Christian Schneider, at twenty-five the youngest of the group, said only that everyone was talking of moving to America and that he had resolved to join them.

Although the men complained of poverty and hunger, they said they had decided to leave only reluctantly. Two mentioned that if there were fewer restrictions on hunting the wild animals that destroyed their fields, they might be able to save their crops as well as feed themselves on the wild beasts. Then, perhaps, they would remain. Peter Ott said he "would in his heart like to stay."[107]

The men may have expressed reluctance to leave, but they had not taken long to decide to join the migration. None of the respondents reported that he had heard of the emigration and the queen's promises more than three weeks earlier. Several had heard of it only in the past week, and one man reported that he had heard of it only the day before. The men's reports indicate that they were caught up in the excitement of the moment. They almost all claimed to suffer from poverty and malnutrition, but apparently they had not seriously considered emigration as a possible solution until a few days before they filed their petitions. Rumors of Queen Anne's generosity and the sight of other emigrants heading for London spurred them to action. They wanted to join the movement before it was too late. They had no time for lengthy deliberations.

The court officials were particularly interested in finding out who had influenced the men's decision to move. They suspected outsiders had been encouraging the people in their foolishness. They were right.

When asked where the idea to emigrate originated, the petitioners seemed wary of implicating anyone in particular. Instead they reported that "everywhere in the country one talks about it."[108] Like other people in the German southwest the villagers of the Westerwald did not live in isolated, closed communities. They moved about and had come in contact with strangers telling strange stories. Two respondents told of Palatines who had spoken of the migration; two others said the idea to emigrate had come from residents of Hesse-Darmstadt. The migration to America had begun in late February or early March in a region near the confluence of the Rhine and Neckar rivers. Two months later, word had spread a hundred kilometers north to the narrow valley of the Lahn River, and the residents of Nassau-Weilburg knew a large-scale emigration was under way.

The emigrants already on their way were not the only factor that swayed the men of Nassau-Weilburg. A small book also influenced their decision. In a period when few other forms of mass communication existed, books could have a powerful effect on the imagination of those who read or heard them.[109] Such was the effect of this book, which told wonderful stories of America's riches and insinuated that German emigrants could share in the New World's wealth. Although the men being interrogated mentioned only one copy of the book, at least two-thirds of them knew its contents.

At first the men seemed reluctant to admit that the book and its wild promises had circulated in the region. Eventually Johannes Flach and Gerhard Stahl admitted to having a copy. Apparently Stahl, a carpenter from Altenkirchen, had traveled to Frankfurt a short while earlier. While there he bought the book from an English agent. Although only one of the petitioners mentioned Stahl by name, it is clear that Stahl had been spreading word of the book's contents around the neighborhood. One man reported that the carpenter in Altenkirchen—almost certainly Stahl—had first told him of the English plan to send German farmers to America. Another man, who had been attending church in the village, also reported that it was in Altenkirchen that he had first heard somebody reading the book with the queen's promises.

Many of the villagers of Nassau-Weilburg may have been illiterate, but they were not immobile. They traveled from village to village to attend church, to work, or to go to market. One literate man with enough money to buy a small book and the willingness to read it aloud in the tavern or outside the church could quickly inform friends and strangers of its contents. Illiterate people returning to their villages could then recount the book's promises. Rapidly the book's message, or rumors of its message, spread throughout the region. Many people decided to move based on the contents of a book that they could not read, that they may not have seen, and that may have been imperfectly reported and perhaps even wildly exaggerated.

When asked how they would pay for the journey, thirteen of the men said they would sell their belongings to cover the initial costs of the trip. The farmers would sell their cattle. The artisans would sell what little they owned. Several admitted to having no idea how they would raise the necessary funds. Yet they all seemed convinced that if they could reach London the queen would pay the rest of their expenses. One reported that "the Queen of England would give the people bread until they could grow it themselves."[110]

The appeal of the queen's offer was so strong that the men were willing to leave without detailed knowledge of their destination. Johannes Flach said he "did not know anything more [about America] than what was read to him from the book."[111] Philips Petri admitted he knew nothing at all. The others said only that they had heard the land was good and that if one worked, one could do well. Adam Hartman gave the most optimistic report. In words that closely echoed the promises made in Kocherthal's *Bericht*—again suggesting the strong influence of the book—Hartman said he had heard "that if one would work, one could grow and harvest so much in a single year that he could live off it for two years."[112]

Clearly the men had not spent long hours reflecting on America's possibilities or the problems that the migration might entail. Instead they seemed caught up in a vast, unthinking movement; their actions betrayed a sense of urgency, an anxiousness that they not be left behind. Like most of the emigrants, the nineteen men from Nassau-Weilburg would never realize their dreams of free land in America. But in May 1709 they did not know what the future held, and they were determined not to allow the opportunity to pursue their dreams pass them by.[113]

In a largely illiterate society, Kocherthal's book worked. Although few could read it, the peasants of the German southwest heard the book read aloud in taverns and churchyards. In this way its message spread much more rapidly than if its transmission had relied on hundreds of peasants buying the book and reading it quietly at home. And the sight of thousands of emigrants already on their way to London surely had a powerful influence on any debate over the book's contents. Whether one could read the book made little difference. Promises that moved so many people must be true.

Eventually around fifteen thousand people from hundreds of small communities throughout the German southwest left their homes and journeyed to London. To many observers the migrants had lost their senses. Officials in Nassau-Dillenburg reported that people had their minds so set on Pennsylvania that attempts to turn them back were useless.[114] Nevertheless most people in the German southwest stayed home. They resisted the temptations spelled out in the golden book and followed the admonitions of the state authorities and their pastors to accept the lot God had given them. They might be poor and suffering, but their occupations were honorable and pleasing to God. They should not allow themselves to be seduced by America's riches.[115] It was an argument that state authorities would repeat throughout the eighteenth century, rebuking potential emigrants by invoking the biblical injunction to "Trust in the Lord and do good; remain in the country and support yourself honestly."[116]

Many people questioned the emigrants' motives. Some suggested the emigrants were laggards looking for an easy life elsewhere. A village pastor complained that "a particularly deceptive spirit" had broken out among some "more or less lazy and indolent fellows" in his parish. They dreamed of going to Carolina, a place where they believed "breakfast bread would rain into their mouths." Although he had tried to change their minds "through a more accurate representation of the facts," the emigrants "would not let themselves be deterred from their calm delusion."[117] The emigrants appeared to be sheer opportunists, defying common sense and the will of God. They sought a life of great riches and little labor.

The pastor's criticism had some truth to it. The colonial propaganda did provide the people of the German southwest with an opportunity. Those who chose to pursue the opportunity had to make the conscious decision to defy authority and to face the possible condemnation of their own communities. But the opportunity made the consequences worthwhile. Most of the emigrants were peasants and artisans teetering on the edge of poverty. They wanted a place of their own free of feudal obligations and far from the everlasting threats of famine and war. And if America's bounty meant less work, all the better. They dreamed the not-so-noble dreams of toiling people, dreams of more time in the home and tavern and less in the shop and fields.

Once they had decided to move, the emigrants could not easily reverse their decision. To make the journey, most of the emigrants had to sell their land and belongings, and sometimes they had to renounce their right to return home. Many also gave up the respect of their friends and neighbors. The high costs of leaving made it crucial that the emigrants achieve their goal. Soon the British would have thousands of determined opportunists on their hands, people not looking for British charity but for what they had convinced themselves was rightfully theirs—land in America.

CHAPTER 2

"The Poor Palatine Refugees"

LONDON, SPRING–SUMMER 1709

The 1709 emigration from the German southwest began in the center of the Palatinate near the confluence of the Rhine and Main rivers, not far from Joshua Kocherthal's home in the Kraichgau. The peasants in that region must have been among the first to hear that Kocherthal's group of fifty settlers had received land in New York at Queen Anne's behest. Word of Kocherthal's good fortune probably reached the German southwest in late 1708, and many Germans, eager to enjoy the same benefits, did not wait for the harsh winter of 1708–9 to end before beginning their own journey. The worst of the severe cold began to subside with February's arrival, and by late February the Rhine was probably sufficiently clear of ice to make travel possible.[1] Soon the emigrants left their homes, and by mid-March they were camping outside Rotterdam, seeking transportation to London.[2]

Upon reaching Rotterdam the emigrants applied to James Dayrolle, the British resident at the Hague, for permission to travel to England. Although he readily granted it, few had enough money to pay their passage.[3] The others remained behind in miserable camps perched on dikes outside Rotterdam's walls, above fields flooded from rain and melting snow.[4] Dutch officials soon discovered that the Germans were intent on sailing to England and hoped the emigrants would be only a temporary presence in their country. Nevertheless, because many of the Germans were starving, Rotterdam officials felt compelled to provide public funds for their relief. Various private groups also raised money to support the Germans and even paid to send some eight hundred emigrants to London in late April.[5]

Thousands more took the place of the eight hundred who left. Johann Wilhelm, the Palatine elector, who kept his court in Düsseldorf safely away from the problems of the Palatinate, grew concerned as boatloads of his subjects floated past on their way to Rotterdam. On April 25 (NS) he issued a decree forbidding unauthorized emigration to America. His subjects ignored the decree. The elector tried more drastic means. He ordered a boat of thirty Palatines to be intercepted near Koblenz and forced back home.[6] Yet Johann Wilhelm's actions proved ineffective, and people continued to leave.

Soon the emigration craze spread beyond the Palatinate. News of Queen Anne's alleged offer moved quickly along the rivers, drawing migrants from throughout the Rhineland. To the east, along the narrow valley of the Lahn, came hundreds of emigrants. Many began the journey near Herborn in the Westerwald, the hometown of Kocherthal's wife, Sibylla, and an area where many heard with interest the news of the 1708 emigrants. These migrants from the Westerwald traveled south to the Lahn and then west to the Rhine. Along the way they attracted more migrants from the villages along the Lahn, including Weilburg, site of the count of Weilburg's newly renovated palace, and Nassau, whose ancient castle had been the seat of a long line of princes. On the opposite side of the Rhine, migrants began their travels deep in the isolated hills of the Hunsrück, leaving towns such as Oberstein, fifty kilometers west of the Rhine, and traveling along the broad valley of the Nahe past vineyards and orchards damaged by the winter's hard, sustained freeze. The short valley of the Wied River, north of the confluence of the Rhine and Mosel rivers, saw a tremendous exodus of migrants from the villages of Niederbieber, Heddesdorf, Rengsdorf, and Segendorf. These villagers must have felt their hopes of a better, more equitable life in America confirmed as they loaded into boats on the banks of the Rhine just outside the local count's capital city of Neuwied. Not more than a hundred yards away stood the count's beautiful new palace, paid for by taxes and levies they could ill afford.

As emigrants continued to drain from the territories throughout May and June, the situation became so desperate that the landgrave of Hesse-Darmstadt, the princes of Nassau-Idstein, Nassau-Dillenburg, and Nassau-Weilburg, the duke of Württemberg, and the count of Sayn all issued decrees designed to stop the flow.[7] As the German princes' concern grew, Queen Anne found herself having to assure them that she had done nothing to encourage the migration.[8]

While the German princes struggled to keep their subjects from fleeing, James Dayrolle, representing British interests in the Netherlands, welcomed the immigrants, believing that the German princes' loss could be Britain's gain. The British government had just passed a new naturalization act that eased the transition of immigrants into British society. Like the Whigs who pushed through the naturalization bill, Dayrolle subscribed to the theory that people are the most important component of a nation's wealth. Therefore increasing a country's population would increase its wealth, and encouraging immigration was a way of reaching that goal. The German migrants had unwittingly stumbled into a situation that ensured them a warm welcome.

With the support of the duke of Marlborough, Dayrolle immediately began to search for ways to transport the Germans to London. The War of the Spanish Succession had been dragging on since 1701, and British troops continued to arrive regularly in Rotterdam to join the duke of Marlborough's army on the Continent. Dayrolle suggested that the troop ships should return to London loaded with German emigrants. By late April the queen had approved the idea, and on May 6 (NS) Dayrolle informed the Germans of the plan.[9] With the next arrival of soldiers they would be on their way to London.

Meanwhile, on April 28 the first boatload of Germans from the small convoy that the Dutch had privately subsidized arrived in London.[10] Within a few days over eight hundred Germans had crowded together in miserable rooms in St. Catherine's parish. The parish, on the city's east side just beyond the Tower, had long been a community of poor English families and foreigners. Already in 1598 it was described as "inclosed about or pestered with small tenements and homely cottages," and it remained so a hundred years later, when its inhabitants consisted "of weavers and other manufacturers and of seamen and such who relate to shipping and are generally very factious and poor."[11]

The British authorities suspected that the Germans would try to contact William Penn, who was known to have previously recruited settlers from the Rhineland for his colony.[12] But the migrants seemed to have had few, if any, contacts with Penn. Instead they approached Anton Boehme, a German Lutheran pastor who had helped Kocherthal's small band of settlers the year before.[13] Boehme had been court pastor to

Prince George of Denmark, Queen Anne's husband. When Prince George died in 1708, he left money to support the Lutheran chapel at St. James Palace, and Boehme remained at his post after his patron's death. Although Boehme was perhaps the most influential leader in London's German-speaking community, he left for a previously planned trip to Germany shortly after the German immigrants arrived in London. The care of the Germans fell to John Tribbeko, a Lutheran chaplain who served with Boehme at St. James Palace, and George Ruperti, the pastor at London's German Lutheran Church in Savoy.[14]

The Board of Trade, which had opened an inquiry on the condition of the new arrivals, employed Ruperti and Tribbeko to visit the German immigrants.[15] On May 9, 1709, the two pastors gave their first report. They had found the Germans crowded together, often twenty to thirty to a room, in St. Catherine's. Most had spent all they had to make the journey. They needed food and clothing. The migrants had emphasized to the two pastors that without support they would soon become sick and weak and "so not be serviceable in the Plantations." They seemed to have no doubt that they would soon be sailing to America, for they asked that they not be so crowded on ships during the voyage to America as they had been on the voyage from Holland.[16]

Ruperti and Tribbeko also began a detailed census of the Germans. They reported that 852 immigrants had arrived in London—390 adults and 462 dependent children. Of the 210 men in the census, 147 were husbandmen or vinedressers. Almost all the rest were rural artisans. Although the two pastors referred to the immigrants as the "poor Protestant Palatines," their census revealed that 24 families consisting of 100 people were Catholic. Of the remaining families, 134 were Reformed, 53 were Lutheran, and 13 were listed as "Baptist."[17] Government officials may have chosen to ignore it, but religious diversity marked the migration from the beginning.

During the early eighteenth century London did not have a strong German community that could support the new arrivals. A dozen men organized by Frederick Slare, a German-speaking physician living in London, undertook the immigrants' care. The group of men, which included Tribbeko, Ruperti, and John Chamberlayne, the secretary of the Society for the Propagation of the Gospel, met during May at the Temple Exchange Coffeehouse.[18] There they considered ways to lodge the Germans, whose filthy condition made them stand out in an already stinking city. The Germans were, according to the understated report of one meeting, "so crowded together that they were offensive to one another as well as those that visited them." One did not need to move far to reach the cleaner air of the countryside. The men rented several barns and houses just a few miles south of London in the villages of Camberwell, Walworth, and Kennington and lodged some of the immigrants there. They also provided the Germans with a diet of bread, cheese, and milk.[19]

On May 3 the secretary of state, Charles Spencer, earl of Sunderland, informed the Board of Trade that, although the immigrants came "with Intentions to settle in Her Majesty's Plantations," the queen was "convinced that it would be much more for the Advantage of Her Kingdoms if a method could be found to settle them here . . . instead of sending them to the West Indys." According to Sunderland, the queen believed "it would be a great Encouragement to others to follow their Example, and that this Addition to the Number of Her Subjects would in all probability produce a proportionable Increase of their Trade & Manufactures." Sunderland therefore directed the Board of Trade to consider how the people might be employed and where they might be settled.[20]

The Debate over Immigration and Naturalization

When the Germans arrived in London, the Whigs controlled Parliament. Sunderland, as secretary of state, and his ally Sydney Godolphin, the lord treasurer and a moderate Tory, served as the government's chief ministers. From the time the Whigs took power in 1708, they had worked to promote measures that encouraged immigration to the island. England's population had grown slowly, and at times had stagnated, during much of the seventeenth century.[21] In the second half of the seventeenth century English economic writers began challenging prevailing assumptions about the dangers of overpopulation. They argued that, instead of bringing scarcity and starvation, a growing population actually increased a nation's wealth.[22] As Daniel Defoe wrote, "The more people, the more trade; the more trade, the more money, the more money; the more strength; and the more strength, the greater the nation."[23]

The new theories on population appealed to the commercially minded Whigs, who proposed bolstering the country's population and wealth by encouraging immigration. Theories linking population growth to national wealth were not limited to England, and the Whigs nervously monitored the actions of their European neighbors. Both the Dutch and the Prussians had adopted policies that encouraged immigration. The Whigs feared that Britain might miss an opportunity to attract skilled laborers to its shores. If the Dutch and the Prussians believed it worthwhile to welcome Huguenots and other displaced people to their lands, surely British commerce would also benefit from such immigrants.

To encourage immigration the Whigs proposed simplifying the process by which foreigners became British subjects, a process known as naturalization. One of the main hardships aliens faced in England was their inability under the law to own real property. Naturalization removed that hardship. Once naturalized, immigrants held the same rights as native-born subjects: they could own real property, inherit it, and pass it on to their children.[24]

Most Tories did not favor easing naturalization laws, and the issue divided the two parties during the late seventeenth and early eighteenth centuries. The Tory landed and High Church interests tended to distrust foreigners and foreign connections.[25] Some worried that naturalizing aliens would rapidly increase the number of Dissenters among British subjects, thus undermining the power of the Church of England. Worse still, some Catholics might slip in. The Tories also worried that immigrants might strain England's social order in other ways. Reflecting on the country's experience with Huguenot immigrants twenty years earlier, they worried that skilled immigrants would displace British workers and lead to unrest among the lower classes. And if the immigrants were unskilled, they might find no work at all and become a burden on the Treasury. From 1704 to 1709 England suffered an economic depression and high unemployment.[26] The Tories could not imagine how welcoming new immigrants would solve these problems.

Despite Tory opposition, the Whigs moved swiftly to pass a naturalization bill after taking power in 1708. The General Naturalization Act was introduced in February 1709, quickly passed the Commons and the Lords, and received the royal assent on March 23. The act allowed foreigners who had received the Sacrament within the past three months in a Protestant church—not just the Church of England—to be naturalized after taking an oath of allegiance and paying a one-shilling fee.[27]

The debate over the passage of the Naturalization Act of 1709 had scarcely died down before the first wave of German emigrants arrived in London. Sunderland and the other Whig leaders had not encouraged the Germans to come to Britain; they had not even mentioned them in the debate over the Naturalization Act. But now that the immigrants had arrived, their numbers compelled the government to formulate a policy to deal with them. After months of proclaiming the advantages of increasing Britain's population, Sunderland could hardly choose any other policy than settling the Germans in Britain. He was glad to do so, however. Sunderland was sure the new arrivals would be model citizens. In a proposal to the Board of Trade written in mid-May, Sunderland described them as "Religious Temperate and hardy Industrious" and concluded that the Palatines were "perhaps the fittest Nation in Europe to be encouraged to come among the Britains."[28] Although Sunderland knew that the Germans hoped to be transported to America, for the good of the country and for Whig policy he was prepared to ignore the Germans' wishes.

The Arrival and Care of the German Migrants

In early May nobody knew the magnitude of the looming German migration. In Rotterdam James Dayrolle continued his efforts to ship more emigrants across the Channel. By mid-May British troop ships were preparing to return from Rotterdam to London. Although Dayrolle anticipated the government's approval to use the ships to send the Germans to England, he still had not been formally advised of the government's intentions. Therefore he sought and received the duke of Marlborough's blessing before allowing the migrants to board the ships. On May 12 the second fleet of German migrants set sail for London with 1,283 people on board.[29]

The ships arrived on the Thames by May 23, and the Board of Trade had to scramble to find lodging for the Germans. On May 24 the board decided to place them, at least temporarily, a few miles east of London in an abandoned ropeyard in Deptford.[30] The landing was poorly coordinated, and the group of men who had privately aided the first arrivals in St. Catherine's had to hire barges to help the second arrivals disembark from their ships. Although some settled in the ropeyard and adjacent warehouses, others were transported to barns that had been leased for them in the farmland just south of London. By late May twenty barns had been rented for the first two waves of migrants.[31]

By mid-June two more convoys of troop ships had ferried an additional 4,700 Germans from Rotterdam to London.[32] In a letter describing the arrangements he had made to transport the Germans across the Channel, Dayrolle noted that many of the recent migrants were Catholics. He had not been certain he should allow them to travel to London, but the duke of Marlborough had told him "there was no great

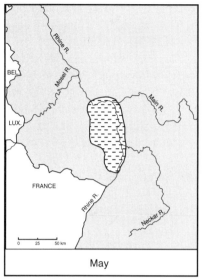

May

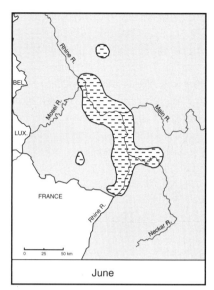

June

July

Map 3. German origins of immigrants arriving in London in May, June, and July 1709. The maps reflect how the propaganda that fueled the migration spread. The first immigrants came from the Rhineland region between Frankfurt, where Kocherthal's book was published, and Kocherthal's home, just south of the confluence of the Rhine and Neckar rivers. By June the migration craze had spread up and down the Rhine as well as to a more re-mote northern region centered on Herborn, the hometown of Kocherthal's wife, Sibylla. By July word had spread to the interior regions of the Palatinate, Hesse, and Nassau, and farther south into Württemberg.

inconveniency to let them go with the rest." Besides, the Protestants and Catholics seemed to get along well, and Dayrolle observed that "several of them mixed together husbands & wifes." Dayrolle also summarized in one sentence the migrants' origins and their reasons for migrating. "They are not all Palatins," he wrote, "a great many of them coming from the Duchy of Deux Ponts and the neighboring countrys and flying not so much for Religion as to shake of[f] the burden they ly[e] under by the hardshipps of their Princes Government and the contributions they must pay to the Enemy."[33] Over the next several months as a fierce debate raged in London over the nature of the German immigrants, Dayrolle's brief, though insightful, observations would be ignored, hidden away in his official correspondence.

Meanwhile, Tribbeko and Ruperti continued to care for the new arrivals, visiting the warehouses and barns where they were housed, holding religious services for them, and compiling censuses of them. Between May 6 and June 15 Ruperti and Tribbeko completed four censuses that listed 6,519 German migrants. The census takers painstakingly listed the names, ages, occupations, and religions of all the adult men. They also showed whether the men were accompanied by their wives and listed the sex and age of any children with them. Widows and single women traveling without their families were listed at the end of each census.[34]

Despite the effort that Ruperti and Tribbeko put into the censuses, the government left certain questions unasked and ignored the answers to others. For example, the censuses revealed nothing about the immigrants' geographic origins. If the government had bothered to ask, it would have found out that the migration did not consist of one large, cohesive group. Instead it was a hodgepodge of hundreds of small groups of families and neighbors from dozens of different principalities. When it came to labeling the immigrants, the British would ignore these complex origins. They would also ignore, at least for a time, one thing that the censuses did reveal: almost a third of the immigrants were Catholics.

By late June the roughly 6,500 German migrants were scattered all around London, living in houses and warehouses in St. Catherine's, Southwark, and Deptford, as well as in barns in Walworth and other areas south of the city. The queen sympathized with the Germans. In the past she had taken action to ensure the religious freedom of her husband's coreligionists in the Palatinate, and she seemed genuinely concerned about the plight of these apparent refugees from French and Catholic aggression.[35] Already in May she had contributed to their subsistence. But as the number of Germans increased, the amount of money needed to support them also rose. The queen's subsidy rose from £16 a day in mid-May to £30 a day in early June and finally to £80 on June 24.[36] The men who had been helping the Germans were having trouble keeping up with the needs of the immigrants. In mid-June they advertised in

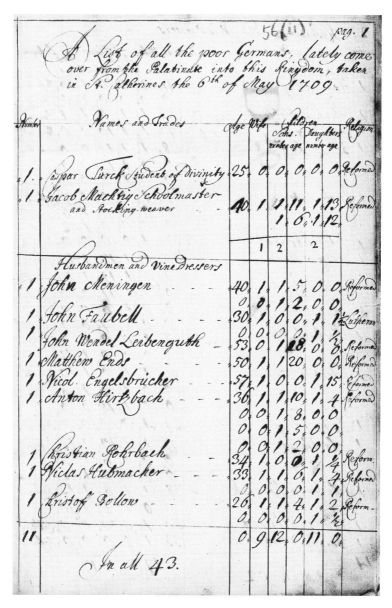

Figure 4. First page of the London census of the German immigrants, May 6, 1709. Four such censuses enumerating over 6,500 immigrants were completed during May and June of 1709. PRO, CO 388/76:56(ii). Courtesy of the Public Record Office, London.

a London newspaper, encouraging "such as are disposed to contribute to the Relief of the Poor Palatines" to bring their contributions to Tribbeko, Ruperti, or one of the other men organizing the immigrants' relief.[37] With their own money and the money they raised, the men bought combs for the migrants' lousy hair and paid the rent on the barns and warehouses housing the poor Germans. But the men noted that the farmers needed their barns back by the beginning of the summer and that the Germans would soon have to move elsewhere.[38]

In late June most of the Germans moved out of the barns and warehouses in Deptford, Walworth, and other areas south of London to large camps established at Blackheath and Camberwell.[39] The government supplied thousands of army tents to house the migrants. The living conditions at Camberwell and Blackheath may have been primitive, but the rural setting was considered beneficial to the migrants and to the people of London, who suspected that the filthy Germans were spreading disease. Blackheath, just south of the grounds of the Royal Observatory at Greenwich, was considered one of the most beautiful places in the London countryside and was a frequent destination for city dwellers making weekend excursions.[40] By July 1, Ruperti and Tribbeko reported 4,541 Germans at Blackheath. Those settled at Camberwell and remaining in St. Catherine's numbered 1,977.[41] The problem of finding temporary homes for the Germans had been solved. The more difficult problem of finding them permanent homes remained.

Until mid-June private groups had administered the care and settlement of the Germans, relying on the queen's charity and a few private donations. These private groups now found themselves overwhelmed. On June 16, at the request of the justices of peace for Middlesex, the queen authorized a nationwide charity drive to raise money for the "relief, subsistence and settlement of the poor distressed Palatines." She meant business. The order decreed that "the minister and Church Wardens of every parish, shall go from house to house, to ask and receive from their parishioners their christian and charitable contributions." Not only householders would be solicited "but also servants, strangers, lodgers, and others in all the City's Towns and villages etc., in our Kingdom etc."[42] At the same time the queen appointed a Commission for the Relief and Settlement of the Poor Palatines, made up of ninety-six men to oversee the immigrants' care. Members of the cabinet led the commission, but it also included Tribbeko, Ruperti, Slare, Chamberlayne, and others already involved in the day-to-day affairs of the Germans.[43]

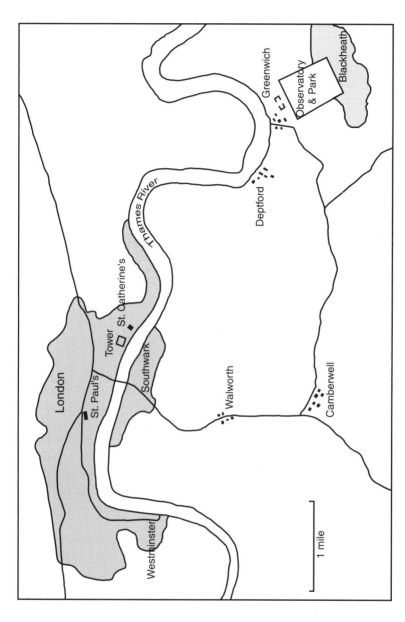

Map 4. Early eighteenth-century London and the sites of the German refugee camps. The map is based, in part, on John Roque, *An Exact Survey of the Citys of London Westminster the Borough of Southwark and the Country near Ten Miles Round* (London, 1746).

Sunderland had originally assigned the Board of Trade the task of finding ways to settle the Germans. In May the board considered a proposal to clear forests and wastelands in England to create new townships for the immigrants.[44] The officials also heard from the United Governors, Assistants and Society of London for Mines Royal, who wanted to send the Germans to Wales, where some would work in silver and copper mines while the rest cultivated the surrounding wasteland.[45] In addition, the marquis of Kent proposed settling twenty families on his estates in Herefordshire and Gloucestershire.[46] The board evidently rejected all three proposals. It noted that the marquis of Kent's proposal would cost over £15,000 for one hundred people and that if the government settled all the others in the same way it would require over £150,000. The board members, reacting to grumbling that the German migrants received better treatment than Britain's poor, noted "that the intention was not to settle these people here upon a better foot than our own."[47]

While the Board of Trade considered formal proposals for settling large numbers of Germans, various members of the government sought ways to settle smaller groups of Germans throughout Great Britain. Sunderland wrote to the mayor of Canterbury in early June, noting the city's "Charity for Strangers" and asking if some Palatine families might be sent there. The mayor replied with regret that the city did not have enough work to employ its own poor and had no good land for the Germans to farm.[48] The Commissioners for the Relief and Settlement of the Poor Palatines also sent letters throughout Britain encouraging towns to find ways to settle the immigrants.[49] Liverpool eventually agreed to take in 130 immigrants, and the parish of Sundrich in Kent reluctantly accepted two families.[50] Yet even though the government later offered to subsidize the settlement of German families in towns and villages throughout the country, this approach saw little success.[51]

During July, the newly appointed commission began its work in earnest, taking over much of the responsibility for settling the German immigrants from the Board of Trade. It held its first public meeting on July 6 at St. Paul's chapter house in the shadow of the newly rebuilt cathedral.[52] The commissioners continued to seek ways to employ the Germans in Great Britain. They encouraged ship captains to recruit German men at Blackheath, where a small booth served as a rudimentary employment office for the migrants.[53] The commissioners also heard a proposal from the lord proprietors of Carolina to settle the Germans in their colony.[54] But before the committee could act on the proposal, two more convoys containing 4,200 Germans arrived in London and joined the camps at Blackheath and Camberwell.[55] Eleven thousand Germans had now settled into camps in and around London.

Efforts to Stop the Migration

By late May Britain's representative at the Hague, James Dayrolle, wondered if perhaps the Germans were becoming too much of a good thing. He had visited the Germans camped outside the gates of Rotterdam and had heard from them that "the whole Palatinate is ready to follow them poor and rich." He suggested that the queen's ministers let him know "what is her Majies pleasure in case the number augment in that manner."[56] Two weeks later he again reported that "upon the continuation of H.M. Bounty or any other encouragement, you may have half Germany if you please, for they are all flying away not only from the Palatinate, but from all other countrys in the neighborhood of the Rhine."[57]

The queen's ministers decided they would prefer not to have half Germany, and on June 24 Secretary of State Henry Boyle informed Dayrolle that he was to send over only those Germans already in Rotterdam and no more. In addition, Boyle told him to send no more Catholics.[58] Dayrolle attempted to slow the migration by sending some Germans back up the Rhine to warn other migrants to turn back. He also placed a notice in the *Cologne Gazette* stating that Britain would accept no more German immigrants.[59] Dayrolle sent the 2,700 Germans already in Rotterdam on to London, but within two weeks another 1,500 Germans were camped outside Rotterdam. These, too, were sent to London in late July at the government's expense.[60]

By August the flow of Germans down the Rhine began to slow but did not stop. Although the British government no longer paid to transport the migrants to London and threatened to send back new arrivals, another thousand still managed to make the journey. Some paid their own fares, and others relied on Dutch charity to pay their way.[61] The Dutch had no desire to support the destitute Germans outside Rotterdam's gates. In August the city's leaders employed two ships to patrol the lower Rhine and force boatloads of Germans to return home. The Dutch States General ordered its ministers in Cologne and Frankfurt to work to prevent further migration.[62]

Despite Dayrolle's efforts and the efforts of various Dutch officials, more Germans arrived in Rotterdam and a few continued to cross the

Channel. In late August Dayrolle was outraged to discover an English-man distributing fliers to the Germans with a translation of the Carolina proprietors' recently presented proposals to settle them in Carolina. The Englishman encouraged the Germans to send the fliers to their friends back home. Since the proprietors' proposal offered one hundred acres rent-free for ten years to each man, woman, and child who would settle in Carolina, it was a powerful countervailing force to Dayrolle's threats that no more migrants would be allowed in England.[63] In late September, fifteen hundred Germans remained camped outside Rotterdam, deter-mined to get to London.

The Germans already in London now realized that the queen had never planned to settle them in America and had been completely un-prepared for their arrival. They were forced to wait for the government to decide their fate. While they waited, the Germans attempted to make their lives as normal as possible. A woodcut of one of the German camps published in 1709 shows the women cooking and hauling wood while children sleep next to the tents. Many of the immigrants were too ill to leave the camps, but others managed to find work on surrounding farms.[64] Queen Anne employed around four hundred to dig a canal near Windsor.[65] Some German men joined the British army.[66] Those Germans remaining in the camps lived on food supplied by the government. To ensure the management of the camps and the proper distribution of food and supplies, the authorities assigned several German men who were able to read and write to serve as camp supervisors. Because the men kept accounts listing the recipients of the queen's bounty, they became known as listmasters.[67] Lutheran and Reformed ministers held services for the migrants at the camps or at the churches in Savoy and Deptford. Ruperti translated the Anglican liturgy into German for the migrants' use, and Tribbeko translated the Church of England catechism, which was printed in parallel columns in English and German so that the mi-grants could also use it to learn English.[68] The Germans continued to marry and to have children. The Lutheran church in Savoy registered thirty-eight German marriages in 1709, and several German marriages and baptisms were recorded at the parish church in Deptford.[69]

The Debate over the Nature of the Immigrants

London, with a population of around 600,000, was the largest city in Europe, but the sudden influx of thirteen thousand Germans still created

The State of the *Palatines*,

FOR

Fifty Years paſt to this preſent Time.

CONTAINING,

I. An Account of the Principality of the Palatinate; and of the Barbarities and Ravages committed by Order of the French King upon the Inhabitants; Burning to the Ground a great Number of their moſt Famous Cities, and throwing the Bones of Emperors, Princes and Prelates, out of their Tombs, &c.

II. The Caſe of the Palatines, Publiſhed by themſelves, and Humbly Offered to the Tradeſmen of England. With a Liſt of them, and the Trades which the Men are brought up to.

III. The Humble Petition of the Juſtices of *Middleſex* to Her Majeſty on their Behalf, with Her Majeſties Order thereupon, and an Abſtract of the Brief graciouſly Granted for their Subſiſtence.

IV. A Letter about Settling and Employing them in other Countries.

V. A Proclamation of the States-General for Naturalizing all Strangers, and receiving them into their Country.

VI. Laſtly, Their preſent Encamping at Camberwell and Black-heath, in many Hundred Tents, by Her Majeſties Grace and Favour, till they can be otherwiſe diſpos'd of, and how they Employ themſelves; with their Marriages, Burials, &c. Alſo the great Kindneſs their Anceſtors ſhew'd to the Engliſh Proteſtants in the bloody Reign of Queen Mary.

Figure 5. Title page of *The State of the Palatines, for Fifty Years Past to This Present Time* (London, 1709) with a depiction of a German refugee camp in London. By permission of the Houghton Library, Harvard University.

a sensation among its people. One Londoner admitted, "The case of the Palatine[s] is all our domestic talk."[70] The camps at Camberwell and Blackheath drew hundreds of curious Londoners.[71] The first thing the Londoners noticed about the immigrants was their raggedness and poverty. One migrant later recalled arriving in London "where the people knew us by our old clothing."[72] But the British noticed more than worn-out clothes, and over the summer they began to define the Germans in ways that would have important consequences for the migrants' future.

The first step in defining a people is naming them. And the first names the British applied to the German-speaking immigrants revealed scant interest in determining their geographic origins or the reasons they had left their homes. In his earliest instructions concerning the migrants, Sunderland referred to them as "poor German Protestants . . . coming from the Palatinate."[73] The journals of the Board of Trade were filled with many similar references.[74] The minutes of the Society for the Propagation of the Gospel referred to "the poor persecuted Palatines lately arrived from Germany," and Daniel Defoe referred to the migrants in his *Review of the State of the British Nation* as "poor Inhabitants" of the Palatinate fleeing "Popish Persecution."[75] The fondness for alliterative terms stuck, although Defoe eventually distilled his description into the more manageable "poor Palatine refugees."

For Defoe, a moderate Whig in the pay of both Godolphin and Sunderland, the newly arrived immigrants served as a test case of the Whig arguments put forward during the naturalization debate.[76] Beginning in late June and continuing through late August, he wrote a series of articles for the *Review* defending the German immigrants and Whig policy pertaining to them.

While emphasizing, as he had done in the debate over naturalization, that people equaled wealth, Defoe attempted to demonstrate how settling the Germans on wasteland and in the forests would make such lands more productive and, without hurting the livelihood of others, would make the kingdom more prosperous.[77] He also argued that the Germans possessed characteristics that would make them valuable subjects. "The People are sober, temperate, modest and courteous," he wrote. "There appears nothing loose, nothing immoral, nothing prophane among them—They are chearful under their Misery, thankful in the Sense of their kind Reception here, perfectly subjected to what the Queen pleases to do for or with them, and behave themselves in all Things without the least Offence."[78]

In an effort to publicize the Whigs' position regarding the German immigrants beyond the *Review*'s London readers, Defoe reorganized and carefully summarized his arguments in a fifty-page book, *A Brief History of the Poor Palatine Refugees*, published in mid-August.[79] Defoe began the book by recognizing that some people opposed allowing the Germans into the country "in a Time when Trading was low, Employment scarce, a long War on our Hands, and all sorts of Provisions at such excessive Rates."[80] But he reminded his readers that "it's the constant and experimented Principle of all the rational part of Mankind, that People are the Riches, Honour, and Strength of a Nation, and that Wealth increases in an equal Proportion to the additional Numbers of Inhabitants."[81] Defoe noted that other countries also accepted the maxim. The duke of Brandenburg had enriched his kingdom by encouraging Huguenots to settle there and by inviting Palatines, like those now in London, to settle in Magdeburg in 1689. Likewise, the Dutch had copied Britain and now had their own naturalization act, which encouraged Protestant immigration. Conversely, France and Spain, two countries that Defoe's readers would not have Britain imitate, were losing wealth by driving people away.[82]

Defoe had to admit that the Germans were generally not skilled artisans like the Huguenots who had arrived two decades earlier, but he argued that the German farmers could help Britain by introducing new and useful plants and farming techniques. The Germans could be settled on wasteland and in the forests, thus making such lands more productive and, without hurting the livelihood of others, making the kingdom more prosperous. According to Defoe, the Germans were perfectly suited for the task. They were "laborious and skillful—Industrious to Labour, and ingenious in working, and exceeding willing to be employ'd in anything—In a word, They every Way recommend themselves as a People, that shall bring a Blessing, and not a Curse to any Place that shall receive them."[83]

Having shown that the Germans could be beneficial to the kingdom, Defoe also worked to demonstrate that they deserved Britain's favor. To allay suspicions that the immigrants had left their homes simply to enjoy England's bounties and the charity of its people, Defoe labeled them as "Palatine refugees." Both parts of the label furthered Defoe's cause. The term *refugee* had entered English parlance to refer to the Huguenots arriving from the Continent and originally referred only to people fleeing religious persecution.[84] Eighteenth-century Britons were keenly aware of the Palatinate as a victim of French Catholicism. Many Britons sympathized with the supposed refugees from the Palatinate, a principality that had the misfortune of lying in close proximity to Britain's greatest enemy, France. Ninety years before, during the Thirty Years' War, English charity drives had helped pay for the defense of the Palatinate, considered a beleaguered bastion of Protestantism in a region dominated by Catholicism.[85] By the late seventeenth century, the French army had reintroduced Catholicism to the Palatinate, and in 1690 a Catholic had succeeded to the position of Palatine elector. A book published in London in 1699 described the hardships and religious persecution the Protestants faced in the Palatinate.[86] The arrival in 1708 of Kocherthal and his immigrant party, all blaming their migration on French barbarity in the Palatinate, had served as a recent reminder of the problems in that territory. As Defoe said, "The Palatinate groans under the Oppression of Popish Persecution, and we see the poor Inhabitants flying hither for the Liberty of Religion."[87] When such long-suffering, God-fearing, and Protestant people sought refuge among the British, Defoe argued, a place should be made for them to share in, and eventually add to, Britain's bounties.

In the process of making the German-speaking immigrants well-suited objects of British charity and the potential beneficiaries of naturalization, Defoe created a new identity for them, one that Londoners could readily understand. These poor Palatine refugees were latter-day Huguenots, skilled, albeit rural, laborers on the run from French and Catholic tyranny. In creating this identity, Defoe simply disregarded the immigrants' varied origins and different religious backgrounds. He overlooked why they had left their homes, and he ignored their wishes to continue on to America. Such distinctions only led to confusing labels that muddied the issues. "Poor Palatine refugees" was much simpler and better suited the purposes of the Whig government.

The description, of course, was wildly misleading. Most of the German-speaking immigrants were not Palatines, few were fleeing French invasions, and almost none—especially the thousands of Catholics among them—were victims of Catholic persecution. The immigrants were not the first or the last victims of simplistic and ill-informed labels. Studies of migration are full of stories of new arrivals coping with the crude categorization of host populations. Thus the white colonists of early America viewed all the forced migrants from the African subcontinent as essentially one people despite the many obvious differences in language and culture among them. And in the eighteenth century Anglo-Americans ignored the differences among immigrants from Sicily, Umbria, and Emilia-Romagna, calling them all Italians. Newcomers are compelled to assume a larger, less differentiated identity because the people they encounter either cannot make such fine distinctions or in fact prefer the simplistic, and often pejorative, labels they have created. Meanwhile, the labels dehumanize the newcomers by forcing them into crude and misleading categories that ignore the immigrants' deeply held sense of who they are.

Defoe created, and the British people quickly adopted, such a label for the "poor Palatines." But rather than resisting the inaccurate and misleading label, the immigrants embraced the identity that the British forced on them, willfully adopting an identity and a history that had not been part of their past. They had good reason to do so. They faced a dilemma. In one way Defoe had labeled them correctly: they were certainly poor. Most had spent all they had to get to London. They now needed British charity to feed and clothe themselves and, with luck, to get to America. They were not refugees, but it seemed a poor strategy to pose as what they really were: peasant opportunists bent on acquiring free land. Better to adopt the British label and use it to their advantage.

CHAPTER 3

"A Parcel of Vagabonds"

LONDON, SUMMER–WINTER 1709

The Germans' first attempt to portray themselves as worthy of British charity relied too heavily on the truth and showed little recognition of the British prejudices that might have proved useful to them. In May, some five hundred Germans, members of the first immigrant convoy to arrive in London, appealed to the queen to help them get to America. In an awkwardly worded petition, with numerous misspelled words and phrasing that was more German than English, the immigrants described the causes of their migration as "war and other hardships, God the Almighty has send over us." Having heard of the queen's charity to their neighbors who came to London in 1708 and were sent "free" to America, they "could not but chose the footsteps of them." Although the petition's tone was one of groveling submissiveness, its message was simple: since the queen had helped their neighbors get to America, they would be sorely disappointed if she did not do the same for them.[1]

In June the German-speaking immigrants wrote a more sophisticated petition for British aid. Determining who authored the petition is difficult. Apparently few, if any, of the immigrants were fluent in English. The authors knew something about the situation in the German southwest but also understood the situation in Britain, which suggests that perhaps the German pastors in London in conjunction with some of the emerging immigrant leaders formulated the Germans' appeals. Whoever the authors were, they obviously understood the desperate straits of the German immigrants and the importance of gaining British sympathy for their plight. They also understood that an outright request for free land in America would do them little good. The authors had a keen sense of the emerging British national identity and of the issues that would appeal to the British people. They used that understanding to craft a petition that focused more on British prejudices than on German greed.[2]

With the Act of Union in 1707 the people of England, Scotland, and Wales began assuming a shared second identity as Britons. The process was a slow one, and it did not mean that the peoples of Great Britain forgot their differences or that they dispensed with older identities. People can adopt any number of identities, and depending on the situation, an eighteenth-century London merchant might have defined himself as a merchant, a Londoner, an Englishman, or, beginning in 1707, a Briton. But in 1709 the people of England, Wales, and Scotland remained keenly aware of their differences; what they had in common was far less apparent. The new British identity was not simply the sum of its parts. In relation to one another, the parts fit together poorly. But if the new Britons turned outward instead of inward, they gained a better sense of who they were. To define who they were, they had to decide who they were not.

Notions of "us" and "them" became critical to British perceptions of themselves, and the "them" that the British people defined themselves in contrast to were their perennial enemies, the French. French politics and religion represented all that the British were not. The British were Protestants—God's elect and the enlightened enemies of French tyranny and Catholic repression.[3] French Catholicism was clearly a religious threat to British Protestantism, but it also represented an important political threat to the British nation. The possibility of a Jacobite invasion remained real—the last had been in 1708—raising the specter of a Catholic ruler in Britain supported by a French and Catholic army. Britain displayed its great mistrust of all Catholics by not allowing British Catholics to vote until 1829, excluding them from Parliament and other state offices, and forbidding them to own weapons.[4]

The authors of the German petition "The State of the Poor Palatines" knew of British sympathy for the Palatinate as a land often overrun by the French. The petitioners drew on this sympathy, not by describing themselves more generally as "German Protestants" or by ascribing their hardships to "God the Almighty" as they had done in their May petition, but by describing themselves specifically as "poor distressed Palatines," whose "utter Ruin was occasion'd by the merciless Cruelty of a Bloody Enemy, the French."[5] Perhaps not wanting to draw too much attention to the fact that a group that called itself Protestant had many Catholic members, the petitioners did not raise the issue of religious persecution directly. Instead they praised Britons' religious principles, which made them a people markedly different from the French. According to the petition, Britain was a land that "abounds . . . with a Religious People, who as freely give to the Distressed for Christ's sake, as it was given to them by the Almighty Donor of all they enjoy." The Germans closed their petition with a collective signature that summed up all the attributes that made them worthy of British charity. They signed themselves the "poor distressed Protestants, The Palatines."[6]

"The State of the Poor Palatines" cleverly used half-truths about the immigrants' background to appeal to people who increasingly defined themselves as anti-Catholic and anti-French. So although the majority of the migrants were not from the French-ravaged Palatinate, they referred to themselves only as Palatines. Although almost a third of the migrants were Catholics, they called themselves the "poor distressed Protestants." And although few of the migrants had complained of French atrocities when they left their homes, in their petition they blamed the migration entirely on the monstrous behavior of the French.

In the end, the Germans' account of their migration had no more basis in reality than Defoe's, but, by appealing to Britons' anti-Catholic and anti-French attitudes, the Germans helped ensure an initial favorable response to the charity drive that Queen Anne had established on their behalf. The appeal raised over £22,000 in London alone; one woman reportedly donated £1,500.[7] The scale of giving over just a few months easily matched earlier English charity to the Huguenots, which had totaled £63,000 for the ten-year period from 1686 through 1695.[8]

Despite the initial success of the charity drive, some people had reservations about the Germans' worthiness. Gilbert Burnet, the bishop of Salisbury, reported that the charity drive "filled our own poor with great indignation; who thought those charities, to which they had a better right, were thus intercepted by strangers."[9] Not only the poor grumbled; few Tory leaders contributed to the drive. They had never agreed with the Whigs' proposition that naturalizing foreigners and encouraging immigration worked to Britain's benefit. Most Tories still defined British Protestantism as Anglicanism and feared that allowing in so many

Lutheran and Reformed immigrants might weaken the Church of England. The charity drive took on political overtones. The bishop of Carlisle wrote that those looking for money would "find charity very Cold in these parts" and noted that if "large contributions on this occasion be the true distinguishing character of Whigs, we shall assuredly pass for rank Tories."[10]

Defoe tried to repudiate the claims of those who argued that charity should go first to Britain's poor. He contended that there was plenty of work for everyone and that many of Britain's poor were simply too lazy to work.[11] To the argument that competition with German labor would lower wages, Defoe countered that the Huguenots' arrival in 1685 had not lowered English wages and that the effect of the Germans would be no different. Defoe admitted that the Germans were generally not skilled artisans like the Huguenots, but he continued to argue that the German farmers would benefit Britain by introducing innovative crops and farming practices.[12]

Just as Defoe relied on economic reasoning to bolster his arguments in favor of the Germans, his opponents did the same. They began by rejecting his central argument that more people meant more wealth. England's poor failed to see how bringing over more impoverished people improved their own lot. They tended to agree with the English artisan who maintained that "our Charity ought to begin at Home, both in Peace and War, before we extend it to our Neighbors."[13]

They also disagreed with Defoe regarding the Germans' potential contributions to Great Britain. Unlike Defoe, they believed the Germans compared poorly with the Huguenot artisans who had arrived two decades earlier bringing new skills and trades. The Germans were farmers, and unless they somehow managed to establish vineyards in Britain's inhospitable climate, there seemed little chance that they would transform British agriculture. Even the Board of Trade expected little from the migrants. Comparing them to the Walloons who had come to England in the time of Elizabeth, the board observed that the Germans "have neither stock nor manufacture, most of them women and children; a great many of them, through age and infirmities past their labour, others (not a small number) not come to it; some of them more fit for almshouses than work-houses."[14] Because the immigrants came as families, much of the board's description of the group's demographic characteristics rang true. As the immigrants soon discovered, when the British evaluated potential subjects or colonists, only working men had much value.

Women, children, and the elderly—people whose labor was overlooked or deemed negligible—did not seem worthy of British favors. Jonathan Swift summed up the economic arguments of those who opposed Whig policy: "The Maxim, That People are the Riches of a Nation, hath been very crudely understood by many Writers and Reasoners upon that Subject. . . . The true way of multiplying Mankind to publick Advantage in such a Country as England, is to invite from abroad only able Handicrafts-Men and Artificers, or such who bring over a sufficient Share of Property to secure them from Want."[15]

Initially most Londoners expressed sympathy for the Germans' plight. They gave generously to the charity drive. Many took an interest in the Germans' customs, and trips to the German camps on the city's outskirts became a popular pastime. The appearance of booklets such as *A Short and Easy Way for the Palatines to Learn English* demonstrated the willingness of at least some Britons to incorporate the Germans into their society.[16] But, as the summer wore on, public perception of the Germans began to change.

At first the British had seen the immigrants as Protestant victims of French aggression. Sharing a common religion and a common enemy created a bond between the two peoples. On closer inspection, however, the British began noting important differences between themselves and the German immigrants. The Germans' poverty was, of course, immediately apparent. Since it was the result of French tyranny, it might have been overlooked, but Londoners grew concerned about the squalor that the Germans' poverty seemed to create. Many Britons feared the refugees were spreading disease.

Soon an alternative image to the "poor Palatine refugees" emerged. John Floyer, a physician in Litchfield, wrote to Lady Dartmouth, who lived near Blackheath: "I wish you the recovery of your health, and a better neighborhood than the Palatines, which I fear have infected your pure air. Our country has whole loads of them and call them gipsies, not knowing the language and seeing their poor clothes."[17] To be identified with Gypsies was a worrisome portent for the Germans. Gypsies were often portrayed in Britain as parasitic intruders who invaded civilized societies while maintaining their own closed and mysterious communities. In 1711 Joseph Addison described them as "this race of Vermin . . . this idle profligate people . . . [who] infest all the Countries of Europe, and live in the Midst of Governments in a kind of Commonwealth by themselves."[18] In the eyes of most Europeans, Gypsies epitomized the other, the mysterious and potentially dangerous unknown.[19] They were not proper subjects of British charity, and they certainly had no claim to the rights and privileges of British citizens.

In the eyes of many Britons, other, less mysterious characteristics began to make the Germans suspect. By late June word had spread through London that many of the Germans were Catholics.[20] The picture of the Germans as refugees fleeing Catholic persecution no longer made sense. In addition, many of the Protestants also seemed unlikely victims of persecution. A visitor to the camp at Blackheath remarked with some surprise that many of the migrants came from territories "under Protestant princes; so religion, or persecution upon that account, was not in the case."[21]

Defoe rose to the Germans' defense by trying to downplay the number and significance of the Catholics. He admitted that "a few" Catholics were mixed in with the other Germans but argued that "they are far from being either Frenchizfi'd or Spanioliz'd Papists, for most of them having been Protestants, or the Children of Protestants, they still retain a Tincture of their Father's Religion, which they had not forsaken, but to avoid Persecution and Contempt, and to obey the Commands, and follow the Example of their Sovereign."[22] Nevertheless some Londoners began to suspect that the migrants might be more similar to the French and Catholic "them" than to the Protestant and charitable, but perhaps gullible, "us" who had allowed the migrants into Britain.

Not only did the Catholic migrants represent a potential threat to Britain's security, but they also tainted the reputation of the Protestants who associated with them. Protestant and Catholic migrants living in harmony, sometimes as husband and wife, did not speak in their favor. British liberties were Protestant liberties. If the German migrants could not maintain the distinctions between Protestant and Catholic worldviews, then it seemed unlikely that they could understand British liberty or ever successfully integrate into British society.

The bishop of Norwich, seeing the Germans as victims of French aggression, wrote that the Germans sought refuge in Britain "being induc'd thereto by the Excellency of our Constitution, and the Justice and Clemency of our Government."[23] In other words they sought the privileges of British subjects. But many British subjects were not sure the Germans deserved those privileges. *The Palatines Catechism or a True Description of Their Camps at Black Heath and Camberwell*, a pamphlet published in 1709, purported to record a conversation between an "English Tradesman and a High-Dutchman." In it the tradesman raised a number of objections to the presence of so many impoverished migrants. His German companion responded by reminding him of the Biblical account of the Gibeonites living "in the land of Canaan among the Israelites, without any disturbance or evil effects." The tradesman replied: "Yes; but then they were hewers of wood and drawers of water to the people and not equal in freedom, trade, liberty, and property as our strangers are like to be."[24]

Both the English tradesman and the bishop of Norwich, like most Britons, took pride in the privileges of British subjects and were wary of sharing them with undeserving strangers. By the beginning of August the people of London had visited the German camps and taken stock of the German migrants. The "poor Palatine refugees" had not lived up to their billing. Rather than being fit objects of charity, they had become, in the words of an anonymous pamphleteer, "a parcel of vagabonds, who might have lived comfortably enough in their native country, had not the laziness of their dispositions and the report of our well-known generosity drawn them out of it."[25] To some Britons, seeing the impoverished migrants suffering and dying in their vast encampments, the Germans seemed to have lost every vestige of civilized humanity. One observer noted that Londoners said of the Germans that "you hit them, but they do not feel it."[26] Far from being the stuff of Britons, the Germans were hardly human at all.

A piece of doggerel, published in 1709, summed up the public's growing contempt for the German migrants. The poem, entitled *Canary-Birds Naturaliz'd in Utopia*, described the problem of Palatine canaries living amid British robins:

> Well! quo' the lesser free-born Birds
> Through all Utopia's Flocks or Herds:
> "Let these good pious Palat'nates,
> And all such strange we know-not-whats,
> In their wise interloping Freak,
> Go to the Devil's Arse a-Peak;
> . . . .
> T'enhance the Mis'ries of poor Robin.
> Must we Canaries all bid welcome,
> That hither do from France or Hell come?
> If this Utopia's kind Intend is,
> Of those Intruders there no End is."[27]

Action eventually caught up with words. In the countryside a mob of peasants rose up against ten Germans, half of whom were children, who had been settled on an estate near Sundrich in Kent. Although the Germans came to no harm, the mob drove them away, threatening that "if they would not be gone by fair means they should by foul."[28] London's artisans and laborers, already smarting from increased competition from the Huguenots, feared that the Germans would add to their misery. In July, English workers had destroyed the looms of Huguenot weavers living in London.[29] Now they threatened to attack the German camps and to slit the throats of another group of foreign interlopers. The Germans began posting guards around their camps.[30] Anton Boehme, the Lutheran chaplain at St. James, later reported that one of the camps was actually attacked, although he blamed British hostility on the presence of Catholics among the migrants. He wrote that "there came more than 1800 English people, on a dark night, with scythes and other weapons to our camp, who desired to cut down all the Catholics. This, indeed, without doubt would have been accomplished had they not been with the Lutherans and Reformed."[31] Boehme's description comes from a tract he wrote in 1711 to discourage further German migration to London, and the size of the attack may have been exaggerated. But by mid-July the Germans clearly no longer enjoyed the sympathy of many Britons.

As British hostility grew, so too did the Germans' frustration with their plight. They tired of life in the camps and worried that the voyage to America would never materialize. Soon they were no longer the cheerful and thankful refugees Defoe had described. An event in late August revealed the Germans' growing testiness. According to the Tory Thomas Hearne, a group of forty German migrants passed an English tavern where "3 or four honest Englishmen" sat drinking "a Pot or two of Ale." The Englishmen saw the Germans walk by "and of course they made some Reflections upon the Receiving of these People into the Kingdom." Having overheard the remarks, the Germans pushed their way into the tavern and beat the men who had insulted them. According to Hearne's report, only the sudden arrival of the constable kept the Germans from cutting the men's throats. The constable managed to break up the attack and to calm the Germans, but to Hearne's obvious dismay, the Germans received no punishment for their behavior. Instead the justice of the peace released them "with a soft Reprimand, & the answer given for this Easy Penaltie was that being Forreigners they were ignorant of our English Laws, & 'twould be a peice of Barbarity to make them subject to it as yet."[32]

Hearne felt little sympathy for the badgered Germans. His account of the event painted the immigrants as inhumane, uncivilized, ignorant of British law, and obviously ill-suited to enjoy British liberties. He and many others were growing increasingly frustrated with those who would overlook the Germans' shortcomings and continue to force the migrants on the British people.

Most Germans probably realized it would do them little good to antagonize their British hosts, including the people who threatened their camps. The immigrants attempted to address the concerns of England's artisans and laborers by drawing up a new petition, this time directed specifically to "the Tradesman of England."[33] The petition paralleled other statements the Germans had made concerning why they had left their homes and come to Britain, a place they praised as a "Blessed Land!, Govern'd by the Mother of Europe, and the best of Queens." But they had little to offer the English tradesman in return for sharing their blessed land. The Germans could only beg that England's workers "lay aside all Reflections and Imprecations, and Ill Language against us, for that is contradictory to a Christian Spirit, and we do assure you, it shall be our Endeavor to act with great Humility and Gratitude, and to Render our prayers for you." But the British had their own prayer, as expressed by the English tradesman visiting the German camps: "We'll pray for them, but wish 'em out o' the Land."[34]

In the eyes of many Britons, the immigrants had changed from "poor Protestant refugees" deserving sympathy to "a parcel of vagabonds" deserving nothing. Despite the German immigrants' appeals to British prejudices against the French and the Catholics, the immigrants had failed to convince their hosts that the similarities between Briton and Palatine outweighed the differences.

The German-speaking immigrants may have failed to become British, but the migration experience did not leave them unchanged. In the early eighteenth century the people of the German southwest had many allegiances and many identities. Some were local and based on ties to one's kin group or village of origin or to the dialect one spoke. Some were broader and included ties to one's principality or religion. Although they sometimes called themselves *Teutschen*, or Germans, this shared cultural identity remained amorphous. It had no corresponding political identity. Despite a common written language, their sense of sameness remained weak. The differences were brought home for many peasants when they sought manumission in order to leave the German southwest. Every German territory had different rules regarding manumission and different fees that had to be paid. A peasant's identity as a Hessian or Nassauer, a Palatine or Hanauer became clear when he or she took this fundamental first step toward greater freedom. Coming from dozens of different territories with different dialects, religious practices, political structures, and all the other variations that exist among small-scale societies, the German emigrants of 1709 would have been much more aware of their differences than their similarities.

Migration forced them to reconsider who they were. People construct identities out of their interactions with others, and migration and the fight for survival forced the many German-speaking emigrants of 1709 to define themselves as one people. The British showed little interest in uncovering the emigrants' varied origins; the Britons just lumped them all together as "poor Palatines." Now the Germans began to do the same. They, too, began calling themselves Palatines and creating for themselves a common history. In front of their British audience they no longer maintained the distinction between Hessian and Hanauer, Nassauer and Württemberger. Instead they were poor, distressed victims of the French. Of course much of what the migrants did with these labels and concocted histories was intended to elicit sympathetic treatment from the British. But when people create for themselves a shared past, whether that past is real or fabricated, they enhance their sense of a common identity.[35] Gradually the German immigrants began to adopt that new identity—an identity that would one day become as meaningful as the identities based on religion, language, and birthplace that they had brought with them to London.

Resettling the German Migrants

It was, however, British definitions of the Germans that shaped the migrants' immediate future. Whatever the Germans might be, they were too poor, too unskilled, too Catholic, and too unenlightened to be British subjects. Settling them in Great Britain had become untenable. By July the government had begun changing its policy concerning the immigrants. Instead of distributing them throughout the parishes of England, it sought to place them on the British periphery. On July 20 the Commission for the Palatines reported its resolution to settle the Germans "in North-Britain, Ireland and the Plantations."[36] Three resettlement plans were already under consideration: two by the commission to settle the

Germans in Ireland and North Carolina and one by the Board of Trade to send them to Jamaica.

When assessing the German immigrants, the English had been alarmed by the many who were Catholics. But Irish politicians, led by Thomas Wharton, the Whig lord lieutenant of Ireland, saw the migrants in a different light. Focusing on the Protestants rather than the Catholics, they saw thousands of potential subjects who could be useful for "strengthening and securing the Protestant Interest in Ireland."[37] On July 7, Ireland's Privy Council requested "as many of the poor German Protestants . . . to be sent into this Kingdom, of whose Sincerity and Steadiness in professing the Protestant Religion there can be noe doubt by reason of the Sufferings they have undergone for the same."[38] The commission quickly approved the plan and agreed to send five hundred families.

In late July Tribbeko and Ruperti visited the German camps, seeking willing settlers who were "entirely Protestants, as nearly related as possible" and skilled in linen making or husbandry.[39] On July 30 the pastors reported that 350 families at Blackheath and 200 at Camberwell were "wel disposed to goe for Ireland."[40] The Germans were divided into groups of 100 to 150 people, and on August 8 the first group set off for Chester. Near Chester, they boarded ships and sailed for Dublin.[41] The ships reached Ireland between September 4 and 7 and carried 2,971 Germans in 794 families. Another 100 Germans arrived on October 14.[42]

The British government agreed to pay a small subsidy to the Germans until they were established in Ireland. Some of the Germans remained in Dublin, where the men were employed building a government arsenal. The remainder were divided into groups and were distributed to forty-three landlords. The Germans seemed attractive tenants. They were Protestants and, because of the subsidy they received, less dependent than their Irish Catholic counterparts. Some of the Germans were settled on manors in Limerick, where a distinct German community existed for many years, but the rest did not remain in Ireland for long. They had not left their homes to become Irish serfs instead of German serfs. Within a year almost a thousand had found passage back to London, and by November 1711 only 1,200 of the more than three thousand Germans who had landed in Ireland remained.[43]

While the commissioners arranged to send a quarter of the migrants to Ireland, they also considered a plan to settle six hundred Germans in North Carolina. In mid-July the Carolina proprietors had proposed giving the migrants "an hundred Acres of Land A Head, for Men, Women and Children, for ten Years gratis, and from thence forwards to pay a Penny an Acre, as the other Inhabitants of the Province."[44] At the same time two Swiss speculators, Franz Louis Michel and Christoph von Graffenried, were in London trying to arrange land deals with various colonial agents. They were working in part to find a home for some Mennonites recently expelled from Bern, but the two men also hoped to find silver in America and had a small number of miners ready to follow their call. The Swiss plan eventually merged with the proprietors' plan. In August and September Graffenried concluded several agreements with the Carolina proprietors whereby he purchased 5,000 acres of land between the Neuse and Cape Fear rivers in North Carolina and received an additional 10,000 acres to settle the Swiss and the Germans. Graffenried was designated the settlement's landgrave. Michel bought 2,500 acres but did not join the Swiss and German settlers.[45]

In October the Commission for the Palatines approved Graffenried's plan to settle the Germans at New Bern and allowed him to choose six hundred Germans for the new settlement.[46] When the proprietors' initial proposal had been publicized, many Germans thought their dream of free land in America was about to come true. They immediately petitioned the Crown to be transported to Carolina.[47] Although Graffenried's plan was slightly less generous than the proprietors', offering 250 acres to each family instead of 100 acres per person, it was still very attractive, and Graffenried could choose settlers from a large number of volunteers. Graffenried chose those Germans he thought would best ensure the settlement's success. "I selected to that object," he later wrote, "young people, healthy and laborious, and of all kind of avocation and handicraft."[48]

Those chosen may have considered themselves lucky, but Graffenried's New Bern settlement was a fiasco. The Germans departed for North Carolina in January 1710. The voyage proved disastrous. During the crossing, the severely overcrowded ships were blown off course and took thirteen weeks to reach America. Over half the passengers died in the squalid conditions aboard the ships. Another sixty died during warfare with the Tuscarora Indians in 1711. In 1713 Graffenried left the colony, and after a series of land disputes the remaining Germans lost title to their property. The Germans worked to secure new land, but it was not until 1748 that the remnant of the original German community finally received grants on North Carolina's western frontier.[49]

Along with the Irish and Carolina proposals, the Commission for the Palatines considered a plan from a group of merchants who wanted to settle two hundred German families in Jamaica. Eventually the commission referred the plan to the Board of Trade, which in 1708 had considered a similar plan for the fifty Germans in Kocherthal's immigrant group. The plan had been rejected then because the board considered Jamaica's climate too hot for the Germans.[50] In 1709, with several thousand Germans encamped around London, the Board of Trade was prepared to overlook questions of climate. On August 30 the board submitted a plan to the Treasury to send one thousand Germans to Jamaica, where they would receive up to six acres each. Their presence would increase the productivity of the island and would make it more secure from foreign attack. The board also said that Jamaica's planters would "not only receive these Palatines and give them land, but help them to settle it, as 'tis their interest so to do, they being sensible how much they want numbers of white people in that place."[51]

Although the board was optimistic about the plan, the Jamaican proposal was expensive and complex. Even as it considered ways to implement the Jamaican plan, the board gradually shifted its attention to a proposal to settle the Germans in New York. Eventually the Jamaican plan seems to have been abandoned along with other plans to settle the Germans in the Scilly Islands or in the Caribbean at either Barbados or Saint Christopher's.[52]

The government's most efficient and least costly resettlement plan took effect in September. Since the British deemed the Catholics the least desirable of the migrants, they had made little effort to find a place for them. The only group that had actively recruited Catholics was the British army, which was willing to send Catholic men to kill other Catholics as part of Britain's war effort in Portugal.[53] Otherwise the government had no use for them. Now it offered the Catholics the choice of converting to Protestantism or being sent home. A few did convert, but, despite Defoe's claims that most of the Catholics had adopted their religion for political reasons, almost 2,200 Catholics refused to convert and were shipped back across the Channel in mid-September.[54]

The thousands of returning Catholics accomplished what government decrees had failed to do: they stopped the flow of German emigrants. Not only did they spread the word that Catholics had no place in Britain, but they also spoke with authority about conditions in London. Prospective migrants might ignore government decrees, but they could not ignore the stories of their returning neighbors. By forcing the Catholics to leave, the government profoundly changed the makeup of the German immigrant community, not just in 1709 but for the next hundred years.

The immediate effect was the creation among the immigrants in London of a common Protestant identity that had not been part of their German past. The long-term effect was that German migration to colonial America would remain a Protestant movement. Britain and its empire would not be a place of refuge for German Catholics, and they would not seek out North America until the nineteenth century.

Only one more large group of Germans made it to England in 1709. When the Catholics arrived back in Rotterdam, some fifteen hundred Protestant German migrants still remained camped around the city. These Germans knew that they had been duped by the propaganda circulating in the German southwest, but they still had not lost hope of reaching America. The return of thousands of Catholics offered an opening. As one of them later wrote, "The return journey of these Catholics . . . opened up to us travelers, who had been laid up in Rotterdam for five weeks, the passage to England."[55] In September the Protestants remaining in Rotterdam sent a petition to Secretary of State Boyle. The Germans admitted they had been "very much Deceived" about Queen Anne's desire for settlers and about promises of free land in America, but "to go back again to our Country, It is Impossible, for we shall not be accepted." They found themselves "in a Most deplorable Condition Being most dismally deceived by others, . . . and are Like to Perish (wth our wives & Children) wth Hunger." [56]

Dayrolle interceded on behalf of the fifteen hundred Protestants. He reported that they were camped on a causeway outside Rotterdam, living in huts made of straw and reeds. They did not have enough money to return home and feared that the rulers of the principalities they had left would not allow them back anyway. The people of Rotterdam wanted them out, and Dayrolle suspected that the Dutch would soon put the Germans on boats to England just to get rid of them. He asked Sunderland to allow the Germans to cross the Channel.[57]

Sunderland refused the request, but by the time his message reached Dayrolle the Germans had already departed for London. A Dutch merchant had arranged their transport, probably with Dayrolle's tacit support. In late October the last large group of German migrants—around 1,100 people—arrived in London.[58] Unlike the earlier arrivals, they were welcomed neither by the public nor by Whig officials. Sunderland realized the practical and political problems that the huge numbers of Germans were causing. In his futile message to Dayrolle to prevent the last group from departing Rotterdam, Sunderland noted "the great Clamour that such numbers do raise at this time of scarcity, and the great Load and Expense it is on the government."[59]

In the six months since the arrival of the first German immigrants, Sunderland's attitude toward them had changed completely. Rather than seeing them as industrious workers likely to add to the wealth of the kingdom, he now described them as "Vagrant destitute people" and was determined to allow no more of them into the country. When another 150 Germans slipped into London in November and December, he had them sent back immediately.[60]

The British government never considered settling the October arrivals in Britain. The government had rid itself of the Catholic migrants and had arranged to send many of the remaining Germans to Ireland and North Carolina. Now the Board of Trade began work on one final plan—a proposal to send the Germans to New York to make tar and pitch.

The possibility of a New York settlement was a logical one. The Germans who had arrived in London in 1708 had all been settled in New York, and many of the German migrants arriving in 1709 clearly considered New York a probable destination.[61] On August 30 the Board of Trade presented a proposal to the Treasury suggesting that the Germans be given land on the Hudson River and that the government pay their subsistence for one year.[62]

The plan revealed a curious mixture of attitudes toward the Germans. On the one hand the board took a realistic view of the Germans' skills. It knew the Germans were farmers, and it proposed supplying them with the necessary tools for that vocation. It even suggested that some Germans might be settled farther south, in Virginia, to plant vineyards. The board believed the Germans would increase Britain's riches by turning some of New York's wastelands into farms, and it proposed rewarding the Germans for their productivity by making them "denizens of this kingdom, that they may enjoy all the privileges and advantages as are enjoyed by the present inhabitants of New York."[63]

The Board of Trade also saw the Germans fulfilling roles that might not be appropriate for British settlers. If the Germans settled on the frontier, they would make a convenient barrier between "H.M. subjects and the French and their Indians." Although the Germans would become British subjects through denization, they would be lesser subjects, expendable in case of attack. Further, the board suggested the Germans might increase the colony's security "by intermarrying with the neighbouring Indians, (as the French do)."[64] Thus the board encouraged the

Germans in behavior befitting Britain's uncivilized enemies but far less acceptable for British subjects. The Germans could serve a useful purpose for Britain, but not as proper Britons.

On September 9, 1709, Robert Hunter, a Scottish officer who, until 1707, had served as Marlborough's aide-de-camp on the Continent and thus had some familiarity with the situation in the German principalities, was appointed governor of New York. He replaced Robert Lovelace, who had died after only five months in office. Building on the Board of Trade's proposals but working independently of the board, Hunter also made plans to settle the Germans in New York. In mid-October he proposed to Lord Somers, lord president of the queen's privy council, that the convoy escorting him to New York carry three thousand Germans.[65] By November Hunter's plan was so far advanced that Sunderland wrote a letter to the Council of New York warning it that three thousand Germans would soon set sail for the colony.[66] On November 30 and December 1 Hunter presented the Board of Trade with his plans.

Hunter's proposal differed considerably from the one the board had first put forth in late August. The primary purpose of the German settlement would no longer be husbandry but instead the production of naval stores, primarily tar and pitch. Sweden had long monopolized the trade in naval stores, and the British government wanted to secure another source for these products, which were essential to Britain's navy and, hence, to the maintenance of its growing empire. Watertight ships could not be built without pitch to caulk the hulls, and tar kept a ship's ropes from rotting on the open seas. New York and New England were thought to have pine trees suitable for pitch and tar production. Although samples of tar and pitch sent from New England to London generally did not meet the standards of the British Navy, which found the tar "of too hot a temper," in the late 1690s several colonial speculators, including Richard Coote, earl of Bellomont and governor of New York and Massachusetts, actively promoted naval stores production in America. As a result the Board of Trade had begun considering measures to encourage the export of tar and pitch from New England and New York. After the price of tar doubled during the last decade of the seventeenth century, Parliament in 1705 passed "An Act for encouraging the Importation of Naval Stores from America."[67] National security and mercantilist concerns lay behind the act, which had the threefold purpose of easing the English navy's reliance on Swedish naval stores, of increasing English shipping, and of keeping English bullion in the country by trading English woolens for American tar.

Hunter expected that the Germans could contribute to the enterprise by working in the forests at the edge of British and Dutch settlement in New York. At the same time, they would help protect the colony by forming a human barrier between the French and the British. Therefore Hunter requested six hundred guns to arm the Germans along with the six hundred tents he needed to house them. Finally Hunter suggested that the board consider how much land should be granted to the settlers and "whether it be not advisable that they be servants to the Crown for a certain Term, or at least 'till they have repaid the Expences the Crown is at in setting them to work, and subsisting them whilst they can not subsist themselves."[68]

The board quickly considered Hunter's suggestions and by December 5 had incorporated almost all of them in a proposal to be presented to the queen. The board proposed that the Germans be settled along New York's frontier, on either the Mohawk River or the Hudson River. There they would serve as a defensive barrier against the French and their Indian allies, but the Germans' main task would be to produce pitch and tar. The board estimated that the Germans soon could make enough of these products to supply the British navy and that there might even be a surplus to trade with Spain or Portugal. Despite the board's optimistic estimates of what the Germans could produce, it admitted that "As these Palatines are ignorant in the production of those stores, it will be necessary that three or four persons well skilled in the doing thereof (if to be had) be sent from hence, to instruct the said Palatines." Eventually the Germans would be allowed to return to farming. The money from the sales of the naval stores would be used to pay off the costs of the Germans' settlement and early subsistence in New York. After the debt was paid, each person would be granted forty acres of land.[69]

Compared with its August proposal, the board's new proposal had little to offer the Germans. The Germans had traveled to London with expectations that they would receive free land in America where they could establish their own farms. The first proposal offered them that opportunity. The second proposal ignored both their wishes and their skills. The Germans would have to work for years at a job for which they were ill-suited before they received the farmland of which they dreamed. The plan did little to ensure a contented and efficient workforce. It did, however, remove three thousand Germans from London. On January 7, 1710, the queen gave the plan her blessing.

Blinded by the potential wealth the plan offered and unsympathetic to the Germans' desires, the government began to implement the scheme. Even before the queen had given the project her approval, the board had chartered ships to carry the Germans to America, and shortly after Christmas the immigrants were moved from the warehouses to the ships.[70] Only one more detail had to be worked out. Realizing the Germans had little to gain from the project, Hunter wanted a contract drawn up that would specify the obligations the Germans would undertake in exchange for their subsistence and transportation to New York.

The board drafted the contract, had it approved by the attorney general, and submitted the draft to Sunderland on December 23.[71] The contract insisted that the migrants were all Palatines, referring to them as "Persons Natives of the Lower Palatinate of the Rhine." Thus, the "Palatine" part of their identity remained intact even if the "Protestant" and "refugee" part of the label had been called into question. Although the contract refers to the "undersigned" Palatines, no document survives actually signed by the Germans. The Germans later remembered only that the contract was read to them. In fact they apparently did not hear its terms until early April 1710, while they sat in ships anchored outside Plymouth, waiting for their long-delayed voyage to begin.[72] After four months on crowded ships inching along England's southern coast, the Germans had no intention of allowing the contract's terms to keep them from America. Hunter thought the contract ensured that the Germans understood and accepted their obligations. The Germans, who later remembered the contract's terms quite differently than Hunter did, saw the document as the last hurdle before their voyage to New York.

Bad weather and poor planning delayed the Germans' departure from winter into spring. As their convoy waited off the southern coast of England, another small convoy passed it in early April, going in the opposite direction. On board were four "Indian kings," supposedly representing the five Iroquois nations of New York. They were sailing to London with colonial officials to lobby Parliament for an invasion of Canada. Although there is no record of the Indians' reaction to the shiploads of German-speaking migrants, the Germans would later remember the encounter, albeit in a much altered form and setting, as one that induced great sympathy from the Indians for the Germans' plight. At the time, however, the Germans had more important matters on their mind, and the chance encounter went almost unnoticed.[73]

Finally, in mid-April 1710, almost a year after the first migrants had arrived in London, the convoy bearing the three thousand Germans and

Governor Hunter left England.[74] With its departure, the British government had finally dealt with most of the German immigrants. A group that had been touted as a potential source of wealth for Great Britain had now been safely resettled on Britain's periphery, where, for various reasons, its members remained appealing additions to society. Ireland welcomed them as Protestants, and Jamaica had wanted them as whites. Only Hunter still primarily valued them as the grateful and hardworking people that Defoe had described.

The British government's problems with the Germans, however, were not entirely over. The camps in Camberwell and Blackheath had been closed with the coming of winter, and the Germans who had not been transported elsewhere crowded back into warehouses in Deptford and Southwark. Eventually most of them gave up hope of ever seeing America and asked the government to help them return home. Hundreds of disgruntled Germans also returned to London from Ireland during 1710. They crowded into warehouses in Southwark bereft of government support and close to starvation. A memorial written in December 1710 stated that "great numbers of poor [German] women and children are now wandering and begging in the streets of London and Westminster to the great annoyance of the Inhabitants."[75] In January a concerned observer noted that "the Constable beates them [the Germans] away from begging at folks Doors, So that their famine, I wish don't bring Sickness, for they are ready to sink."[76] Twice in 1710 and once in early 1711 the British sent convoys carrying a total of over two thousand Germans back to Rotterdam.[77]

A few hundred Germans remained in England, a pitiful reminder of the mass immigration of 1709. An English diarist writing in 1712 noted, "In my return [from Kensington to London] I saw a number of the Palatines, the most poor ragged creatures that I ever saw, and great objects of charity if real exiles for religion." Three years after the Germans had first arrived and two years after most had left, Britons were still puzzling over the migrants' true identity and their proper treatment.[78]

Soon after the convoy of Germans left for New York, the British government took measures to ensure that another wave of immigrants would not wash up on Britain's shore. By late 1710 the Whigs, who had initially supported the German immigrants, were out of office. Many people blamed the Naturalization Act for encouraging the Germans to come to Britain. Although few, if any, of the German migrants took advantage of the act, Parliament repealed it in 1711.[79] Hunter left for New

York confident that the naval stores project would enrich the nation, but the new Tory government took no interest in the plan. Britain's rulers, unlike their Prussian and Austrian counterparts, would never again contemplate a government plan to settle its empire with willing emigrants from the German southwest.

A Final Reckoning

The German pastors in London, who perhaps came closest to understanding who the 1709 emigrants were and what they wanted, also questioned the migrants' identity and motives. Anton Boehme, the Lutheran chaplain at St. James, had returned to London from Germany by October 1709. Reflecting his Pietist biases, Boehme worried that the migrants seemed more concerned with material betterment than with their spiritual well-being. In a letter written soon after his return, Boehme lamented that "the poor people are not willing to recognize that this is a time of divine judgment which must be removed not with outward flight but with the eradication of inner sinfulness."[80] In 1711 he published *Das verlangte, nicht erlangte Canaan* (*The Longed for, but Unattained Canaan*), a book that painted a grim picture of the 1709 migration. In Boehme's view, the 1709 emigrants, whether they longed for material success or for spiritual fulfillment, would not find either across the Atlantic. America was not the promised land. The 1709 emigrants had sought God's kingdom in America when they should have been seeking it within themselves.[81]

John Tribbeko, who had helped care for the Germans throughout their stay in London, also understood the German migrants and their aspirations. In a final sermon that he preached to the Germans before they embarked for New York, he compared their flight from home to the Israelites' exodus from Egypt. Tribbeko said that whereas the Israelites' exodus had been commanded by God, the Germans had begun their flight "with vain hopes of obtaining great things, extensive lands, rich property. . . . Some were indeed forced to emigrate, from their extreme necessities but others, from needless . . . sinful curiousity." Tribbeko then reminded the Germans of the charity of Queen Anne and many of her subjects. He hoped the migrants would remember these kindnesses, but he was not sure they would. "No injustice would be done," Tribbeko concluded, "if, like Moses, I were to call you an obstinate, and stiff-necked people, who walk after the thoughts of your hearts, and will not learn the ways of God, even when He has chastened you sore."[82]

If Robert Hunter had been sitting in the congregation, he might have had second thoughts about his new settlers. Instead he set sail for America with an optimism untempered by Tribbeko's judgment of the three thousand Germans who accompanied him.

CHAPTER 4

"A Deplorable Sickly Condition"

NEW YORK CITY, 1710

On June 13, 1710, after a two-month voyage, the *Lyon of Leith* with 330 Germans on board arrived in New York. During the next two weeks, seven of the nine other ships carrying Germans arrived. The *Medford*, separated from the convoy by bad weather, arrived in July, and the *Berkeley Castle*, which ran aground soon after leaving England, did not reach New York until August.[1] The passage had been typical of eighteenth-century transatlantic crossings—a two- to three-month voyage marked by delay, disease, and death. Thomas Benson, a doctor serving on the *Lyon of Leith*, reported that all 330 of its passengers were sick at one time or another on the voyage.[2]

Before Governor Hunter and the Germans set sail, Sunderland had instructed the New York colonial council to prepare for the immigrants. In late April the council began securing supplies to feed the Germans, and by early May it was restricting the export of foodstuffs that would be needed for the immigrants.[3] The influx of three thousand new settlers threatened to overwhelm New York City, a town of fewer than six thousand inhabitants. The townspeople feared that the new arrivals might "have many Contagious distempers among them" that would endanger the health of the city's residents and hurt trade "by detering the Country People and Others from Resorting & Coming hither as usual."[4] The council was sympathetic to these medical and commercial concerns and decided to settle the Germans on Nutten Island, where they could be safely quarantined. The council assigned three doctors to check the immigrants' health and two carpenters to build shelters for the new arrivals.[5] The two carpenters faced a daunting task building temporary homes for almost three thousand people, and many of the Germans must have spent their time on Nutten Island in the army tents that had been brought with the convoy. Their initial settlement in New York would have appeared very similar to the one they left behind at Blackheath.

The city of New York might have looked familiar, too. With its Dutch-style architecture, it must have reminded the Germans of the small towns they passed on the upper Rhine during the initial leg of their journey. Unfortunately, their life on Nutten Island may also have reminded them of their miserable existence on the dikes outside Rotterdam. Shortly after they reached New York, Hunter reported that the people were "in a deplorable sickly condition." A third of them required medical care.[6] The Germans had been living in close quarters since they boarded their ships in late December—a period of almost six months. They had suffered terribly on board the ships and did not recover quickly during the New York summer, described by one emigrant as "excessive hot."[7] A carpenter submitted a bill to the government for 250 caskets he built over the next few months for the Germans.[8] Only at summer's end did the death rate begin to fall.

The exact number of immigrants who died on the voyage or during their first months in New York is difficult to determine. The naval stores plan called for the British government to send six hundred families, or upwards of three thousand people, to New York. The Board of Trade had chartered enough ships to carry 3,300, but Governor Hunter later reported that only 2,814 Germans departed for New York.[9] If Hunter's statement is roughly accurate, at least two hundred and perhaps as many as five hundred people perished from late December, when the Germans boarded ships near London, until mid-April, when the ships finally set off across the Atlantic. James du Pré, the commissary of stores for the Germans, estimated that around 2,400 arrived in New York. Hunter corroborated du Pré's estimate, reporting that around 470 people died on the voyage or during the first month in New York.[10] When drawing up a budget for the naval stores project after he arrived in New York, Hunter estimated he would be supporting 2,300 immigrants.[11] Du Pré reported 2,227 immigrants receiving support in late 1710. If du Pré re-

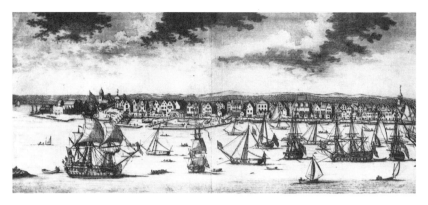

Figure 6. A view of New York City, 1717, by William Burgis. Detail showing southeastern portion of the city (negative no. 43057). © Collection of The New-York Historical Society.

ported correctly and if at least 3,000 Germans boarded ships in London in December 1709, then one-quarter of their number had died in just less than a year.[12]

The loss of life had a profound impact on the Germans. When the emigrants set sail from Rotterdam for London in 1709 each family averaged 4.7 people. By mid-1711 family size averaged only 3.6 people.[13] The emigration had been particularly deadly for children; the Germans remembered a decade later "the loss of most of their young children at their going from home to America."[14] Children who did survive often found themselves orphans. Hunter had no desire to support people who would not contribute to the naval stores project. He expected men to be the chief laborers in the project, and orphans and widows who had no familial ties to the men making pitch and tar risked losing government support. Du Pré lumped orphans and widows together with "other useless people" who could be "left at their own disposal" when the rest of the Germans moved to the naval stores camps.[15] The colonial authorities wanted to support as few of the "useless people" as possible. Therefore, on June 20, the colonial council decided to take proposals "for Placing out the Orphans and other Children whose Parents have a numerous family."[16]

A list of the children apprenticed by Governor Hunter shows that at least seventy children were apprenticed from August 1710 through June 1711, by which time most of the Germans had moved from New York City to the naval stores camps.[17] The children were young. The average age was just under eleven, and the list included orphans as young as three and four. Over half of the children were apprenticed to people living in New York City. Most of the rest went to people in the surrounding areas of northern New Jersey and Long Island, but Paul Schmidt, age twelve, and Jacob Berliman, age eleven, were bound to a master in Rhode Island. The apprenticed children, cut off from relatives and friends, had to make the difficult adjustment to life in America with little support from the German-speaking community in which they had grown up.

Of the seventy apprenticed children, forty-one were orphans. Nineteen others were children of widows, who were more likely to have their children apprenticed than widowed men. Hanah Zenger, whose husband died on the voyage to New York, lost her only surviving child, who was apprenticed to the New York printer William Bradford. Although John Peter Zenger would eventually become a successful printer (and the defendant in a famous libel suit affecting freedom of the press), parents had no guarantees of their children's futures and mourned their loss. Love explains the parents' reaction, but adults also realized the importance of children's labor in the family-based farm economy. Years later the Germans remembered how Governor Hunter "without and against their Consent [took] many children from them, and bound them to severall of the Inhabitants of that province till they should arrive to the age of 21 years . . . by which means they were depriv'd of the Comfort of the Childrens' Company and education as well as the assistance and Support they might in a small time have reasonably expected from them."[18]

The issue of apprenticing orphans and other children was one of the first to divide Hunter and the Germans. Among the migrants, it created strong feelings of distrust of Hunter's motives and exposed important differences between Hunter's view of the Germans' role in the New World and the view the Germans held of themselves. Such differences would plague relations between the governor and the immigrants over the next decade. Hunter always viewed the Germans as part of a commercial venture. He seemed sympathetic to the Germans' plight as an impoverished people fleeing their homes and like others initially referred to them as the "poor Palatines," but their value lay chiefly in the labor they contributed to the naval stores project. By binding orphans and other children as apprentices, Hunter reduced the cost of the project. He realized he could not bind children indiscriminately; the German community might refuse to work if all its children were taken away. But Hunter apparently believed that orphans and children of widows—children with no direct ties to the men who would labor in the naval stores project—could be apprenticed with little adverse effect on the venture's success.

The new immigrants, on the other hand, had come to America for farmland. They saw the naval stores scheme as a means to that end. Making pitch and tar might help pay the costs of transportation, but the Germans planned to devote as little time to the project as possible. They wanted to be farmers, and successful farms depended on the cooperative labor of members of a nuclear family. They valued their children in part for their "assistance and Support." With so many children already lost on the voyage, the Germans were distressed when Hunter took away even more.

The death of a spouse also threatened the emotional and economic stability of immigrant families. Because women were not expected to make naval stores, Governor Hunter hoped to keep widows off the support rolls just as he had orphans. Therefore, widowed women risked hunger and isolation if they did not remarry. At the same time, men depended on women to care for the children and to till the small plots each family received in the naval stores camps. So men and women remarried quickly. Of the fifty marriages recorded in 1710 and 1711 in the surviving German church records, thirty-nine involved people who had been widowed during the migration or shortly after arriving in New York.[19] Seven of the remaining eleven marriages involved previously unmarried women whose fathers had died. Thus 92 percent of the marriages represented attempts to reestablish nuclear family households headed by husband and wife. In this difficult period of adjustment, the Germans used marriage not so much to create new households as to ensure that all the immigrants had the protection provided by the nuclear family.[20]

Remarriage affected the community in another important way by breaking down regional and religious differences among the emigrants. Those who were married before emigrating had generally married someone from their own village or a village nearby. Once they were in New York, widows and widowers often married people from different German territories—people who did not necessarily share the same customs or speak the same dialect. Of the twenty-three marriages recorded in 1710 in which the origin of both bride and groom can be determined, only six were between people from the same village or from villages within twenty kilometers of each other. Often the bride and groom came from different principalities. The English rarely distinguished between the various territorial backgrounds of the emigrants—they were all

"Palatines." By 1712 these regional distinctions began to break down within the German-speaking community itself.

Before the German-speaking immigrants could define themselves as Germans rather than as Palatines, Hessians, Swiss, or Nassauers, a transformation had to take place. Some changes began in London, where the diverse group of emigrants felt compelled to speak with one voice to improve their chances of sailing to America. British policy also forced some changes to the emigrant group's identity. When the Catholic emigrants were forced home, the remaining emigrants found themselves sharing a common Protestantism that had not been part of their German past.

The transformation continued gradually in New York. When the German-speaking immigrants arrived in New York in 1710, they did not forget their dialects, local customs, or the names of the principalities where they had once lived. Kocherthal carefully noted in the Lutheran church records the villages and territories where church members had resided before emigrating. As late as 1749, Anna Maria Müller, one of the 1710 immigrants, remained interested enough in the affairs of her principality's ruling family that she devoted a few lines to the topic in her first letter home in four decades.[21] Place of origin remained part of each immigrant's identity, but, as the settlers remarried, questions of dialect and territorial origin were far less important than the survival of the family. Over the next decade changes imposed by the British colonial authorities or exacted by the American environment gradually reshaped the identity of the German immigrants. It was not just the nature of the German southwest but also the immigrants' reaction to the challenges they faced in America that eventually blurred their territorial identities and helped clear the way for the development of a German-American identity based on language and religion.

The Immigrants' Stay in New York City

The Germans remained in New York City until late September, waiting for Hunter to purchase land for the naval stores. During the three and a half months they lived in New York City, they began to piece together a new community. They accomplished this in part by creating new families through remarriage. Governor Hunter and the colonial council also dictated part of the process. They arranged for the Germans to be fed and established courts to govern them. Initially the immigrants were grouped together according to the ships they arrived on. One German-speaking member of each ship, the listmaster, headed each group and divided provisions among the other immigrants on his ship.[22] After the Germans left their ships, the listmasters continued to facilitate the distribution of supplies and also emerged as the chief intermediaries between the German immigrants and the colonial authorities.

Most of the Germans apparently lived on Nutten Island before being transferred to the naval stores camps, but they were allowed to travel in the surrounding region. Their pastors held church services for them in New York's city hall. Johann Friedrich Haeger, the Reformed minister, reported six hundred people attending his services.[23] Those who were not too ill sometimes looked for work. Hunter hired two Germans to be his gardeners. Several found work in the surrounding countryside, and some earned enough to purchase cattle, which they later brought with them to the naval stores camps. A few even took on permanent positions as farm laborers or perhaps tenant farmers and did not join the others when they moved to the camps.[24] But many of the men had no interest in working as laborers on somebody else's farm. They had come to America for farms of their own. Hunter had to use force to get a contingent of men to go to Lewis Morris's nearby manor to chop wood, even though the men were paid.[25]

The first few months in New York saw the German-speaking emigrants organizing themselves into their old denominational groups. Although the British government had forced most of the Catholics to return to the Continent, members of the Reformed and Lutheran churches continued to live side by side just as they had in many parts of the German southwest. The two ministers who had accompanied the migration served the two denominations. The Reformed minister, Haeger, arrived in New York with the backing of the Society for the Propagation of the Gospel, which paid his salary and in return expected him to introduce the Germans to the Book of Common Prayer and, if possible, to bring them into the Church of England.[26] Joshua Kocherthal, who had returned to London in late 1709 and then sailed back to New York with the convoy of German migrants in 1710, ministered to the Lutherans.

Despite his training in the Reformed Church, Haeger seemed willing to support the aims of his Anglican backers in the SPG. When he reached New York, he hoped to unite all the Germans—both Reformed and Lutheran—in a single religious community that would use the Book of Common Prayer and follow the rites of the Church of England. Unfortunately for Haeger, his was not among the first ships to arrive in New

York's harbor. By the time Haeger came ashore, Justus Falckner, the Lutheran pastor serving the Dutch congregation in New York, had already held Lutheran services for the earlier arrivals. In the services Falckner had encouraged the Lutherans to remain true to their denomination.[27] When Kocherthal arrived, he echoed Falckner's sentiments, and Haeger's plans were frustrated. He was limited to introducing only his Reformed congregation to the Book of Common Prayer.

Although Haeger wanted to please his benefactors, his querulous congregation saw no reason why it had to adopt an Anglican liturgy. The members asked why they had to conform to the Church of England when the Lutherans did not.[28] The situation was made more difficult because many of the translated prayer books provided by the SPG had been destroyed on the voyage. Without them Haeger's congregation could not join together in the congregational responses that were part of the familiar rhythm of the liturgy. Haeger pleaded for more prayer books so that his congregation could "answer according to custom."[29] The words of the service may have been changed, but the congregation wanted the form unaltered.

By October Haeger was able to write, "In our congregational prayers I have caused my people to conform to such an extent, that they themselves take great pleasure in them and desire nothing more ardently but to obtain such books (of prayer) in some manner."[30] He also reported that his congregation was growing. He had instructed fifty-two new members, using the Anglican catechism. Among the fifty-two were thirteen Catholics, evidence that some of the Catholics had evaded the orders given earlier in London to convert to Protestantism or return home.

Kocherthal also claimed that his congregation of Lutherans was adopting the liturgical forms of the Church of England. Ever the opportunist, Kocherthal hoped in this way to convince the SPG to supplement his salary. He did not offer to tamper with Lutheran theology, but he wrote that he was having some success, despite strong opposition, in changing church ceremonies to resemble more closely those of the Church of England. For instance, he said he had convinced his parishioners to take Communion on their knees rather than standing.[31] Ironically the German Protestants found themselves adopting a practice they found distinctly Catholic to satisfy the demands of their anti-Catholic benefactors in the SPG.[32]

Although Haeger and Kocherthal hoped to convince the SPG that the German settlers were conforming to the Church of England, in the end they made only superficial changes. Haeger emphasized his use of the Book of Common Prayer but never mentioned the content of his sermons. Neither he nor Kocherthal admitted to any changes in theology, and their congregations did not become Anglican.

When Haeger attempted to change Reformed services, his parishioners resisted and the Lutherans laughed. Few immigrants wished to adopt the religious practices of their Anglican benefactors. In the immigrants' efforts to preserve Lutheran and Reformed liturgy and religious ceremony, they exhibited an independent streak that the established churches of the German southwest might have found troublesome. The immigrants resisted the authority of their pastors and displayed an independence in church affairs that would become common among the Lutheran and Reformed laity in colonial America. Yet their resistance to church authority did not mean the rejection of their Lutheran or Reformed identities. The root of their discontent was, after all, their pastors' attempts to impose English ways.

Establishing the Naval Stores Project

While the Germans struggled to reestablish their families and churches in New York, Governor Hunter searched for land suitable for the naval stores project. Before Hunter left London, the Board of Trade had suggested that he settle the Germans on land along the Schoharie River, a region twenty miles southwest of Schenectady on the edge of English and Dutch settlement in New York. The Schoharie tract had belonged to Nicholas Bayard, a member of the governor's council, who claimed to have bought it from the Mohawks in 1696. Governor Benjamin Fletcher had confirmed the purchase and issued a patent for the land. But when Richard Coote, earl of Bellomont, replaced Fletcher as governor, Bayard found himself out of political favor. In 1699 Governor Bellomont annulled the patent along with a number of other "extravagant grants" given by Fletcher. The Schoharie land reverted back to the Mohawks. In August, Hunter sent John Bridger, Her Majesty's surveyor general in the American colonies and the man chosen to supervise the naval stores project, to survey the land. The Mohawks would not allow Bridger to carry out the survey, however, until Hunter confirmed their title to the land. After Hunter complied, the Mohawks, who desired English trade and wanted to curry the favor of the new governor, presented the land as a gift to the queen.[33]

Figure 7. Governor Robert Hunter. Portrait attributed to Sir Godfrey Kneller (negative no. 7221). © Collection of The New-York Historical Society.

Despite Hunter's efforts to obtain land in Schoharie, he decided to settle the Germans elsewhere. The Schoharie lands actually proved too fertile for Hunter's intended use; pitch pine tends to grow on poor and rocky soil.[34] Although the Schoharie lands were good for farming, the trees necessary for naval stores production did not grow abundantly on their soil. While he negotiated with the Mohawks for the Schoharie tract, Hunter began considering other sites.

On October 3, 1710, Hunter reported to London that he had bought six thousand acres along the Hudson River from Robert Livingston.[35] He reported that the land had good soil for farming with pine forests nearby. He also noted the deep landings along the river that would allow ships to supply the Germans and to carry away naval stores. Because the land purchased from Livingston could not support all the German families, Hunter also allocated to the project another 6,300 acres just across the river from lands that had reverted to the Crown under the 1699 Vacating Act.[36]

The deed of sale between Hunter and Livingston makes clear that Hunter expected the Germans to use the land for farming.[37] The pine trees intended for making naval stores stood about three miles inland on property that still belonged to Livingston.[38] The deed gave the Germans liberty to enter Livingston's manor to prepare trees for pitch and tar production. The sale had obvious advantages for Livingston. Although he would not receive money directly from the sale of naval stores, the Germans would be clearing his land, building roads, and erecting bridges. In addition, Livingston would retain possession of any trees the Germans cut that were suitable for sawing into boards.[39] Livingston also signed a victualing contract to provide the settlers with bread and beer.[40] Not surprisingly, he had a flour mill and a brewery on the manor that could easily provide these products. By having the Germans settled nearby, Livingston spurred the development of his yet unproductive manor.[41] He and Hunter completed the sale on October 5, by which time the first Palatine group was already beginning to settle on the land.[42]

CHAPTER 5

"They Will Not Listen to Tar Making"

THE HUDSON VALLEY, 1710–1712

During the last week in September the Germans who were well enough to travel began moving from New York City to camps along the Hudson. By the beginning of November almost fifteen hundred people had settled in five rude villages.[1] Two more villages, one on each side of the river, were added in the spring. The villages of Haysbury, Queensbury, Annsbury, and Hunterstown, known collectively as East Camp, stood on the east side of the river on the land purchased from Livingston. They were laid out on the hillsides leading down to the Hudson in an area stretching three miles south from Livingston's manor house. Livingston's home, built in 1699, stood just north of the point where Roeliff Jansen Kill emptied into the Hudson. The creek cut a small valley between his manor and the German settlements. On the west side of the Hudson, set back from the river on a small rise, stood West Camp, consisting of Elizabethtown, Georgetown, and Newtown.[2] John Bridger, the surveyor general, laid out forty-by-fifty-foot plots for each of the German families.[3] With winter settling in, it was too late to begin work on the naval stores project or to plant crops. The Germans built their huts and began clearing land for spring planting.

Hunter appointed several men to supervise and provision the Germans. Because Livingston had procured the contract to supply the Ger-

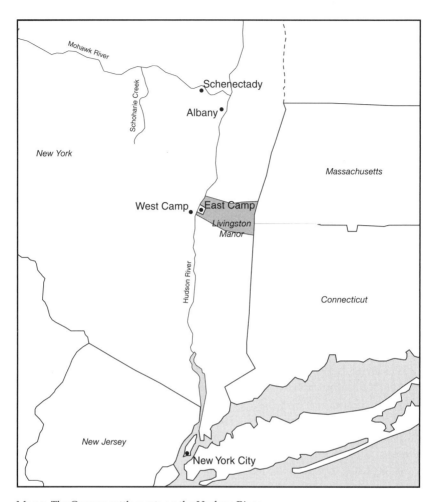

Map 5. The German settlements on the Hudson River

mans with bread and beer, he was deeply involved in the project and often reported to Hunter on its progress. George Clarke, secretary of the colony, served as the project's treasurer and commissary of provisions. He helped procure meat and other food around New York City and arranged for its delivery to the Germans. James du Pré served as the commissary of stores and spent considerable time moving between New York City and the German villages, coordinating the project's administration. Andrew Bagge worked as undercommissary of stores for the villages on the west bank of the river. Jean Cast, one of the migrants, held the same position for the villages across the river, near Livingston's manor.[4]

Of all the 1709 migrants, Cast held the highest administrative post within the naval stores project. He came from Strasbourg and spoke French and German, allowing him to communicate both with Hunter (in French) and with his fellow immigrants. He served as Hunter's interpreter to the Germans. When Hunter sent du Pré to London in late 1710 to secure further financing for the project, Cast took over as the operation's principal commissary and accountant.[5]

Each village appointed one of its own to serve as listmaster.[6] Just as they had done in London and on board the ships to America, the listmasters distributed provisions to the immigrants and kept accounts of how much each family received. They also represented the villages in meetings with Cast or whenever Hunter visited the settlements. Hunter enhanced their authority by giving them military commissions and paying them a salary.[7] Although they had the backing of military commissions, their positions were not secure if they performed badly. In at least one case, a village petitioned to have its listmaster removed, accusing him of improperly distributing provisions.[8]

No records reveal how the villagers chose the listmasters; the only obvious requirement was that the leaders could read and write. Two of the seven listmasters had been soldiers in Europe. Johann Conrad Weiser had served as a corporal in the Württemberg Blue Dragoons.[9] Perhaps the villagers exhibited a certain deference to such figures while valuing their leadership skills. Several of the men had been listmasters in London and New York City, and that experience also made them logical candidates. All were married. They tended to be young; at least four were thirty-five or younger. They came from small towns throughout the German southwest. Some, like Johann Christopher Fuchs of Niederbieber, came from towns that had contributed a large number of people to the 1709 emigration. Others, such as Johann Gerlach of Laudenbach in Hesse-Kassel, came from towns on the periphery of the migration. Ironically, none of the six listmasters whose villages of origin are known actually came from the Palatinate.[10]

Besides the beer and bread provided by Livingston, each family was to receive beef or pork three times a week, and fish, cheese, flour, or peas the other four days.[11] The Board of Trade had instructed Hunter to provision the settlers at a rate of six pence a day for all people age ten and over and four pence a day for children under age ten. Hunter used these amounts to calculate a monthly budget of £1,641 to provision the entire group. He prided himself on paying from this budget for both the Germans' food and the salaries of the commissaries and listmasters.[12] Still, Hunter realized that keeping the Germans well-supplied would make them better workers. He asked for additional funds to provide the Germans with six hundred dairy cattle (one cow per family), three hundred horses, six hundred pigs, and the farm implements they needed, including harnesses, plows, horseshoes, and saws.[13] In addition, he provided the Germans with six hundred guns that the Board of Trade had sent with the immigrant convoy, on the assumption that the Germans would be settled on New York's frontier.

Hunter believed that the British government would not allow the potentially profitable venture to fail. Still, the government had advanced only £8,000 for the plan, and by October Hunter had spent most of the money. He dispatched du Pré to London to lobby for more. Originally the government had approved funding the project for one year. But the Germans had not moved into their settlements until late 1710, and it would take another two years before they could produce tar and pitch in meaningful quantities. Hunter estimated he needed another £35,000 to support the Germans for two more years.[14] By that time, he believed, the project would be profitable and the Germans would be self-supporting.

Meanwhile Hunter used his own money and took out personal loans to support the Germans, trusting the British government to repay him. Over the winter he made sure the Germans in the naval stores camps had enough food and warm clothing. Andrew Bagge reported that the two villages on the west side of the river received 280 pairs of shoes, 263 pairs of stockings, and ninety-one hats, as well as cloth and soap.[15]

Discontent and Confrontation

Despite Hunter's efforts, the Germans grumbled. Because they could not begin preparing trees to make tar and pitch until late spring, they had the long winter to reflect on what migration had gained for them. They had left their homes expecting rich farmland and prosperity in America. Now, almost two years later, all they had to show for their efforts was a mere two thousand square feet of desolate land for each family and a contract to produce naval stores.

The lands Hunter had abandoned in Schoharie weighed heavily on their minds. The Germans knew of Hunter's original plan to settle them in Schoharie and of his initial reports on the land's fertility. Now that Hunter had placed them on Livingston's land instead, the Germans suspected that their interests had been abandoned in favor of the interests of a powerful landlord. Looking back on the events of early 1711, Hunter wrote that he had "met with great opposition from many of the ill disposed Inhabitants, who dayly insinuated that there were better lands for them on the Fronteers and that they were ill used in being planted there [on the Hudson]."[16]

As winter drew to a close, the Germans became, in Hunter's words, "idle and backwards" and refused to prepare their plots for cultivation.[17] The Germans' resentment of their treatment at the hands of petty rulers and stingy landlords—the sort of officials they thought they had left behind in Europe—was so strong that it overcame one of the strongest peasant impulses: planting the land. The Germans' actions, or, more accurately, their lack of action, marked the beginning of a contentious three-month period for the Germans and Hunter. If Hunter had expected obedience from the Germans in thankfulness for the queen's generosity and in recognition of his authority as the queen's representative, he was to be sorely disappointed.

Rather than remembering the generosity of those who had fed them, the Germans remembered the promises of free land in America. The immigrants began to suspect that the British government was no different from the governments of the petty princes they had known in the German southwest. The immigrants came from village communities that had long distrusted outside authority. Such authority seemed the source of war and taxes, religious persecution and economic instability. During the Thirty Years' War and other wars of the seventeenth century, when local rulers proved utterly incapable of protecting peasant communities, peasant self-reliance and disregard for authority grew.[18] The Germans whom Hunter faced had a long tradition of subverting illegitimate control over their lives, sometimes through outright revolt but more often through subtle and understated acts of resistance.[19] As they grew disgruntled with their situation in New York, the Germans began to direct their anger and resistance toward the latest prince who would try to control them—Governor Hunter.

All the labels and counter-labels, all the made-up stories and careless histories, all the hastily made plans and hastily sought agreements had created a situation in which neither side understood where it stood or how it should react to the other. In England, the Germans had relied on Londoners' charitable impulses to protect them. Those impulses were already beginning to fade when they left England, and by 1711 the Germans were resorting more and more to forms of resistance rather than to appeals for charity in their dealings with the British colonial authorities. In the confusion that the immigrants had helped to create, their resistance to the naval stores scheme often seemed erratic and inconsistent. They made threats and demands, then backed down when challenged. For every act of boldness, there was one of abject submission.

Several reasons help explain the Germans' actions. First, many acts of resistance were spontaneous; they do not appear well planned because they were not. In addition, the Germans still depended absolutely on Hunter for their survival. He could demand their obedience because he fed them. Like other peoples trapped in such uneven power relationships, the Germans realized that resistance carried great risks. Their resistance took on a schizophrenic and indirect character as they looked for ways to mitigate their situation without provoking an overwhelming and possibly fatal response.[20] Finally, the Germans did not agree among themselves about the proper course of action. The Germans' struggle was not just with Hunter but also with one another. Although oppression and acts of resistance can pull people together, they can also reveal divisions that might not otherwise be apparent. The risks associated with resistance are not the same for all members of a community, and people possess bravery or recklessness in different portions.[21] In London and at the beginning of their stay in New York, the Germans had faced situations that led them to overcome their differences and even to create stories that pretended that their backgrounds and motives were all the same. In their struggles with Hunter, however, there were hints that instead of always pulling together, they might instead begin pulling apart.

The struggle between the Germans and Hunter was not completely one-sided. The Germans may have depended on Hunter for their survival, but Hunter depended on the Germans for the success of the naval stores project, a project he hoped would enrich him as much as the British government. He was just as confused by the Germans' actions as they were frustrated by his. What had happened to the grateful, compliant settlers whom he had shepherded from London to New York?

In March 1711, when Hunter learned the Germans were refusing to plant their gardens and were murmuring about the abandoned lands in Schoharie, he hurried to the camps to discover the Germans' intentions. Hunter thought the Germans' discontent was minor and hoped that reasoned argument would quiet them. When he arrived at the German villages, he called the villagers together and reminded them that their first task was to make naval stores, something they could not do in Schoharie because the proper trees did not grow there. He also told them that even if the naval stores contract were not an issue, the Schoharie region would be a poor spot to settle. It was isolated and difficult to supply. In addition it was vulnerable to attack from the French and their Indian allies. If the Germans went there, Hunter explained, they would have to labor "as the Israelites did of old, with a sword in one hand and the Axe in the other."[22]

Underestimating the Germans' frustration and willingness to resist, Hunter started back home certain that he had convinced the Germans to stay put. In truth, he had accomplished little. A messenger overtook him before he reached New York City with a report that the Germans were again threatening to mutiny. Hunter quickly returned and demanded a meeting with the German leaders. Instead, the whole community came out to meet him. Ignoring the threat implied by the mass gathering, Hunter ordered Cast to read the naval stores contract in German and then asked whether the villagers were going to abide by it. Betraying a lack of resolve and perhaps an underlying split in the community, the Germans gave in. Hunter wrote, "After some small deliberation they returned me for answer, that they were resolv'd to keep their Contract & would for the future be directed Intirely by me, Soe wee parted good Friends."[23]

The Germans' short-lived and poorly organized rebellion was unsuccessful, but at least the community had not been punished and the Germans had a better idea of how the governor would react to their demands. They had also made Hunter aware of their discontent. For the time being, that was enough. Those who emphasized the group's dependence on provisions supplied by Hunter encouraged submission, and the rest agreed temporarily to comply with Hunter's demands.[24]

After Hunter returned to New York City, Cast sent reports describing a change in the Germans' attitudes. They went about their work without complaint, and when Cast met them to distribute tools from New York City, "they all, without exception, evinced a modesty, civility and respect which surprized, as much as it delighted me,"[25] They cleared their land and asked for seeds to plant their gardens. Yet within Cast's cheerful reports lurked hints that all was not well. The stresses felt by a group of people living on land they did not like and facing a task they did not want began to take their toll. Episodes of jealousy and violence broke out in the German settlements. The people of Elizabethtown resented it when Georgetown's residents received tools before they did. In Queensbury people fought over newly appropriated land, attacking each other with axes. Haeger reported that two couples were seeking divorces.[26] Some immigrants wanted a more effective judicial system to govern their affairs. According to Cast, they claimed that "our affairs will never prosper as long as we are our own masters; each follows his own evil inclinations."[27]

Yet the main issue that split the Germans was whether they should remain in the camps or attempt to move to Schoharie. Cast reported that the artisans seemed satisfied to stay put. Only "the agricultural portion . . . contemplate the possession of a large quantity of land."[28] But, according to Cast, most of the farmers seemed resigned to staying in their present settlements for a year or two. They hoped they would eventually get the land in Schoharie when the French threat to the region was removed.

One night five Germans gathered around a fire to discuss their future.[29] They all agreed that their present settlement possessed some advantages: it fronted on a navigable river, it stood between New York and Albany, and it seemed safe from attack. Yet the men had migrated for much more. They had not forgotten their dreams of rich and plentiful land, and they knew such land lay tantalizingly nearby in Schoharie. Despite the advantages of their present location, they found it difficult to forget the land that they thought by right should be theirs.

One man tried to calm the others with reasoned argument: "What, if, in return for all your pretended rights, the Governor will not give you any other lands than those in the rear of our villages, and be determined that we pass our whole lives here? What can you do? Nothing . . . but draw down by the displeasure of the Governor, evils we do not experience here, and deprive ourselves of the good we now enjoy." He remained convinced the queen would not forget them. "For in fine . . . as it is our duty, and we must absolutely work for the Queen, it cannot be otherwise than that Her Majesty will put us in a position to earn our bread; for she will not keep us always in this way."

But one of his companions would have nothing of it. "Earn our bread," he said in disgust. He reminded the others of why they had moved, reiterating the reason one emigrant after another had given the German authorities when seeking permission to leave their homes: "We came to America to establish our families—to secure lands for our children, on which they will be able to support themselves after we die." In its simplest terms, that had been their goal. Unfortunately, he concluded, "that we cannot do here."

Still his companion saw few options. "What is to be done in that case," he replied, "but to have patience?"

To which the other responded with a German saying: "Patience and Hope make fools of those who fill their bellies with them."

At that the group broke into laughter and, realizing late-night conversation could not solve their dilemma, moved on to another topic.

Settling along the Hudson

Shortly after their March confrontation with Hunter, the Germans in the naval stores settlements were joined by those migrants who had been too sick to leave New York City in the fall. The number of Germans depending on government support in New York City fell from 358 in April to 124 in May and finally to 102 in June. Only the very elderly and a few widows and orphans remained in the city.[30] Hunter had to buy an additional eight hundred acres on the west bank of the Hudson to settle some of the later arrivals. He realized "the extent of ground [was] a great encouragement to the people," so he instructed the surveyors laying out the two new villages on either side of the Hudson to make the plots somewhat larger, but not so large that the people from other villages would discover it.[31]

By May 1711 the four settlements east of the Hudson had a total population of just under 1,800; the villages across the river had 583 inhabitants.[32] Just as the remarriage of widows and widowers began to break down territorial distinctions among the emigrants, the way the emigrants were settled in the camps also eroded regional differences. Each of the seven villages was made up of people from all regions of the German southwest. Neighbors who had traveled together from the Rhineland often managed to stay together in New York, but there was no strong concentration of people from one region or territory in any village. In Haysbury a number of families had emigrated from near Neuwied, and in Annsbury most of the settlers came from areas north and east of the Rhine and Main rivers. Even in these two villages, however, the concentration of people from any one territory was not strong.[33] People from territories spread across the German southwest had become neighbors. Differences might have remained, but the settlers faced Hunter and his naval stores scheme together.

When the weather warmed and before the naval stores' work started, the immigrants cleared their small lots and began planting crops. Instead of growing familiar crops such as grapes, oats, or spelt, the Germans received corn to plant as their primary field crop. In addition they received seeds for a wide variety of garden crops, including peas, onions, carrots, beets, turnips, and cabbage.[34] Despite the variety, Cast reported that the settlers were anxious to get more seed and that they also wanted to grow flax. Flax was a common crop in the German southwest, and the immigrants relied on it to produce their linen clothing.[35] Some of the Germans had earned enough money while in New York City to buy a few cattle, but most owned no livestock when they moved to the Hudson River settlements.[36] Although Hunter planned to provide the Germans with cows, horses, and pigs, it is not clear how much of the livestock the Germans ever received.

The immigrants' gardens and livestock could not feed the people, and the settlers continued to rely on food provided by Hunter's commissaries. The quality of the food was a constant source of complaint. Much of the meat was packed in salt and was sent up from New York City. In early May, Cast complained to Hunter about the quality of the pork. "I never saw salted meat so poor nor packed with so much salt as this pork was. In truth, almost one eighth of it was salt."[37] Although Hunter was not yet getting rich from the naval stores project, clearly others were reaping a profit from the scheme. The pork suppliers were not the only ones cheating the immigrants. The Germans received flour in barrels, which was credited to their accounts by weight. To calculate the amount of flour the Germans received, the tare, an amount representing the weight of the empty barrel, was subtracted from the total weight of the barrel and its contents. The Germans complained that suppliers consistently understated the tare and returned several barrels of flour to Cast for reweighing. After weighing the empty barrels, Cast found that one barrel that had been tared seventeen pounds actually weighed twenty-one. Similar discrepancies existed for other barrels.[38] The Germans learned not to trust their European neighbors in New York, and many continued to dream of a Canaan in the Schoharie Valley where they could live beyond the reach of those who would enslave and cheat them.

Although the Germans agreed to cultivate their gardens, they clearly had not resigned themselves to the naval stores plan. In late March, Kocherthal reported to Cast on the attitude of the Germans living on the west side of the Hudson. According to the Lutheran minister, his parishioners worked hard but "manifestly with repugnance, and merely temporarily." They believed that the land in Schoharie, which they were convinced had been intended for them, was "a Land of Canaan." They realized that settling there now was too dangerous, so they agreed to remain on the Hudson for a couple of years. But they had not changed their mind about the naval stores project. The Germans might farm their land, Kocherthal reported, but "they will not listen to Tar making."[39] The problems that Hunter thought he had dealt with in early March still festered in the German camps.

A Second Confrontation with Hunter

In early May when the naval stores work was to begin at last, the Germans once more refused to work and threatened to strike out for Schoharie. Hunter found himself again sailing up the Hudson to the German camps. Having no desire for prolonged discussions, Hunter ordered a detachment of sixty soldiers from Albany to join him.[40]

When Hunter arrived the Germans were hampering surveyors' efforts to lay out additional lots for them along the Hudson. Hunter called the German listmasters to a meeting at Livingston's manor house and demanded to know why the people were hindering the surveyors' work. The listmasters sullenly replied that the land being laid out was no good; it was not even worth surveying. They still wanted the Schoharie lands, which they claimed had been granted to them by their contract with the queen. Whether the Germans were aware that the Board of Trade had suggested in 1709 that the Schoharie Valley be considered as a place to settle them, they certainly knew that Hunter had negotiated with the Indians to obtain the lands for the naval stores project. By settling them along the Hudson, the Germans believed, Hunter had cheated them of the lands they had been promised.

Hunter tried at first to be conciliatory. He announced that any settlers who were unhappy with their land in the camps or who had already cultivated what had been granted them could have more. He insisted, however, that the Germans could not avoid their obligation to make naval stores, and they could not move to Schoharie. He reiterated the old arguments. There were no pine trees in Schoharie. The land was too remote, and the settlers could not be provisioned. Besides, if they settled there, they would be in great danger from the French and their Indian allies.

Despite Hunter's arguments the deputies insisted on the Schoharie lands. Exasperated, Hunter reminded them of how the queen had saved them from starvation and of the contract they had signed in England. He then ordered the minutes of their meeting to be written down so that the deputies could take them back to the villages for the people's consideration. Hunter wanted to ensure that everyone understood he was requiring their absolute adherence to the contract. He told the deputies to return the next day at 4:00 P.M. with an answer.

Some of the Germans, however, were ready to answer much sooner. Shortly after the meeting ended, three hundred to four hundred German men, armed with the guns they had been given by Hunter to guard their frontier settlement, assembled on a hill overlooking the manor house. The guns intended to defend the frontier against the French and Indians were now being used to defend German claims against Hunter and the British. The German men had evidently gathered while the meeting was taking place, moved by fears that Hunter was holding their leaders hostage. The armed men planned to free them. When Hunter learned of the gathering, he called his military detachment and marched out to meet the Germans. Faced with sixty professional soldiers and seeing that their leaders were free, the German farmers backed off.

Many of the German men probably sighed with relief. Although a few had served in European armies, most probably had little experience with guns and did not care for their chances against the British troops. The sheepish German farmers now claimed they had simply come to pay their compliments to the governor. They were sorry if they had caused alarm. Hunter noted the peculiarity of the Germans' welcome but sent them home without taking further action. In a feeble attempt to save face, the German men stopped when safely out of reach of the British detachment and fired their guns into the air.[41]

The next day, as ordered, the village deputies returned to the manor house to meet Hunter. Although they began in a "humble stile," they continued to demand land in Schoharie and even claimed "they had rather lose their lives immediately" than remain in the camps along the Hudson.[42] They argued that the naval stores contract Hunter had presented them differed from the one read to them in England. They claimed that the contract they had agreed to in London provided them each with forty acres from the time they arrived in New York. It gave them seven years to repay their London expenses and the costs of transporting them to America. The contract allowed them to work their new farms while they also made naval stores. Under such an arrangement, they argued, their families would not suffer while the debt was being repaid. They agreed to be obedient to the queen, but only if the contract read to them in England were kept. If Hunter refused to honor the contract, they wished to send representatives to plead their case directly before the queen.

Whether they remembered the contract correctly, the Germans had good reason to feel cheated. The contract had not been finalized until early April 1710. By that time they had been sitting on ships off the coast of England for almost four months, waiting for their convoy to leave for America. It is unknown what they thought the conditions for their resettlement were when they boarded the ships in December, but by April they probably felt compelled to accept any terms. They had waited too long and suffered too much. Any contract that would get them to America would be acceptable.

Nevertheless the contract they chose to remember in 1711 clearly differed from the English version of the document.[43] Because Hunter apparently did not have a German copy of the contract with the men's signatures, he could not easily counter the Germans' arguments. In fact, such a document may not have existed. The German deputies referred to a contract being "read" to them, rather than referring to one they had signed. Reading may have been necessary since many of the Germans were illiterate, but there is no evidence that Cast carried to New York a document in German actually signed by the immigrants. Without it, the Germans' recollection of the contract could not be disproved.

The Germans' refusal to accept Hunter's version of the contract represented a relatively risk-free form of resistance, by which the Germans could seek to demonstrate the legitimacy of their claim to land in Schoharie while frustrating Hunter's counterclaims. Moreover, by asking to take their case directly to the queen, they explicitly questioned Hunter's authority and implicitly questioned his loyalty to the Crown. Was he carrying out the queen's instructions or had he developed a new plan that would benefit only him? The Germans' tactics outraged Hunter. The Germans later reported that Hunter "in a passion stamped upon the ground and said, here is your land (meaning the almost barren Rocks) where you must live and die."[44] The Germans may have out-argued Hunter, but because their survival depended on British subsistence, it did not matter.

As the meeting was taking place, a large group of Germans again gathered across the creek and ravine separating their settlements from the manor. After the previous day's events Hunter had sent for reinforcements from Albany; he had perhaps been more intimidated by earlier events than the Germans realized. He now had a force of 130 men, and with them he marched out to confront the Germans. Again the Germans dispersed, but this time Hunter marched on to their northernmost village and disarmed the men. Hunter was determined to remove the German threat. The next morning he continued his march through the other three villages on the east side of the Hudson, collecting the residents' guns. He returned to the manor house and sent word to the villagers in West Camp that they too must turn in their guns or he would send his detachment to take them. Finally Hunter revoked the military commissions he had previously granted the German listmasters and established a court to govern the Germans' affairs.[45]

George Clarke, who apparently accompanied Hunter to the German settlements, detected a split in the German community. As one of the plan's administrators, he preferred to believe that the Germans had been incited by only a few rebels who gave the people unrealistic visions of Schoharie and then intimidated them into refusing to make tar and pitch. He reported that once Hunter had disarmed the settlers, "the sober and better sort of people, who are likewise the Majority, being secured from the rage of the hot headed, unthinking, and misguided" asked Hunter's pardon. In a ritual of humiliation the Germans returned to Hunter, some on their knees, and promised "a thorrough Reformation of their behaviour, and an entire Resignation to his orders."[46]

Because Hunter needed the Germans' labor if the naval stores project was to be a success, his options, like those of the Germans, were limited. He could do nothing more than accept their apologies, with a warning that further disobedience would be severely punished. According to Clarke, the Germans received the pardon "with great joy." He wrote to the Board of Trade that "now they begin to demonstrate their sincerity by inquiring when they shall be set to work, and show a great desire to make a good beginning in it."[47]

Appearances can be deceiving. Even though the community split over the methods and degree of resistance, it never acceded to the naval stores project. Although the Germans did not again risk armed confrontation, they resisted in other ways, by dawdling and through various minor acts of insubordination. It may have appeared to Hunter and his aides that only a few "hot headed" men opposed the project, but the "sober and better sort of people" were unhappy, too. Hunter later admitted as much when he wrote that he found "it hard to keep the generality of them to their duty."[48] Yet despite their unhappiness, by the summer of 1711 the generality understood that open protest had gained little for them. Unlike their more volatile neighbors, they apparently believed discretion would better suit their purposes in the short run.

Making Tar and Pitch

In late May, almost a year after their arrival in New York, the German men at last began the long process of making naval stores. Even after the delay, the project remained poorly organized. John Bridger, who had been assigned to teach the Germans how to make tar and pitch, had gone to New England and refused to return to New York. Frustrated with Bridger's insubordination and suspicious of his method for making naval stores, Hunter appointed Richard Sackett to take Bridger's place. Sackett, a local landowner, claimed to know a superior method for making naval stores and willingly took Bridger's post as the project's director.[49]

In truth Hunter lacked the knowledge to judge either Bridger's or Sackett's methods for making tar and pitch. Britain did not manufacture these products, relying instead on Swedish imports, and few Britons understood the methods of tar and pitch production. The matter left the board so confused that, two years after it had approved the German project, it admitted that it still did not know whether tar and pitch could be made in one season or if it took at least two years, as Bridger and Hunter were reporting.[50] The Board of Trade finally instructed the British ambassador in Russia to find out how the Russians made the stuff.[51]

Broadly defined, naval stores include all products used in making ships, including timber for masts and hulls, hemp for ropes, flax for sails, and various resinous products of the pine tree, such as turpentine, tar, and pitch. The German project concerned itself only with the production of pitch and tar. The technology for making the two products was crude. First, bark was stripped from the pine trees. The resulting wound opened up gum ducts in the tree, triggering gum production until the wound sealed and pressure in the gum ducts was restored.[52] Over a two-year period the trees would be "barked" periodically to stimulate further gum production. In the process, the wounded areas would become saturated with gum. The trees were then cut down, and the sections that had been barked were cut into smaller pieces for burning. The wood was stacked in piles and slowly burned in a large earthen kiln. Tar seeped from the burning wood onto the kiln's clay floor and then down a drain into a barrel placed below the kiln. To make pitch, the tar was boiled in large cauldrons until the liquid evaporated. The resulting pitch was used to caulk ships' hulls and decks. When it dried it formed a hard and watertight seal. Tar was painted on ships' hulls to protect them from the corrosive effects of salt water, and ropes were soaked in tar to keep them from rotting.[53] Although turpentine and rosin could have been made from pine trees too, the technology required a more sophisticated distillation process. The British had little enough experience with tar and pitch and evidently made no plans for turpentine and rosin production among the Germans.[54]

On May 20, 1711, the German men hiked into the pine woods on Livingston's manor and began stripping bark from the trees. Two wagons accompanied them, carrying tents and the men's baggage. The woods stood about six miles from the settlements, and the men apparently spent weeks at a time away from their families. On May 29, the German girls and boys followed the men into the woods to gather pine knots, the gum-soaked stubs of fallen branches.[55] The women remained in the villages, where they cared for the livestock and maintained the fields that had been sown during the spring.

By the first week of June the men had stripped the bark from thousands of trees, while their children busily collected several wagon loads of pine knots.[56] Unlike the trees, which had to stand for two years before they could be processed into tar and pitch, pine knots could be used immediately to produce naval stores. Although the men were carrying out their task, the knowledge that nothing would result from their labor for such a long time weighed heavily on their minds. It would be years before they could pay off their debt and gain their independence. Seeing their children outperform them also must have been difficult. Virtually all the pitch and tar produced while the Germans were employed in the naval stores scheme came from pine knots that the children gathered.[57]

Another reason might explain why the men resented their task. The British ambassador observing tar making in Russia remarked on its similarity to making charcoal.[58] In fact, charcoal was a by-product of tar production. Charcoal burners occupied the lowest level of the social scale in the German southwest.[59] They lived mysterious lives alone in the forest, beyond the control of surrounding communities. A common element in German folklore is the forest's association with demons, iniquity, and terror.[60] The Grimms' fairy tales, with their stories of children lost in the woods and set upon by witches, robbers, or wolves, are perhaps the best-known examples of the dread the forest might inspire.[61] Now the German men had to disappear into the forest for weeks at a time doing work similar to that of the wretched charcoal burners. It is no wonder that Hunter was forced to station a detachment of troops at the German settlements to keep the men at their task.

The court Hunter established after the May rebellion served as another tool for controlling the Germans. Even though the court limited the Germans' autonomy, the makeup of the court and the way it functioned show that Hunter realized cooperation rather than coercion would better suit his plans. Robert Livingston and Richard Sackett presided over the court, which also included the commander of the detachment of soldiers stationed near the German villages, the commissaries Bagge and Cast, and two overseers, Godfrey Wulfen and Herman Schuneman.[62] Wulfen had been part of the 1709 emigration, but was apparently a man of some means who managed to procure administrative powers over his fellow emigrants shortly after they reached London. Schuneman came from Hamburg and had been a member of the 1708 emigration. Their inclusion along with Cast meant the court had three German-speaking members. These men could serve as intermediaries between the English-speaking authorities and the villagers as well as give the impression that the immigrants had some representation on the court.

But Cast, Wulfen, and Schuneman came from the economic and geographic peripheries of the migration and never seemed to have gained the trust of the bulk of the people. The village listmasters, whom the villagers themselves had chosen, were still their principal leaders—a fact the court recognized when it assigned the listmasters to carry out the court's instructions.[63] Yet the listmasters were the same men who had served as the Germans' leaders during the May rebellion. The court apparently realized it had to recognize the village leaders if it wished to be successful, and perhaps it hoped to co-opt the listmasters by giving them close access to the court.

Still, Hunter's instructions to the court signaled a change in his attitude toward the Germans. He specified that any person who refused to work or otherwise caused trouble could be punished "by confinement or Corporal punishment, not Extending to life or mutilation." The court was to be guided by similar cases involving "overseers over Servants."[64] In other words, the Germans would be treated as servants and nothing more.

At least some of the Germans were pleased to have a court set over them. They hoped it would lead to a more orderly government and would lessen the intimidation they felt from those who favored continued resistance to Hunter's plans. But Hunter's instructions to the court show that a fundamental difference in outlook existed between Hunter and the Germans. Hunter remained focused on the success of the naval stores project and saw the Germans as servants hired to carry out the work rather than as adults struggling to support their families. In Britain servitude was a condition common to many girls and boys and young, unmarried men and women. Because marriage depended on some degree of economic independence, most servants were not married. The German adults did not fit the servant model, but Hunter ignored that reality, focusing only on the men and seeing in them servants of the Crown.

The Germans' outlook differed considerably from Hunter's. They linked servitude to serfdom. Serfdom was not temporary, and it represented a system of land ownership that the Germans wanted to escape. As the German farmer sitting by the fire had put it, "We came to America to establish our families—to secure lands for our children." As long as Hunter and the Germans had such different conceptions of the immigrants' role in New York, the Germans were bound to resist Hunter's plans regardless of how he ruled them.

Reports from the camps revealed that resistance continued. Coopers and their assistants refused to make the barrels necessary to store pitch and tar. Several men balked at building a bridge to convey barrels of tar and pitch to the river.[65] Although Cast assured Hunter that the Germans would be kept at their labor, the Germans' endless foot-dragging and obstruction hindered the smooth operation of the naval stores project. The Germans did not resort to outright rebellion, but their actions betrayed their underlying discontent.[66]

A "Turbulent Race of Men"

Hunter faced another problem besides his discontented workforce. He was running out of money. Hunter's pet project had taken a hard blow as early as October 1710, when the Tories gained power in Britain. The Tories had never cared for the German masses who had invaded Britain the year before. They accused the Whigs of inviting them and began an investigation of the Whigs' involvement in the affair. Although the Board of Trade continued to back the naval stores project and tried to keep it from becoming a political issue, Hunter lost many of his allies in the government, and his chances of receiving further funding for the project diminished considerably.[67]

In June 1711 the Board of Trade assured Hunter it was pressuring the Treasury to cover his expenditures.[68] Meanwhile, Hunter continued to use his personal credit to provision the settlers. In August he considered disbanding the settlements and allowing the Germans to shift for themselves, but his enthusiasm for the project and his belief that it would soon be profitable kept him from closing it down.[69]

The Germans realized that not all was going well. By July Hunter had run out of money for their bread and beer, and Robert Livingston refused to provide food without payment. He instructed his wife, who ran the manor during his long absences in New York City and Albany, to stop baking bread.[70] Alida Livingston, forced to contend with discontent among the Germans and Sackett's demands that his workers be fed, confessed, "I wish the Palatines had never come here."[71]

Just as the Germans began feeling the pinch of dwindling food supplies, the departure of three hundred men recruited for a campaign against Canada caused further disruption in the community. In a cruel twist of fate, the Germans found themselves enlisted to fight in the same war they thought they had left behind in Europe. The War of the Spanish Succession had passed over to North America as Queen Anne's War, and in late June Hunter learned that a combined force of British and American troops was to invade Canada. The British planned a two-pronged attack. While its fleet sailed from Boston to Quebec, troops from New York, New Jersey, and New England would march from Albany to Montreal.[72]

Hunter needed to find men to fill New York's and New Jersey's troop quotas. In his report to the New York Assembly about the planned expedition, Hunter revealed an interesting sense of how the Germans fit into New York society. Hunter wrote that he had "resolved to raise [the needed troops] . . . in this manner, 350 Cristians, 150 Long Island Indians and 100 Palatines." He clearly did not group the German immigrants with the rest of New York's white citizenry.[73] Along with the one hundred German soldiers paid for by New York, the New Jersey Assembly agreed to pay for an additional two hundred. On July 10 Hunter instructed Cast to call for volunteers from among those Germans "who are able to bear arms and endure the fatigue of a long march."[74] Most of the men probably did not mind leaving behind the business of making tar and pitch, but they feared abandoning their families when the supply of food seemed so insecure. Nevertheless, three hundred men volunteered.[75] In a letter to the SPG, Haeger revealed why the German men who had resisted Hunter's every move had volunteered to fight for the British. The Germans, he wrote, "were all joyful in hopes of their liberty and settlement."[76] They believed a British victory would ensure the security of Schoharie, leaving it open for German settlement.

Over seven hundred Indians, mostly Iroquois, also joined the expedition. The German men had the opportunity to observe these allies and to consider what they represented in terms of the possibilities for other ways of living in colonial New York. When, as Haeger reported, the German men thought of "their liberty and settlement," perhaps they considered the Iroquois example. Although the Iroquois tribes faced threats from British expansion and power, they remained independent allies of the British, not their servants. Schoharie, a land that bordered Iroquois land and that remained untouched by Hunter and his men, may have seemed a place where the Germans could enjoy the same kind of liberty their Iroquois neighbors enjoyed.

The men joined the expedition in early August. At the same time, Alida Livingston stopped delivering bread and beer to the villages. The men who joined the expedition were fed, but the people who remained behind, mainly women, children, and old men, suffered from hunger. Alida wrote to her husband on August 7 that "there is a great crying among the wives and children that their men have gone and [they] have no bread or beer [for themselves]."[77]

Luckily for the villagers the expedition was short-lived. Before the colonial forces reached Lake Champlain, news arrived that ten ships sailing from Boston to Quebec had run aground in the St. Lawrence. Admiral Hovenden Walker, the expedition's commander, had already been dreading a winter campaign in Canada. Now fearing further losses on the treacherous St. Lawrence, he turned the remainder of his fleet around and sailed back to Boston.[78] The New York troops had no hope of success on their own, and Hunter ordered them to abandon the campaign. In late September the German volunteers returned to their villages, but not before Hunter once again disarmed them.[79]

The German men, witnesses to an incompetent military campaign, now came home to find "their familys allmost starv'd, no provision having been given them during their absence."[80] Their disillusion with the British colonial authorities continued to grow. The Livingstons eventually began baking bread again after receiving assurances that the British Treasury would pay the project's bills, but few of the Germans would ever trust them to look out for their interests.[81] Hunter also felt frustrated by the situation. By year's end he had received no further payments for the project. In January 1712 he wrote to the Board of Trade, begging for money. Yet he refused to stop the naval stores operation, "judging it impossible that this, so univercally beneficial project shoud be dropt when it is carried on so far, and in so fair a way."[82]

During the fall some Germans managed to supplement their incomes when Hunter allowed them to leave the camps to help with the harvest on nearby farms. A few apparently left their villages permanently. Alida Livingston noted that nine German families from west of the Hudson had crossed the river and settled on Henry Beekman's manor, which lay south of the Livingston manor. They had agreed to rent land for twenty-five bushels of wheat a year. She also mentioned that several families wished to become tenants on the Livingston manor.[83] The slow breakup of the 1710 immigrant community had begun.

Most of the Germans remained in the camps, where they suffered through another winter. Food supplies ran low, and the people remained unruly. In late December fourteen men broke into the storehouse on the west side of the Hudson and stole several items.[84] Hunter grew increasingly disgusted with the Germans' behavior, and in January requested more troops to help police the camps. In his request he no longer referred sympathetically to "the poor Palatines"; instead, he complained, "There is no doing with that turbulent race of men but a strong hand and severe discipline."[85] Hunter's view of his obstinate charges had changed completely from the view he had expressed in 1709. The picture of a grateful and hardworking people, which Defoe had drawn and Hunter had admired, faded away forever on the New York frontier.

Despite the Germans' recalcitrance and his own lack of money, Hunter remained convinced the naval stores project could be successful. In March 1712 he laid out plans for the year's work. He was concerned that German labor be available and organized for the final preparation of the trees. He instructed the commissaries to post thirty soldiers from Albany near the German settlements to keep the Germans at their work. Hunter no longer referred to a court to govern the Germans' affairs. Instead he instructed the commissaries to meet weekly and to dispense punishment if needed. He wanted the project administered in a military style with a strict chain of command and little input from the enlisted. Hunter put Sackett in charge and gave him authority to punish any who appeared negligent or lazy.[86]

In May, with the second year of work in the pine forests about to begin, the commissaries forwarded Hunter's instructions to Albany and requested that troops be sent immediately since "there is no good to be done with these people who will obey no orders without compulsion."[87] A detachment of thirty men arrived on May 9.[88] With the troops in place, the work on the naval stores project went forward. The German men stripped more bark from the trees. They made staves for barrels and worked to complete the road between the warehouse and the pine woods.[89] They made pitch and tar from the pine knots gathered by the children. Although the tar had a "burning quality," Hunter contended that the pitch was as good as any other. Hunter even reported to the Board of Trade that the Germans were "working chearfully."[90] Their cheerfulness was due in part to a proposed change in the way they were paid. Instead of crediting all the profits from the tar they produced to their debt to the Crown, Hunter agreed to pay the workers half of the profits directly while the other half would be credited to their subsistence accounts.

The German community remained much quieter in 1712 than it had been in 1711. The Germans had tested Hunter's resolve and had learned that little could be accomplished in the short term to change their situation. The men settled into the routine of preparing trees for naval stores. They worked in shifts and probably did not remain away from their families for more than a week at a time. Since the Germans had cleared their plots the previous year, they found planting simpler, and some probably managed to expand their small fields. With a year's experience, the women understood better how to raise gardens in New York's soil and climate and how to cultivate previously unfamiliar crops like corn. The children had finished collecting pine knots, and many probably attended classes in the schoolhouse built the year before.[91] The ministers kept busy with the cycle of baptism and burial. Some of the pressures on the German community may have been relieved by the opportunities to leave the villages temporarily and to work nearby. Haeger reported to the SPG that he could not get an accurate count of the people in the settlements because they had "dispersed themselves up and down the country."[92] Hunter did not mind a few people departing since their absence meant fewer mouths to feed.

Although the spring and summer of 1712 passed uneventfully in the camps, Hunter's financial problems continued. By May he was having difficulty buying provisions on credit. Robert Livingston noted that "one cannot get merchants who are willing to advance money on the governor's bills."[93] In July, Hunter instructed Livingston to provide beer only to the men actually working in the pine woods. In addition, he asked if something might be done with the widows and orphans so that he would not have to support them.[94]

Realizing Hunter's difficulties, Livingston constantly worried about whether he would be paid for the bread and beer he provided the Germans. His own costs had gone up over the winter. It seemed everything that went wrong could be blamed on the Germans. In February an ice pack built up behind a bridge the Germans had built on Livingston's property. The bridge eventually gave away, crashing downstream along with the ice and destroying both Livingston's flour mill and sawmill.[95] Livingston had to ship his wheat twenty-eight miles down the Hudson to be ground. Any profits he hoped to make by supplying the Germans seemed to be quickly slipping away.

As his worries increased, Livingston quarreled constantly with Cast and Sackett over supplies. He found Cast's presence particularly galling. Cast often chose to bypass Livingston and to communicate directly with Hunter concerning affairs at the camps. Cast, an Alsatian, wrote his reports in French, a language Hunter understood but Livingston did not. When Hunter revealed one of these reports to Livingston, he was doubly irritated, first because the report was critical of him and second because he had to wait two days to get it translated.[96] By August Livingston was insinuating that Cast might be a French spy.[97] Tensions mounted as Hunter and Livingston awaited du Pré's return from London. Hunter wanted to keep the naval stores project going until he heard directly from du Pré whether the government intended to pay his bills.

In the end Hunter could wait no longer. By September he had run out of money and could get no further credit. Although he was convinced the tar and pitch works were almost at the point of profitability, he had to shut down the project. On September 6, 1712, Hunter instructed Cast to inform the Germans that the government could no longer support them.[98] The naval stores project had come to an end.

The Germans' first two years in New York had been marked by tumult and change. The deadly Atlantic crossing and the forced resettlement on the Hudson had first torn families apart and then led to the creation of a new German community—a community forced to ignore differences of territorial origin and dialect as it struggled for survival. The immigrants' opposition to the naval stores scheme increased their sense of unity and common cause, but that opposition also led to splits in the newly formed community. The Germans soon discovered that a common goal did not ensure a common means to that goal. Their lack of a shared strategy, coupled with their dependence on Hunter for food and clothing, led to sporadic and seemingly ineffective resistance. Every time Hunter demanded their compliance, the Germans backed down. Yet even though they lost every battle, they eventually won the war. The

German men never made a single barrel of tar. Only the pine knots gathered by the immigrant children—the children whom Hunter had hoped to apprentice rather than feed—produced a tangible result. The few barrels of tar resulting from the children's labor constituted the total yield of Hunter's grand scheme.

CHAPTER 6

"The Promis'd Land"

THE SCHOHARIE VALLEY, 1712–1722

With the end of the naval stores project, the Germans seemed at last free to pursue their American dreams. Yet the end of the project also revealed the extent of the Germans' dependence on Governor Hunter. Although they no longer had to make naval stores or live in the naval stores camps, life did not become noticeably easier. Famine still threatened them, and they had not yet found the farmland they desired. Over the next decade the Germans' sense of themselves and their place in New York would remain in flux as they resorted to Old World tactics and adopted New World allies in their struggle to rebuild their lives in America.

Although Hunter could no longer personally finance the naval stores project, he had no intention of permanently abandoning the potentially lucrative scheme. He hoped the Board of Trade would still convince the government of the plan's usefulness. If not, he thought he might find enough private investors in London to support the project.[1] Hunter instructed Cast to tell the Germans that they were allowed to find employment elsewhere in New York or New Jersey but that they must be prepared to return to the camps in the spring. "You must remind them of their contract with her Majesty and assure them there is not the least intention to abandon the Tar works, or to recede from any part of their agreement."[2] Those Germans who found work elsewhere were required to register their destinations with Cast. Hunter wanted to make sure all hands could be found and called back quickly to the camps.

Hunter had good reason to believe the project might soon be profitable. The German men had stripped bark from over seventy thousand trees. Little additional work was necessary before the trees could be cut and burned. Hunter had enough confidence in the eventual success of the project to continue to support the German coopers. He wanted to have plenty of barrels to store the tar once it began to flow.[3]

Despite the importance of German labor for the success of the naval stores project, Hunter showed little concern for the Germans' plight when he cut off their subsistence. With winter approaching and with little to harvest from their meager plots, the Germans found themselves struggling to survive. Over the winter food supplies ran short, and spring brought little improvement. The Germans' Reformed minister, Johann Haeger, whose parishioners' misery had thrown him into "a fit of melancholy," described to the SPG the condition of the Germans remaining in the camps: "There has been a great famine among them this winter, and does hold on still, in so much that they boil grass and the children eat the leaves of the trees. Such amongst them have most suffered of hunger as are advanced in years and too weak to go out laboring. I have seen old men and women crie that it should have almost moved a stone."[4]

As Haeger's letter suggests, many of the Germans wisely left the camps before winter arrived. Beginning in late 1712 and continuing over the next two decades, the 1710 German immigrants would spread throughout the middle colonies, eventually spilling south into the Shenandoah Valley. The migrants, who had come from all over the German southwest, had slowly formed a shared sense of identity through the stories that they told about themselves and the experiences that they shared together. Now they began to pull apart as they pursued the different opportunities that the failure of the naval stores project seemed to present. The first steps in this new migration were taken by a cautious few who found work in nearby and familiar settings. Some took jobs with farmers living near the German camps. A few found work in New York City, perhaps relying on contacts they had made when they first arrived in America. Others moved to New Jersey, settling near Hackensack or along the Raritan River.[5]

The more adventurous, led by the listmasters who had served as the confrontational spokesmen of the group from the beginning, looked west rather than south. Although Hunter had left the Germans in desperate straits when he cut off their subsistence, he had also presented them with the opportunity they had been waiting for. The way to Schoharie at last seemed open. In the fall of 1712 several hundred Germans began making plans to move to the promised land.

The move to Schoharie would not be easy. The Germans faced the practical problems of clearing a road to Schoharie and then feeding themselves once they arrived there. The latter would be particularly difficult since the Germans were determined to move before winter trapped them in the naval stores camps. But, as they had learned during the three years since they had left the German southwest, human obstacles could be as great a hindrance to movement as physical constraints. They were not moving to unoccupied land.

The Germans and the Indians

In the early seventeenth century, Schoharie Creek marked the approximate boundary between the territory controlled by the Mohawks and that controlled by the Mahicans of the Hudson River valley.[6] The arrival of Dutch traders and the establishment of Fort Orange in 1624 destabilized the region. In a bid for unobstructed access to the Dutch traders, the Mohawks carried out a series of attacks against the Mahicans between 1624 and 1628, eventually pushing the Mahicans east of the Hudson River.[7]

In the 1630s European diseases began sweeping through the Iroquois tribes. A massive smallpox epidemic had killed as many as 75 percent of the Mohawks by 1640.[8] European soldiers followed European diseases. In 1666, when the Mohawks did not quickly agree to a treaty between the French and the other Iroquois tribes, French soldiers destroyed the Mohawks' two largest villages. As a condition of the ensuing peace, Jesuit missionaries came to live among the Mohawks, eventually converting hundreds to Catholicism. To counteract the influence of unconverted Mohawks on the newly won souls, the Jesuits enticed several hundred Catholic Mohawks to move to mission reservations near Montreal, further weakening the Mohawks' strength in their traditional territory. Near the end of the century the Iroquois found themselves caught up in French and English colonial struggles, and in 1693 French troops again destroyed the principal Mohawk villages.[9]

By the late seventeenth century the Mohawks who remained in New York were struggling to survive in a world increasingly shaped by the

French and English colonial powers. Although many Mohawks tried to maintain a position of neutrality, others cast their lot with the English. Some Mohawks became Protestants, converted by Dutch ministers who had supplanted the Jesuits as French influence among the Mohawks waned. In return for their support against the French, pro-English Mohawks asked the English to build forts on the Mohawk River to help defend Indian villages against French attacks and to send missionaries to serve the Protestant Mohawks.[10]

The Iroquois may have been weakened by the presence of the French and British in New York, but both colonial powers needed them as allies. With the outbreak of Queen Anne's War, New York's colonial leaders asked the Iroquois for support in pressuring Parliament to approve an invasion of Canada. In 1710 four Anglophile Indians were found to accompany a New York delegation to London, where they were passed off as kings of the five Iroquois nations. These were the same Indians whose convoy had passed the Germans' ships while they were anchored off the south coast of England, waiting to set sail for New York. The delegation, actually three Mohawks and a Mahican with little power or influence among the Iroquois, reiterated past requests for the establishment of British forts along the Mohawk River and for Anglican missionaries to serve the Mohawk communities.[11]

The British did not want to lose their somewhat reluctant allies and eventually fulfilled the Indians' requests. In 1711 the British began building Fort Hunter near Tiononderoge, a Mohawk village at the confluence of Schoharie Creek and the Mohawk River. A year later, as the Germans formulated plans to move to Schoharie, the pro-English and Protestant Mohawks who predominated in Tiononderoge welcomed the SPG missionary William Andrews to Fort Hunter.[12]

The Mohawks continued to control the Schoharie Valley, but they no longer possessed the power they had a hundred years earlier. It appears that by 1712 just over six hundred Mohawks lived in New York. About 360 lived in Tiononderoge, while another two hundred lived in Canajoharie, a Mohawk village fifteen miles west. The rest inhabited a few much smaller settlements, including two along Schoharie Creek—Eskahare, about twenty miles south of Tiononderoge, and another settlement eight miles south of Eskahare. Across the creek from the southernmost hamlet stood a small, predominantly Mahican settlement (see map 6).[13]

Despite the precarious position of the Iroquois in New York, the Germans realized the Mohawks remained the principal power in Schoharie. Hunter had repeatedly emphasized the threat of the French and Indians to Schoharie and the lack of British power in the region. The Germans knew they could not survive in Schoharie without Mohawk support. Therefore, when they decided to settle along Schoharie Creek, they did not simply occupy the land; rather, they sought permission to settle as the Mohawks' neighbors.

The Germans probably formed their earliest impressions of the Indians from the promotional literature that had encouraged them to emigrate. Daniel Falckner's *Curieuse Nachricht von Pennsylvania*, written in a question-and-answer format, devoted 46 of 103 questions to describing the Indians. Falckner used the term *Wilden*—savages—to refer to the Indians, but the Indians he described were not particularly savage.[14] Falckner depicted them as simple and unsophisticated. Although most Indians were not Christians, Falckner admitted they were not immoral, marveling that this could be so since they "almost always go naked." Falckner recommended winning the goodwill of the Indians "by all kinds of repeated friendly allurement and offerings of love; being careful not to hold them so fast as to arouse their suspicion, as if we wanted to curtail their liberty." Falckner believed that once a few Indians understood English or German, they could be led to an understanding of Christianity through divinely guided conversation. Although Falckner's description of the Indians was condescending and simplistic, it was not unsympathetic. The Indians he described were not ruthless beasts, and the Europeans had little reason to fear them.[15]

In his promotional tract on Carolina, Kocherthal also emphasized the nonthreatening character of the Indians. He played down the stereotypes of Indian savagery by referring to Carolina's native peoples as *Indianer* rather than *Wilden*. Kocherthal claimed that the Indians knew little about war except what they had learned from the Europeans. He emphasized that, unlike the German southwest, Carolina was a land of peace.[16] The Palatines, who were terrorized by marauding armies at home, would not face such threats from their American neighbors.

In an appendix to Kocherthal's book, an essay translated from English continued the same theme. The English and Indians lived in "complete friendship and good understanding," it argued.[17] Although the Indians did occasionally carry out attacks, such attacks were against other Indians, not the English. The essay portrayed Indian warfare as limited and not particularly brutal. The Indians were simply too divided and weak to present a substantial threat to the European colonists.

The Germans brought to America images of the Indians as a simple, generally peaceful, and childlike people. The images mirrored those that the English had carried to America a century earlier. English writers had emphasized many of the same Indian attributes that the Germans read about in Falckner's and Kocherthal's books. They also found themselves caught in contradictions as they described the Indians and their behavior. For instance, like the German writers, the English referred to Indian savagery and nakedness. Yet they described Indian warfare as non-threatening and emphasized Indian modesty. Although they noted many differences between themselves and the Indians, the English writers did not dismiss the Indians as subhuman, nor did they use race to explain the differences. They portrayed the Indians as less sophisticated than the English but argued that the Indians could learn English ways, just as Falckner felt certain the Indians could be converted to Christianity.[18]

But the image the English brought with them to America began to fade as they came in closer contact with the Native Americans. At the same time their understanding and appreciation of Indian culture increased.[19] When the Germans settled in the naval stores camps, they also had the opportunity to test some of their preconceptions. From time to time various Indians, probably Mahicans, visited the German camps. Some knew Dutch and used it to communicate with the Germans. At least one Indian attended German church services. In his reports to the SPG Haeger mentioned that he had baptized an Indian who "spoke Dutch, and thus made his confession of faith publicly before the congregation."[20]

The German immigrants extended their contacts with the Indians during the failed expedition against Canada in 1711. Besides the three hundred German men in the expedition, over a hundred Mahican and River Indians joined the march.[21] The Iroquois provided around seven hundred warriors, about a quarter of whom were Mohawks.[22] After the expedition, a few German men were occasionally stationed at Albany to help guard the colonial frontier. They probably had further contacts with the Indians and perhaps gained some knowledge of the Mohawk settlements to the west. They may have also noticed the growing disdain among the Iroquois for British military power. The miserably planned attempt to take Canada in 1711 was not the first campaign that the Iroquois had joined. They had also been part of a failed attempt in 1709. Here were potential neighbors who had reason to share the Germans' contempt for British authority.

During their first two years in New York, the Germans had the chance to develop a deeper understanding of Indian culture and society and of the Indians' stake in colonial politics. Their contacts with the Indians and observations of their behavior would have taught them that the Indians were not as childlike, unsophisticated, or peaceful as some of the promotional literature for colonies might have led them to believe. Certainly the Germans would have learned to respect the strength of the Iroquois in New York. Despite the many setbacks the Iroquois had suffered during the last century, they remained an independent force in New York that could make treaties, fight wars, and control territory—all powers that the Germans lacked.

Nothing that the Germans had learned about the Indians would have prevented them from considering the Indians as potential allies. Unlike the English or the Dutch, the Germans in New York had never suffered from Indian attacks.[23] Instead a few tenuous links had formed between the Germans and some of the Indians as a result of their common participation in the failed expedition of 1711, their shared Christianity, and their ability to communicate with one another in Dutch. The majority of people on both sides may not have shared these links and the two sides probably interpreted the shared experiences in very different ways, but neither side would have seemed as alien to the other as it had before.

In October 1712 the Germans sent a delegation to the Mohawks "by whom they were kindly receiv'd, and to whom they open'd their miserable Condition, and that being wholly Cast of[f] by the said Governour, and left destituted of the means of living elsewhere, they intreated them to give 'em permission to settle on the tract of land call'd Schorie."[24] The Germans entreaties were similar to those they had made in London a few years earlier. In their "miserable Condition" they could make no demands. Once again they were forced to beg for charity from a foreign people.

The Mohawks may have been surprised by the Germans' request. They had already granted the lands the Germans sought to the British in 1710, when Hunter was looking for a site for the naval stores operation. In any event the Mohawks pretended no claim to the land and did not attempt to hinder the Germans. The Germans later claimed that the Mohawks granted their request, "saying they had formarly given that said land to Queen Anne for them to possess, and that no body should hinder them of it, and they would assist them as farr as they were able."[25]

As soon as the Mohawks indicated they would not hinder the Germans' proposed settlement, "all hands fell to work and in 2 weeks time Clear'd a way thro' the woods of 15 miles long with the utmost toyle and labour, tho' almost starv'd and without bread."[26] The Germans probably traveled halfway along the existing road between Albany and Schenectady and then headed west about five miles on a well-traveled Indian path to an area near present-day Altamont where a few Europeans had already settled. From there they probably widened an Indian trail the remaining fifteen miles to the Schoharie Valley.[27] Fifty families moved immediately to Schoharie, while the others spent the winter in Albany or Schenectady.

Johann Conrad Weiser had served as a listmaster in the naval stores camps and had emerged as one of the principal leaders of the Germans during their disputes with Hunter. He had long supported a move to Schoharie and played a key role in planning the German migration there in 1712, although his own family spent the winter in Schenectady. Sometime in November Weiser met with a Mohawk leader named Quainant and made a remarkable agreement that showed the extent to which the Germans in Schoharie had rejected the possibility of assimilation into British colonial society. Rather than sending his children to colonial schools, Weiser arranged for his sixteen-year-old son to move to Quainant's village and to live with his family.[28] Weiser saw the Mohawks as powerful allies and realized that good relations with them depended on clear communication. It was more important for his son to learn the Mohawks' language than to learn English. Weiser had already lost two sons in 1710, when Hunter apprenticed them in New York City; now he would risk another to ensure a strong alliance with the Mohawks. Weiser sent his son Conrad from their cabin in Schenectady to spend the next eight months in a Mohawk village. During that time Conrad mastered the Mohawks' language and gained an understanding of their culture. Following Iroquois custom, the Mohawks formally adopted Conrad as a member of their community. Although the boy returned to the German settlements the following year, he moved easily between Indian and European communities for the rest of his life, serving, as his father had hoped, as translator, negotiator, and cultural broker between German and Indian.

By allowing one of their children to be adopted by the Mohawks, the Germans took a different approach to New York's Indians than had the Dutch and the English before them. The Dutch brought from Holland a trader's sense of the world and viewed Indian villages as nodes on the paths of commerce. Because the Dutch wanted to control trade, not land, they did not need to occupy Indian villages.[29] When the trade nexus was absent, as in the predominantly agricultural village of Schenectady, the Dutch had little social contact with the Indians.[30] One historian has noted that "as seventeenth-century sojourners or colonists from the urban, commercial Low Countries, [the Dutch] proved better prepared to become the Five Nations' trading partners than to become their kinspeople."[31]

The English, on the other hand, carried to America visions of extending the king's dominion. They viewed New York as a battleground, a place to fight the French for the domination of North America. The English could not possess New York without controlling the land.[32] Although they lacked the power to make the Iroquois their subjects, they refused to accept them on equal terms. In 1688 New York's governor, Edmund Andros, instructed the Iroquois to stop addressing the English as "brethren." The Iroquois were but "children" to the English, and Andros, as England's representative in New York, was their father. Although the Iroquois did not follow the convention for long, the exchange illustrates the English colonists' growing sense of authority.[33]

Just as Dutch and English attitudes had been shaped by their European roots, the Germans' attitude toward the Mohawks and the chaotic conditions of the Schoharie Valley may have been shaped by their experiences in the German southwest. Perhaps the Germans, coming from an area subject to continual invasion and to ever-changing rulers, had replaced a worldview consisting of conqueror and conquered with one of constantly changing allies and enemies, in which power was never absolute and always short-lived. Since conquest was an illusion, one sought allies who might help secure short-term gains. The Indians could be enemies or allies; the Germans needed the latter.

There were, of course, also plenty of practical New World reasons why the Germans entered the Mohawk's world the way they did. The Germans no longer possessed firearms; even if they had wanted to attack the Mohawks, their chances of success were slim. They also did not have enough food to survive the winter and needed the Mohawks' support to keep from starving. Nobody else seemed prepared to help them settle in Schoharie. Hunter had made it clear that he did not want them there. The Germans realized that in an environment where several forces contended for power but where none possessed overwhelming strength, the judicious choice of allies would be crucial to their success.

As the Germans feared, winter brought many hardships. Those in Albany and Schenectady sometimes found work and also received food from the towns' citizens, but the Germans in Schoharie depended on the Mohawks for much of their sustenance.[34] Although the Mohawks had little food of their own, they helped the new settlers find something to eat. The Germans later recorded their experience in terms reminiscent of accounts of the Pilgrims' first winter at Plymouth: "Upon the first settlement of this land the miserys those poor and allmost famish'd Creatures underwent were incredible, and had it not been for the Charity of the Indians who shew'd them where to gather some eatable roots and herbs, must inevitably have perish'd every soul of them."[35]

The Germans did not deceive themselves about their reliance on the Mohawks. When British and Dutch land speculators later attempted to enlist the Mohawks' aid in pushing the Germans from Schoharie, the Germans pointed out their childlike dependence. They begged the Mohawks that "since they had so long sukled them at their breast, not to wean them so soon and Cast them of[f]."[36] The Germans defined their relationship with the Indians in striking contrast to the relationship defined by Governor Andros. Andros had insisted he was the English father to the Indian children. The Germans inverted the relationship and changed the sex of the parent. As children, the Germans recognized their dependence on a nurturing Mohawk mother. The Mohawk mother cared for and fed her children, while the English father demanded respect and obedience and offered little in return.

The Germans' early dependence on the Mohawks is clear, but it less clear why the Mohawks decided to help the German-speaking settlers. Certainly the Mohawks had no desire to lose more land to Europeans. It is possible that the Mohawks, like the British, hoped to use the Germans as a buffer to shield them from the encroachments of their enemies. The British feared French and Indian advances; the Indians feared the British. In the standoff the Germans could serve a useful role for both sides.

The Mohawks probably also realized the difficulty of keeping European colonists out of Schoharie and perhaps decided that the Germans would make better neighbors than the other Europeans in New York. The Germans, after all, were not nearly as powerful as the British or Dutch and would perhaps be less of a threat. The Mohawks probably also appreciated the Germans' deferential manner and their willingness to send a child to live with a Mohawk family. The Iroquois had a long tradition of adopting outsiders into their families and of considering them as full-fledged members of their communities. Weiser may not have fully understood the significance to the Mohawks of sending his son to live with them, but his action, which had no parallels among the leading English families of New York, no doubt enhanced the Mohawks' view of the Germans.[37]

Settling in Schoharie

Before winter ended the German families living in Schenectady and Albany joined the fifty families in Schoharie. Just as Hunter had once compared the Germans to the Israelites, the Germans drew the same comparison: "In the same year in March, did the remainder of the people (tho' treated by the Governour as Pharao treated the Israelites) proceed on their Journey, and by God's Assistance, travell'd in fourtnight with sledges thro' the snow which there Cover'd the ground above 3 foot deep, Cold and hunger, Joyn'd their friends and Countrymen in the promis'd land of *Schorie*."[38] By early 1713 between 450 and 500 Germans lived in Schoharie.

The Mohawks helped support them through the winter, but during 1713, when the German population in Schoharie doubled, the Germans needed additional help to survive until the land could be cultivated and crops harvested. On at least two occasions the Dutch Reformed Church in New York sent food to Schenectady to supply the Schoharie settlers. In July 1713 it sent eighty bushels of corn, five hundred pounds of smoked pork, and one hundred pounds of bread—enough to fill five wagons.[39] With the additional help, the Germans managed to survive until they could harvest their own food in the fall.

Hunter had intended that the Germans either stay in the naval stores camps or find work with other settlers in New York or New Jersey. He was irritated when they persisted in moving to Schoharie and sent orders forbidding them to cultivate the land. In a letter to Cast, Hunter said that he would attempt to reward those who stayed in the camps with grants of land, but "as for the other [those who moved to Schoharie], I only pray God to turn away the Vengeance that menaces them and which they have richly deserved."[40] Hunter managed to present the bright side of the matter in a report to the Board of Trade. By going as a group to Schoharie, the Germans at least kept together. It would be easier to round them up to work on the tar works when funds arrived. In fact, Hunter planned to put the Schoharie Germans to work in pine woods near Albany, not so far from where they were settling. He also noted that the Schoharie settlers helped provide a defensive buffer for Schenectady and Albany, although he doubted they would be of much help if trouble came. For the time, Hunter decided to let the Germans remain where they were.[41]

Despite Hunter's orders forbidding them to do so, the Germans began building homes and cultivating the Schoharie lands. Eventually

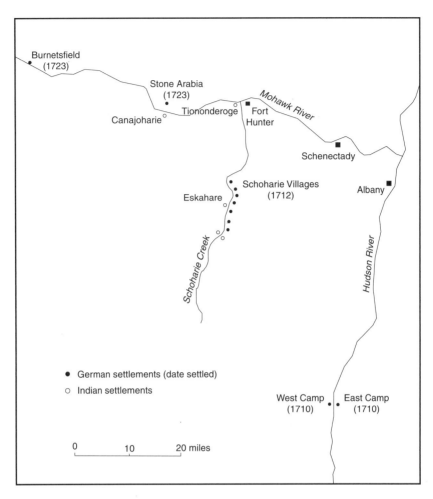

Map 6. Settlements of the 1710 German immigrants in New York

they established seven villages along the east bank of Schoharie Creek, each named after a German leader living in the village. From north to south stood the villages of Kneskerndorf, Gerlachsdorf, Fuchsendorf, Schmidtsdorf, Weisersdorf (or Brunnendorf), Hartmannsdorf, and Oberweisersdorf.[42] The village names reflect a remarkable continuity of leadership among the Germans. Four villages were named after men who had been listmasters on the ships crossing to New York (Johann Peter Kneskern, Johann Christian Gerlach, Johann Christopher Fuchs, and Johann Georg Schmidt). The other villages bore the names of listmasters from the naval stores camps (Hartmann Windecker and Johann Conrad Weiser).[43] The men who served as the German leaders consistently sought ways to gain the land that had drawn them to America. They challenged Hunter's authority and refused to become other men's tenants. The people who moved with them to Schoharie shared their outlook and perseverance. They would be the least assimilative of the various groups of 1710 migrants spreading across the middle colonies, always following their own peculiar path toward realizing the promises of the golden book.

The word *dorf* is usually translated as *village,* but the German settlements were no more than loosely formed clusters of family farms.[44] They had no churches, stores, or mills. The Germans had to take their grain to Schenectady or Albany to be ground and remained dependent on the two towns for many of their supplies. Although the Germans wanted to avoid the intrusion of colonial authorities into their lives, they found independence difficult to attain even on the colonial frontier.

Still the Germans attempted to insulate their settlements from the incursions of other New York colonists. They began buying land from the Mohawks, partly because they did not have enough room for the 120 families now living in Schoharie and partly to prevent other colonists from claiming the land.[45] For the colonial government to recognize a purchase of Indian land, a buyer first had to petition the government for a license to acquire the land from the Indians. Once the government issued the license, the buyer could purchase the land, but ownership was not confirmed until the land was surveyed by the surveyor general's office and the governor issued letters patent. The Germans dispensed with the formalities. Perhaps they did not understand New York land law, or perhaps they realized that the government would never grant them licenses to purchase land. They needed land, and they did not dare alienate the Mohawks. The colonial government might not recognize the land purchase, but the Indians would. For the short term, it was the best the Germans could expect.

The Germans' attempt to preempt the claims of other colonists was not successful for long. In 1714 Nicholas Bayard, the grandson of the man whose Schoharie claims had been disallowed as an "extravagant grant" under the 1699 Vacating Act, traveled to Schoharie. He offered a deed in the name of Queen Anne to any German settlers who brought him descriptions of the land they occupied.[46] Bayard no longer had a legitimate claim to the land, but he had petitioned the government to reconfirm his grandfather's patent. He probably hoped to strengthen his case by showing that the land had been settled and improved.[47]

The Germans would not take the bait. After endless difficulties in obtaining land of their own, they were suspicious when Bayard suddenly offered to confirm the claims that everyone else denied. According to a later account, the Germans suspected that Bayard wanted to make them tenants. Instead of accepting his offer, they drove him from their settlements.[48] The Germans would attempt to establish their claims through possession and improvement, not through legal documents.

In May 1714 five men from Albany petitioned for a grant of ten thousand acres of land in Schoharie including Bayard's vacated grant.[49] In November Hunter issued the patent. A short time later two more men received a patent for land just north of the ten-thousand-acre grant. Together the seven men held all the land in Schoharie on which the Germans had settled. The new landowners, known as the Seven Partners, included representatives of the Schuyler, Livingston, and Morris families, all wealthy families and prominent political allies of Hunter.[50] One of the Seven Partners, Henry Wileman, served as trustee for George Clarke, the colonial secretary who had helped oversee the naval stores project and who now saw the opportunity to profit again from the Germans' labor.[51]

In 1715, three years after the first Germans had moved to Schoharie, the Seven Partners informed the settlers that they would have to purchase the land from its new owners or move away. The Germans adopted a strategy that emphasized their loyalty to the British Crown and recognized the difficulties of controlling the colonial periphery from a distant center. Rather than asserting their own claim to the land, the Germans argued that "the land was the King's and that the[y] were the Kings Subjects and had no power to agree to any thing about his Majesty's lands without his special order." When the Seven Partners replied that they were kings of this land, the Germans answered that "their King was in England, and that the land shou'd not be taken from them without his Majesty's particular order."[52]

The Germans' account of the affair appeared in a 1720 petition to the Board of Trade, part of their continuing effort to gain title to the Schoharie land. At the time the Germans were concerned with presenting themselves as loyal subjects of the king, but the arguments they outlined would have been effective in 1715 as well. The Germans said they did not have to deal with the Seven Partners because the partners had no authority over them. The Germans realized that, unlike in the Old

World, where some authority was always nearby, in the New World the power of the colonial government was limited. Since the Seven Partners apparently did not have the strength to drive them from Schoharie, the Germans could claim the high ground as loyal subjects of the king while ignoring the Seven Partners' demands.

Although the partners could not force the Germans to recognize their claims, they did manage to disrupt the settlers' lives. According to the Germans, the Seven Partners attempted to win over the Indians and "if possible to persuade them (for money or Rumm) to put them in possession of the land and declare them rightfull owners thereof."[53] The Germans discovered that some Mohawks had no idealized notions of a special alliance with the German-speaking immigrants, and the Germans were forced to make presents of what little they owned to keep the Mohawks on their side.[54]

The Germans resisted much more directly the activities of another outsider who owned land in the Schoharie. Adam Vrooman, a Dutch settler from Schenectady, following standard British procedures had purchased 340 acres in Schoharie in 1714.[55] In the spring of 1715 he traveled to Schoharie, cleared some land, and planted crops. Vrooman's land lay just south of the German settlements in an area that the Germans evidently considered their own. They suspected that Hunter had sent Vrooman to disrupt their settlement, and they decided to drive Vrooman from the land.[56] As soon as his crops began to grow, the Germans let their cattle graze on Vrooman's fields. On one occasion, when Vrooman's son drove the Germans' cattle from the field, Conrad Weiser ran to a nearby Mohawk village and enlisted his Indian friends to help drive the cattle back on to Vrooman's land.[57]

Vrooman returned to Schenectady but soon came back to Schoharie, determined to settle on the land. In June he began building a stone house with the help of his son and some workmen, including a slave. The Germans waited until Vrooman's men had built the walls and laid the ceiling beams before taking action. In the middle of the night, while Vrooman and his workmen slept two hundred yards away, the Germans pulled the house down using horses with bells tied to their necks. When Vrooman confronted the Germans the next day "they used such Rebelious Expressions that was never heard off" and indicated they could act with impunity because they could "Run among the Indians." Vrooman returned to Schenectady, leaving his son behind to guard the property. Not long afterward the Germans pulled his son from a wagon, beat him badly, and threatened to kill him if he remained in Schoharie.[58]

The Germans carefully staged their attack on Vrooman's property. Drawing on ideas they brought from the Old World, they sought to make a clear statement of their intention to protect their community but to do it in a way that shielded them from arrest. The Germans attacked at night, thus keeping the identities of the individual culprits hidden. At the same time, they tied bells to their horses. The Germans wanted to be heard but not seen. Unlike the resistance they aimed at Hunter in the naval stores camps, the Germans carried out this act of defiance with an almost gleeful realization that the victim could do little to apprehend the perpetrators. If the colonial authorities sought them out, the Germans would hide among their New World neighbors.

Vrooman immediately recognized the importance of Weiser's ties to the Indians. In his letters to Hunter, Vrooman reported that Johann Conrad Weiser had established himself as the German "Ring Leader" and that Weiser's power was directly tied to the personal link he had established to the Mohawks through his son. Vrooman noted that father and son negotiated directly with the Indians. They made treaties for land with the Mohawks in direct contravention of government orders, and Weiser's son "every day tells the Indians many Lyes, whereby much mischeife may Ensue more than we now think off and is much to be feared."[59]

Hunter shared Vrooman's concern. The Germans' alliance with the Mohawks threatened British control of the region. By settling in Schoharie and purchasing land directly from the Mohawks, the Germans denied the authority of the British colonial state in their affairs. Not only did the Germans live among the Indians, but they also acted like the Indians. They seemed to think they could govern their own affairs and live outside the laws of colonial New York.

Hunter decided to act. On July 22, 1715, he issued a warrant for Weiser's arrest, describing him as "a Covenanted Servant of his Majesty, who had been Guilty of Several Mutinous Riotous and other disobedient & illegal practices." What seemed to concern Hunter most were Weiser's ties with the Indians. He described Weiser as "skulking" in the woods, a description the British often used to characterize what they considered the Indians' devious ways. Rather than facing his punishment, Weiser behaved like his Indian friends, lurking on the edge of civilized society and refusing to play by European rules.[60]

That summer Hunter wrote to the Board of Trade about other troubles created by the Germans' close ties to the Indians. Hunter had just been to Albany to meet with the Iroquois. One of the matters he had to deal with was "some confusion Created amongst them by some turbulent Palatines settled near them." In the same report, Hunter warned the Board of Trade that Weiser claimed to be bound for England "instructed by the Indians."[61] Somehow Hunter convinced himself that the Germans, who had come to America as wards of the British Crown, were now so closely allied to the Iroquois that they would rely on Iroquois advice in their negotiations with their former benefactors. By moving to the colonial frontier the Germans seemed to have slipped from British control.

Hunter must have had his worst suspicions confirmed when he heard news of the bungled attempt to arrest Weiser. Sometime in 1715 Albany officials dispatched a sheriff to the German settlements in Schoharie. The Germans gave only a short public account of his visit, saying the community had been forewarned and the sheriff and his deputies "were prevented" from making any arrests.[62] But the Germans preserved a fuller account of the day's events that they shared with one another and passed on to future generations.[63] In the mid-eighteenth century John Brown, the grandson of one of the German immigrants, heard the story from participants in the day's events, including the sheriff himself. In 1823 he included the story in his history of Schoharie County.[64]

The tale is one of female resistance that went far beyond any acts carried out by the German men against Governor Hunter. In Brown's account, the sheriff, a Mr. Adams, arrived in the German settlement alone. As he attempted to arrest one of the men, "a mob of women rose, of which Magdalene Zee was captain." The women attacked the surprised sheriff, knocking him to the ground, tying him up, and dragging him through the mud. They then paraded their prize hanging from a rail for four painful miles through the German settlements along the Schoharie. The women finally arrived at a bridge on Schoharie Creek, the symbolic gate to the German community, where they dumped the unwelcome and badly battered visitor. Still, the women had not finished. Magdalene Zee yanked out a fence stake and beat the sheriff, breaking two of his ribs and poking out an eye. In a final act of triumph she stood astride her victim, lifted her skirt, and "pissed in his face." Having safely deposited the sheriff beyond the settlement's boundary, the women returned to their work. Somehow Adams survived. When nobody came to his aid, he forced himself to his feet and hobbled slowly back to Albany.[65]

Jeptha Simms, who wrote two decades after Brown, captured the essence of the episode when he called Adams's trip through the settlements a "skimmington ride."[66] The word *skimmington* had seventeenth-century origins and referred to a man who allowed his wife to dominate him. The community mocked him for his weak will and his inability to maintain the order of the patriarchal household. In shaming rituals of seventeenth- and eighteenth-century Europe such men were often forced to ride through town facing backward on a donkey. Over time such processions evolved into a rough form of peasant justice used to punish anyone who upset the social order of everyday life.[67] Although skimmingtons and other forms of peasant justice were usually aimed at people within a community, they could also be directed against outsiders who threatened the community's traditional rights.[68]

The underlying significance of Adams's treatment would have been well understood by all involved. Adams threatened to disrupt the German community by arresting those who most actively defended the Germans' claims to the Schoharie lands. The Germans could expect little sympathy if they appealed Adams's actions to the colonial government, so the German women took the matter into their own hands, using a familiar, Old World means of peasant justice to punish the intruder.

Early nineteenth-century historians found the form of German country justice familiar, but they seemed surprised that the women were the sole actors (other than Adams) in the event. Brown felt compelled to vouch for the story's accuracy, writing, "I have myself seen this very Adams, and have the relation from his own mouth, together with the confirmation of several of the old Schoharie people."[69] He need not have been so defensive. The history of early modern Europe is full of accounts of women's violence. When the defense of family or community required it, "unruly women" throughout western Europe incited riots, attacked government authorities, and chased the clergy from their towns.[70]

The German immigrants grew up in a world where women were considered socially and legally subordinate to men. There were many limits on women's activities, and under normal conditions pummeling the local sheriff and then urinating on him were not within those limits. When women engaged in such violence, they were clearly violating the norms of early modern European society.[71] Because they broke with convention, disorderly women sent a particularly powerful message, and when such messages were needed, communities often relied on women to deliver them.[72] In 1715 Magdalene Zee and the other German women delivered their message to Governor Hunter. By attacking the government's representative, they rebuked the governor and his greedy friends, warning them that they could not easily deprive the Germans of their promised land. The episode proves that the cantankerous behavior that served as a hallmark of the Schoharie settlers was shared by the whole group—male and female alike.

But the intention of delivering a strong message was not the only reason the women dealt with Adams alone. The community might have faced serious retribution if the men, rather than the women, had carried out the attack. The legal system of early modern Europe assumed women could not be trusted to act rationally. By nature they fell prey to their emotions and could not always be held responsible for their actions. On these grounds, the law often punished women less severely than men, and on many occasions women, or men dressed as women, led protests by the lower orders against those in authority.[73] The Germans carried the tactic with them to New York. The Germans' later actions make it clear that the tactic was consciously followed. As Brown put it, "After this circumstance [the attack on Adams], the Schoharie people got very shy to go to Albany—made the practice to send their wives for salt, or not to enter Albany but on Sundays, and then out again."[74]

Women were not immune from arrest, however. The Schoharie settlers later complained that a German woman had been detained and held in the Albany jail.[75] They did not mention the charges; for a woman to be jailed was reason enough to complain. Living on the edge of the European colonial world, the Germans still felt aggrieved when the colonial authorities did not play by Old World rules.

Despite the disruptions, the Germans managed to survive and even to prosper. In October 1715 Hunter reported that the Germans in Schoharie and on the Hudson "subsist pretty comfortably for new beginners having been blest with very plentiful Crops."[76] Still the Germans in the Schoharie settlements remained an irritant to Hunter, especially as they continued to refuse to purchase their land from the Seven Partners. Finally in 1717 Hunter decided to investigate the problem. He traveled to Albany and instructed the Schoharie settlers to send three men from every village to meet him. When the German representatives arrived, Hunter asked three questions: why had they settled in Schoharie without his permission, why hadn't they reached an agreement with the men from Albany who owned the land, and why did they concern themselves so much with the Indians?[77]

The only account of the meeting is contained in a petition that the Schoharie Germans addressed to the Board of Trade in 1720.[78] The petition portrayed Hunter in the worst possible light and hinted that he

Figure 8. German house built in the mid-eighteenth century in Schoharie. The house's present rustic appearance belies what would have been a fine frontier home, with a whitewashed exterior of sawn boards and an interior that was plastered and painted. Courtesy of the Old Stone Fort Museum, Schoharie, New York.

placed his own interests above those of the Crown. In calling Hunter's loyalty into question, the Germans repeated an accusation that had been part of their strategy to discredit Hunter ever since he had settled them in the naval stores camps. Despite its obvious biases, the petition presents the Germans' view of the situation in Schoharie and explains their actions toward the Seven Partners and the Indians.

According to the Germans' account, their deputies replied to Hunter's first question that Hunter himself had told the Germans to shift for themselves after the naval stores project had been suspended. They argued that "the utmost necessity and poverty forc'd them to remove thither to earn their bread for the maintenance of their Wifes and Children." The Germans' goals had changed little since they had left the German southwest—they were intent on gaining land in America to support themselves and their heirs—and they continued to pretend that the

British monarch had every intention of helping them. Queen Anne's death did not dampen their optimism. With King George I on the throne, they were dealing again with one of the German princes they had left behind in 1709, but this time they claimed confidence that the German-speaking monarch would look out for their interests. The men told Hunter that they had remained on their Schoharie lands "in expectation of His Majesty's Grace and His Excell. favour."[79]

The Germans reported that Hunter grew furious when they continued to assign plans to the monarch that contradicted his own. Livingston, who accompanied Hunter, agreed with the governor, pointing to Hunter and saying, "Here is your King."[80]

The Germans were not deterred and answered the second question in a similar manner. First they argued that the Seven Partners wanted too much money, especially since the Germans had invested a great deal of money and labor in improving the land. Besides, the Germans argued, the Indians had given the land to the Crown specifically for the use of the Germans. Only if the king himself acknowledged that the land was intended for the men in Albany would the Germans agree to the terms. "If they serv'd any body, it must be the King and not a privat person."[81]

Regarding the third question, the Germans pointed out that their Indian policy was the only reasonable policy they could pursue. They lived on a frontier threatened by the French, and the Germans could not withstand the French alone. Therefore, "they were oblig'd to keep fair with the friendly Indians amongst Whom, they dwelt, which was the only way to be protected and live in peace."[82] In other words, since Hunter and the other colonial authorities could not protect the Germans, they had to rely on the Indians, who could.

Hunter, tired of the Germans' evasive arguments, ordered them to buy or lease their land from the owners in Albany or to leave. He promised to send assessors to examine the land and to value the Germans' improvements, but he prohibited the Germans from planting new crops until they had settled with the Seven Partners. When the assessors did not arrive, the Germans asked Hunter's permission to plow land for the following year. He refused, but the Germans, fearing starvation, planted their fields anyway.[83]

By 1718 the Germans had lived in Schoharie for five years but still had not secured title to their land. The people once again were divided over what step to take next. Some were ready to purchase or lease the land from the Seven Partners. Hunter believed that "the greatest part" had already accepted the partners' conditions.[84] Conrad Weiser later admitted that the German community had indeed split over the issue, but he noted that the "strongest party would not submit."[85] This party was determined to hang on to their Schoharie farms and even sought to gain additional lands in New York for their families. Finally the Schoharie settlers did what Hunter had feared they would do three years earlier—they sent a delegation to London in hopes of dealing directly with King George.[86]

The Germans selected three men to represent them: Johann Conrad Weiser, Wilhelm Scheff, and Gerhardt Walrath. Since Hunter did not sanction their mission and had threatened earlier to arrest Weiser, the three men avoided New York City and went instead to Philadelphia. Sometime in 1718 they set sail for London. Soon after the men left port, pirates raided their ship, robbing the passengers and crew. Weiser and Scheff managed to keep a small amount of money by convincing the pirates that they shared a single purse. After the raid the ship sailed to Boston for more supplies before continuing to London.[87]

The men arrived in London before the year was out, but their luck did not improve. Queen Anne had died, and few of the German benefactors of 1709 could be found. Although they had earlier claimed that they anticipated King George's support for their cause, the Germans could expect little sympathy from the monarch. Why should he support disloyal peasants who had fled the territories of Germanic princes? After all, he, too, was a German prince. No evidence indicates that he took any interest in the men's case. The representatives of the Schoharie settlers made little progress. Walrath became homesick and left for New York, dying on the return voyage. Weiser and Scheff soon ran out of money and found themselves in debtors' prison. Eventually money arrived from New York and the men were released, but it was not until July 1720, two years after their arrival, that the men were able to place a petition before the Board of Trade.[88]

The Germans began their petition with a rambling history of their trials in New York. They criticized Hunter for withholding clothing and tools from them and for never granting each person forty acres of land, as the Germans contended they had been promised. They complained of being settled on Livingston's lands, where "the profits of building and improving the lands fell to a private person." They spoke of their desire to settle in Schoharie, which they insisted "the Indians had given to the late Queen Ann for their use."[89] With their penchant for created histories, which had helped support and define them since they had initially passed through London in 1709, the petitioners may have elaborated on this claim by arguing that the Indian kings who had visited London in 1710 had offered the land for the Germans' use after seeing the thousands of German refugees living in camps around the city. Certainly Conrad Weiser later spread this story, conveniently overlooking the fact that the German settlers bound for New York had left London before the Indians arrived.[90] In any case, when the naval stores program failed and Hunter would no longer feed them, the Germans were forced to find a place to support themselves. They moved to Schoharie, where the Indians granted them land, saying that they had already given the property "to Queen Anne for them to possess, and that no body should hinder them of it."[91] Through hard work the settlers had improved the land and built houses. Now they faced the prospect of losing all they had labored so hard to achieve. Hunter had sold the Schoharie land to seven men from Albany and ordered the Germans to buy the land at the new owners' terms or leave. In light of all that had happened, the petitioners requested that the Germans "be secured in the Land they now do inhabit or in some near adjoining lands remaining in the right of the Crown in the said Province of New York."[92] Despite their many problems, the Germans wanted to stay in New York.

By the time the German delegation managed to place its petition before the Board of Trade, Hunter had returned to London and was able to refute the Germans' arguments in person. Eleven years after he had appeared before the Board of Trade asking to take three thousand Germans with him to make naval stores in New York, Hunter was back before the board, detailing the headaches the Germans had caused his administration. He blamed the trouble on a few men, not on an inadequately funded or poorly conceived plan. Hunter argued that when the naval stores project was suspended, the Germans had plenty of good land on which to support themselves, but "that Weiser, who is a very seditious and turbulent man, and a great ringleader, came at the head of about 40 families of the Palatines, who, notwithstanding an order and proclamation against it, took possession by force of certain lands, called Schories, which had been granted to others." Although the Germans did not deserve it, Hunter claimed that he had prevailed upon the rightful owners of the land to lease it to the Germans on very good terms. Hunter said that most of the Germans had agreed to the terms and no longer wished for Weiser to represent them.[93]

It must have galled Hunter to have to defend his administration against a man who had caused him endless trouble and who had arrived in London only after eluding arrest in New York. Furthermore the Board of Trade seemed to take the Germans' charges seriously. On August 27 the board granted the Germans' request that Francis Nicholson be brought in to corroborate the Germans' story.[94] Nicholson had commanded the New York troops, including the three hundred German volunteers, in the failed campaign against Canada in 1711.

Unfortunately for the Germans, Nicholson said he did not know enough about the Germans' situation in New York to comment on their complaints. Nevertheless the Board of Trade agreed to refer the Germans' grievances to New York's new governor, William Burnet, who had arrived in the colony in 1720. The board advised Burnet to find lands "for such of [the Palatines], as desire to remove to proper places," although the board observed "that it seemed several of the Palatines had behaved themselves very undutifully to His Majesty and his late Governor of that province."[95]

Weiser and Scheff remained in London, trying to gain further guarantees for their countrymen, but they began arguing with each other and accomplished nothing. Scheff left for New York in 1721. Weiser followed two years later, arriving in New York in November 1723.[96] By the time Weiser returned to Schoharie, the Germans were again on the move. The strategies the Germans had pursued in Schoharie were only good enough to ensure the Germans' short-term survival, not their long-term success. The colonial government never recognized the Germans' claim to the Schoharie lands, and most families who remained in Schoharie had to buy or rent land from the Seven Partners.

Yet many of the Germans would still not submit to British colonial authority. They remained determined to find the land that had been promised to them first by Kocherthal's golden book, then by the charity of Queen Anne, and finally by the Iroquois sachems who had allegedly taken pity on them in London. No matter that none of these promises had much basis in reality. Neither had the Germans' petitions in London when they claimed to be refugees fleeing the cruelty of the French. It was time to move again. Their long, frustrating search for land had not yet come to an end.

CHAPTER 7

"A Nation Which Is Neither French, Nor English, Nor Indian"

THE MOHAWK VALLEY, 1723–1757

The German immigrants who arrived in New York in 1710 had left their homes believing that Queen Anne would give them free land in America. When they realized their faith in the queen's generosity was misplaced, they split over what to do next. In the process, the group's coherence and its sense of common identity, which had developed from the time the immigrants had first arrived in London, began to fade. Many of them would no longer engage in the kind of creative resistance that had pulled the disparate migrants into a coherent group while simultaneously setting them apart from the societies into which they would not assimilate. After the failure of the naval stores project, some immigrants no longer believed that constant resistance to colonial authority and insistence on free farmland was worthwhile. Many of them remained in the Hudson River valley or moved south to central New Jersey. But others, including the influential listmasters, seemed to revel in their muleheadedness. They resisted longer, took greater risks, and held out for ten years or more in their quest for free land. Many of these Germans first moved to Schoharie, and when powerful land speculators booted them from their promised land, they moved to more distant settlements on the periphery of colonial New York and Pennsylvania. Life on the colonial frontier may have been more uncertain and less secure than along the

Hudson River, but the possibilities for creating new worlds were more numerous in regions far removed from the control of the colonial governments.[1]

When Hunter halted the naval stores project, the more pragmatic Germans quickly gained farmland by becoming tenants of the Livingstons, Beekmans, and other nearby landowners.[2] Although they had to abandon dreams of free land, tenancy provided some benefits to the impoverished settlers. They obtained farmland quickly and cheaply. Manor lords provided tenants with easy access to capital, farming equipment, mills, and markets—all vital to a farmer's success but often not available to new immigrants.[3]

Despite the benefits tenancy offered, many Germans who remained along the Hudson still wanted farms of their own. Although the Germans had groused about the poor quality of the land in the naval stores camps, at least sixty-three families decided to stay where they had been settled. Since so many other immigrants had moved away, the remaining families could each hold almost one hundred acres of land. The quality of the land may have been poor, but it was plentiful. After the failure of the naval stores project, Robert Livingston demanded the return of the six thousand acres he had sold to the Crown for the Germans' use, but the Germans secured title to the land in 1724 and gradually established the successful farming community known simply as The Camp (present-day Germantown).[4]

Plenty of unsettled and undisputed land lay between The Camp and New York City, and many of the 1710 immigrants moved southward. By 1714, thirty-five German families had created a small farming community in the vicinity of Rhinebeck.[5] One group settled across the Hudson River near Kingston. Many of the men in this group became naturalized citizens in 1715, and some of them later bought land thirty miles southwest of Kingston in the Wallkill River valley, where they created a small German community.[6] Some Germans left New York entirely and moved to New Jersey. A few settled near Hackensack, while forty-five to fifty families established farms along the Raritan and Millstone rivers in Somerset County.[7]

Other immigrants, such as Jost and Anna Hite, moved to Pennsylvania, where they joined the growing German community northwest of Philadelphia.[8] Jost Hite engaged in land speculation, selling land to German migrants who were just beginning to arrive in large numbers in Philadelphia. By 1731 he had managed to use his gains to become co-owner of 140,000 acres in Virginia's northern Shenandoah Valley—the equivalent of one of the small principalities of the German southwest. The Virginia government granted the land to Hite and his partner, Alexander Ross, an Irish Quaker from Pennsylvania, with the condition that they settle one hundred families on the land within two years. In 1732 Jost and Anna Hite led the earliest European settlers into the valley, including at least four other members of the 1710 migration.[9] There they oversaw the development of a prosperous farming settlement, which anchored the southern end of a line of communities founded by the 1710 immigrants stretching from northern Virginia to central New York.[10]

It is among the settlers who moved to Schoharie, however, that one sees most clearly the single-minded determination of the 1710 immigrants to create communities on their own terms with as little outside interference as possible. Although they had seen Schoharie as their promised land, after a decade of land disputes, they began to lose faith in its promise. Many Schoharie settlers left the disputed lands, moving even farther from the vexing interference of large landowners and colonial authorities. In 1718, 680 Germans lived in Schoharie; within a few years the settlement had lost over half of its German population.[11]

Some of the Schoharie Germans left New York altogether. In the early 1720s five German men traveled south from Schoharie to Pennsylvania to explore possible settlement sites near the Susquehanna River. When Pennsylvania's governor, William Keith, visited Albany in 1722, the Germans secured his permission to settle near Tulpehocken Creek on Pennsylvania's western periphery.[12] In 1723 sixteen families moved from Schoharie to Pennsylvania. Unlike other European settlers in Pennsylvania, the Schoharie Germans approached their new settlement from the west rather than the east, moving through Indian lands. Seemingly intent on avoiding New York City and other centers of British settlement, they traveled west from Schoharie to a tributary of the Susquehanna River. There they stopped to build canoes before journeying three hundred miles downriver to Swatara Creek, just south of present-day Harrisburg. The Germans paddled east up Swatara Creek and then trekked a few miles overland to Tulpehocken.[13] Unlike other European settlements in Pennsylvania, their new community was not tethered to Philadelphia but, like the Schoharie settlement, hung suspended between European and Indian worlds.

The Delaware Indians living near Tulpehocken argued, however, that the Germans had not settled between the Indians and the Europeans but directly on Indian lands. Governor Keith, who knew he had granted lands that were not his to give away, hoped to appease the Delawares by

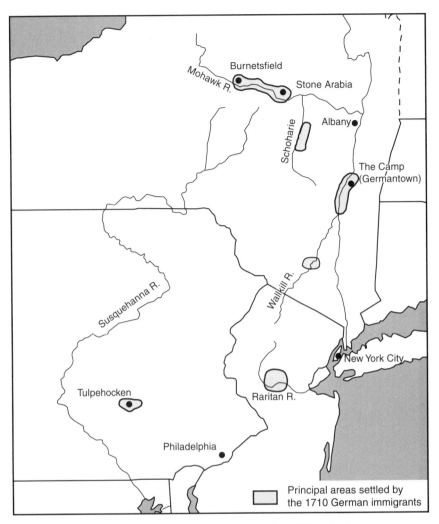

Map 7. Settlements of the 1710 German immigrants in the middle colonies

limiting the amount of land the Germans occupied. He ordered the settlers to "make their Settlements nearer together that they might thereby
give the less uneasiness to the Indians."[14] A few Germans who had settled on the Swatara moved east to join those along Tulpehocken Creek.

The Delaware leader Sassoonan still protested the Germans' presence.
The Germans' cattle were trampling the Indians' corn, and the Indians
were being driven from their lands. Eventually the Delawares, realizing

the uneven odds they faced, left the region and moved west to the Allegheny River. Sassoonan, who remained behind living among the Iroquois, finally ceded his lost lands in 1732.[15] In New York, the 1710 immigrants had been forced to coexist peacefully with the Mohawks because they had no other allies in the colony. In Pennsylvania, where they settled at the governor's invitation, they could simply push the Indians off the land. By 1725 at least thirty-three German families, mostly from the Schoharie villages of Hartmannsdorf and Weisersdorf, lived in the farming community of Tulpehocken.[16] After spending much of his youth and early adult life among his German and Iroquois relatives in Schoharie, Conrad Weiser also moved to Pennsylvania. In 1729, he and his wife, along with their four children, joined the Tulpehocken settlers.[17]

Most of the Schoharie Germans remained in New York, where they soon found themselves dealing with a new governor. Governor William Burnet, who replaced Hunter in 1720, was the son of Bishop Gilbert Burnet, who had been one of the principal church leaders seeking charity for the Germans when they arrived in London in 1709. Governor Burnet, who had not lost a fortune on the naval stores project and who supported the colony's western expansion, proved more willing to help the Germans procure land than had Hunter. In late 1720 the Board of Trade instructed Burnet "to settle those among [the Germans] who behave themselves with dutiful submission to his Majesty's Authority and are destitute of means of subsistence upon such convenient lands as are not already disposed of."[18] Although the Schoharie Germans were clearly the least submissive of all the Germans who had arrived in New York in 1710, Burnet believed there was a way to satisfy the Germans' desires, the Board of Trade's demand, and the colony's needs. He resurrected the old plan of placing the Germans as a defensive barrier along the colony's northwest frontier.

He initially hoped to settle the Germans "as far as [he] could in the middle of our Indians," but when he presented the plan to the Germans in 1721 they found the suggested site too remote. They may have wished to distance themselves from the control of the colonial government, but they also wanted to ensure their prosperity. They could not afford to isolate themselves from their fellow immigrants or to cut their economic ties with New York's markets. The Germans persuaded Burnet to let them settle along the Mohawk River. Burnet agreed to the request but insisted that their settlement "be not nearer than a fall in the Mohocks River which is forty miles above Fort Hunter & four score from Albany." He reported to the Board of Trade that his stipulations had led to an agreement "by which the frontier will be so much extended" and that the Germans "seem very well pleased and satisfyed with what I have done."[19] The agreement also pleased Burnet. He had solved his German problem and had found the human shield he desired to protect the colony from French incursions.

As usual the Germans upset the government's well-laid plans. In 1722 Burnet agreed to purchase land on the Mohawk River about sixty miles west of Schenectady, but the Germans, who were on the verge of receiving the land they had so long sought, now argued that there was not enough land for all the settlers. Burnet reported that the Germans were squabbling among themselves and that "the cunningest among them [were] fomenting their Divisions on purpose that the greatest number might leave the Province and the great Tract of Land lately purchas'd would make so many considerable estates to the few Familys that should remain." The Germans did in fact split into two groups, with one group refusing to settle with the other. Although Burnet remained suspicious about their divisions, he allowed the splinter group to find land of its own since it consisted of people who "had all along been most hearty for the Government."[20] In his desire to rid himself of the annoying Germans, Burnet was willing to overlook the board's instructions to find land only for those Germans who showed "dutiful submission to his Majesty's Authority."

In 1723 the more factious Germans moved to the lands Burnet had purchased on the Mohawk River. Over thirty families established the village of Burnetsfield in a region that became known as German Flats.[21] In 1725 the Germans received a patent for ninety-four thousand acres, which allocated one hundred acres to "every person Man Woman and Child as are Desirous to settle within the Limitts of the said Tract of Land."[22] The settlers clustered their homes together in a small village near the center of the patent. They re-created the familiar field patterns of the German southwest by dividing the patent into 115 lots distributed on the fertile plains north and south of the river and in long, narrow strips extending into the wooded hills north of the village. Each family held several strips of land scattered across the patent, including at least one strip of land fronting on the river.[23]

Meanwhile the Germans whom Burnet had deemed "hearty for the Government" purchased Iroquois lands north of the Mohawk River, about twenty-five miles closer to Schenectady than the Burnetsfield settlement. There they established the farming community of Stone Arabia. Although Burnet had allowed the Stone Arabia group to settle closer to

Schenectady, the land they purchased lay several miles north of the river; more convenient and fertile lands along the Mohawk River were reserved for the colony's powerful and politically connected families. The Stone Arabia patent, issued to twenty-seven persons, consisted of 12,700 acres. Each family received fifty acres; they held the rest of the land in common for future distribution.[24]

As they laid out their new communities along the Mohawk River, the German immigrants recognized the possibilities for organizing their settlements in ways that fit the American environment. Rather than blindly replicating the traditional layout of southwest German farm communities, they assessed the variety and value of land at their disposal and distributed it in a manner that promoted agricultural efficiency while ensuring that all settlers received land of roughly equal value.[25] Settlers on the Burnetsfield patent divided their land into over a hundred lots to ensure that each family had access to land on the Mohawk River and to forest land above the village. Because the land at Stone Arabia varied little—none of it was on the river, and wooded areas probably extended across the patent—the settlers saw little reason for a complex division of property. Each family held its fifty acres in one piece. Unlike Burnetsfield, the Stone Arabia patent did not straddle a major trade route. The Stone Arabia settlers did not need a central village where they could store and protect goods for trade. Rather than grouping their homes in a village, they built their houses where they worked, on their own farmsteads.[26]

By 1725 the German immigrants' search for farmland and the disputes their quest engendered had come to an end. The Germans had learned that it did them little good to ignore colonial land policies or to challenge the power of New York's powerful land speculators. In 1712 the Germans had attempted to obtain land directly from the Indians without the involvement of the colonial government, but after the loss of their Schoharie property, they realized the dangers of farming land without holding proper title to it. Rather than circumventing the law, they now mastered the complexities of the New York land market.

The Germans used their growing prosperity and their knowledge of the land market to spread beyond the bounds of the land initially granted to them. In 1722 Peter and Margaretha Wagner, who had fled their debts in Dachsenhausen in 1709, had enough money to buy land from Francis Harrison along the Mohawk River just south of the Stone Arabia settlement. Harrison, a former sheriff of New York City, also sold lots to several other 1710 immigrants.[27] Other Germans bought land for

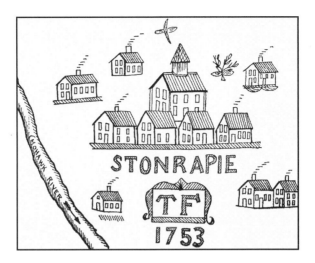

Figure 9. Drawing of Stone Arabia. Copy of the original etched on a powder horn by Timothy Frank in 1753. The simple sketch, with the church in the center and the river along the side, shares its layout with Merian's etching of Oppenheim (figure 1) while portraying a simple frontier existence that seems far removed from the bustle of the Rhineland town. Perhaps the main difference the emigrants would have noticed is the lack of a lord's castle overlooking Stone Arabia. Courtesy of the Palatine Society, Upstate New York Synod, Evangelical Lutheran Church in America. Photo courtesy of the New York State Historical Association, Research Library.

settlement or speculation in the New York backcountry. In 1725 Peter Wagner, Conrad Weiser, and Johannes Lawyer received a patent for land they had purchased from the Mohawks in 1723.[28] Anna Kast, Hartmann Windecker, Johann Peter Kneskern, and other Schoharie Germans also purchased land and received patents along the Schoharie and Mohawk rivers.[29] Johannes Lawyer held land in Stone Arabia, apparently for speculation, while remaining on his prosperous farm in Schoharie.[30]

Eventually the region between Stone Arabia and Burnetsfield became one of the richest farming regions in the northern colonies. With rich soil and efficient farming techniques, the Germans along the Mohawk River soon outproduced the long-established farmers of New England as well as the farms of those who had remained behind on the Hudson. The settlers established a profitable trade in wheat, which was transported from the Mohawk down the Hudson to New York City and shipped as far away as the West Indies. Because of the profits it earned, wheat practically became a staple crop, although the Germans also sold flax, rye, and livestock to their European and Indian neighbors. In addition, they traded rum to the Indians, a profitable exchange for the Germans but a source of contention with the Mohawk leaders.[31]

Although New York did not attract as many settlers as its leading politicians and land speculators had hoped, immigrants continued to trickle into the colony. In 1717, 1722, and 1726 immigrant ships arrived from the German southwest.[32] One result of the new migration was a partial and short-term disruption in the amalgamation of the peoples of the German southwest in New York and New Jersey. The conditions of the 1710 migration had forced the earlier immigrants to create ties among themselves that subsumed regional identities. Later immigrants, however, often came in groups drawn from a much narrower region of the German southwest, and when they arrived in New York they were not forced by high mortality rates and controlled settlement to live among and marry people from different regions. To some extent the newer German immigrant groups often split back into their regional components after disembarking from their ships in New York. Unlike the 1710 immigrants, they managed to retain some semblance of their regional identities. So, for example, nearly 95 percent of the Germans who settled near Montgomery in Orange County from 1726 to 1750 came from Neuwied and nearby villages in the Westerwald. Similar concentrations of Westerwalders settled in Hunterdon County, New Jersey, while Württembergers congregated near Rhinebeck.[33]

Where other German-speaking immigrants settled with the 1710 immigrants, the two groups gradually merged, but the 1710 immigrants generally distanced themselves from non-German colonists. Their children almost always married other Germans. In the records of the Lutheran church at West Camp, Joshua Kocherthal listed ninety-two marriages from 1709 to 1719; eighty-seven of the ninety-two involved Germans marrying Germans.[34] In Pennsylvania and Virginia, all of Jost Hite's daughters married German men.[35] Such marriage patterns were by necessity common among the isolated German settlements on the Mohawk or at Tulpehocken, but even in New York City and near Hackensack, where the 1710 immigrants lived surrounded by non-Germans, they still married other Germans.[36]

Although new arrivals changed the character of some of the communities founded by the 1710 immigrants, the more distant settlements of The Camp, Schoharie, Stone Arabia, Burnetsfield, and Tulpehocken retained a strong 1710 identity. One sign of the earlier settlers' distinct identity was a holiday they created that was all their own. Each June they celebrated "Immigration Day," marking the anniversary of their arrival in New York. In so doing, they celebrated their sense of a shared past and a common identity. Forty years after the immigrants had crossed the Atlantic and after many of them had died, the pastor for these distant congregations continued to mark the service celebrating the day in his journal.[37]

"A Headstrong Ignorant People"

If the 1710 immigrants had maintained their distinctiveness simply by celebrating special holidays and by marrying people from their German homelands, their neighbors and the colonial authorities probably would have ignored them. In fact, most of the German immigrants who settled in the middle colonies during the first half of the eighteenth century were ignored as generally hardworking but rather stupid and politically complacent settlers existing quietly on the periphery of colonial life. Benjamin Franklin referred to them as "Palatine boors," and William Smith, the provost of the College of Philadelphia, described them as "extremely ignorant, and think a large Farm the greatest Blessing in Life."[38] Although many of the 1710 settlers certainly desired large farms, the settlers did not fit the picture of complacency that Franklin and Smith painted of the Germans living in Pennsylvania before 1750. The 1710 immigrants continued to threaten the social order by needling the colonial elite and by challenging conventions of proper behavior.

Robert Hunter, who had left the colony in 1719 suffering from rheumatoid arthritis and "weary of this life," remained a target of German insubordination.[39] The British Treasury still owed him over £20,000 for expenses he had incurred while supporting the naval stores project. To bolster his claim for repayment, Hunter requested an affidavit signed by thirty Germans confirming that he had supported them. Although they would not have survived their first two years in New York without Hunter's support, when the Germans received the affidavit in 1722, they refused to sign. Governor Burnet threatened to remove his offer of land on the Mohawk River if the Germans did not support Hunter's claim, but his threats only caused more of the 1710 immigrants to forsake New York for Pennsylvania.[40] Hunter apparently never secured the thirty signatures, and Parliament never paid his claim.[41]

The Germans showed no more respect for Hunter's successor William Burnet or for their powerful Hudson River neighbor, Robert Livingston. Livingston had long believed the Germans to be "rascals," "worse than northern savages," and "liars and imposters."[42] Pondering his failed attempt to regain the six thousand acres he had sold for the naval stores camps, he criticized the lack of respect that the belligerent, almost haughty, Germans displayed toward him. Rather than showing proper deference, Livingston complained, "the High Germans are in the habit of bragging a lot."[43] Governor Burnet, reflecting on the difficulties he faced settling the Germans on the Mohawk River, called the German immigrants "a laborious and honest but a headstrong ignorant people."[44]

As the 1710 immigrants settled apart in their own communities, memories of their direct, face-to-face challenges to Governor Hunter, Robert Livingston, and other British colonial authorities began to fade. Yet in the less direct, more mundane affairs of their daily lives, the 1710 immigrants continued to challenge the social conventions of both the Old World and the worlds the Dutch and British had established in New York. Discerning what behaviors were peculiar to the 1710 immigrants is sometimes difficult because as they settled throughout the middle colonies, their communities gradually became mixed with later-arriving Germans. Yet almost everywhere the 1710 immigrants settled, especially those who had first moved to Schoharie after the naval stores fiasco, a level of unruliness existed that hardly fit William Smith's picture of dull German farmers sitting in self-satisfied complacency on their large farms. By observing their relations with slaves and ex-slaves, their attitudes toward religion, and their interactions with Indians, one can see how the 1710 immigrants continued to follow a path of their own.

The Dutch had introduced African slavery to New York, and when the English conquered the colony in 1664 about three hundred slaves lived in New York City, along with seventy-five free blacks.[45] In 1712, not long after Hunter had suppressed the rebellious Germans in the naval stores camps, two dozen African slaves set fire to a small building in New York City and then attacked the men who came to extinguish the blaze. They killed nine white men and wounded seven more. The militia combed the island and eventually captured and jailed far more slaves than had been involved in the uprising. Eighteen were executed. In the wake of the uprising, the New York assembly passed "An Act for Preventing, Suppressing, and Punishing the Conspiracy and Insurrection of Negroes, and other Slaves." Hunter feared that the law was more severe than necessary but conceded that "nothing less could please the people." After the attack many New Yorkers began condemning efforts by Elias Neau, the catechist at Trinity Church, to educate African slaves and to convert them to Christianity.[46]

Few Europeans questioned slavery's role in New York society. Although the 1710 immigrants often complained about being treated like slaves in the naval stores camps, once they left the camps they, too, never explicitly challenged the institution of African slavery. Yet neither did they adopt entirely the attitudes of their European neighbors. The Lutheran churches in New York, unlike other New York denominations, accepted Africans, both free and slave, as full members of the church.[47] Justus Falckner, the German pastor in charge of New York's Lutheran churches when the 1710 immigrants arrived, seems to have maintained close ties with his congregations' African members. Falckner had been trained for the ministry at the University of Halle, the center of Lutheran pietism.[48] Halle's pietist leaders were very critical of African slavery in America. They deplored the way it dehumanized both slave and master and condemned its effect on the development of self-sufficient and skilled persons in the service of God.[49] New York's Lutheran church records do not indicate any trouble between its European and African members, and the 1710 immigrants, many of whom had pietist leanings, apparently accepted the Africans in their churches.

The 1710 immigrants who moved to New Jersey's Raritan River valley also shared their church with Africans. In fact, the first Lutheran service held in the valley was at the home of Aree and Jora van Guinee, free blacks who had moved from New York City. The van Guinees had been members of Falckner's church in New York City and invited him to New Jersey to baptize their granddaughter. Falckner traveled from New York for a special service held on August 1, 1714.[50] The congregation consisted of ten free Africans and twenty-six members of the 1710 German migration. This was not a one-time event. The free Africans and Germans living in the Raritan River valley continued to worship together for many years. Aree van Guinee remained an active member in the Raritan church and in 1749 signed the church's call for a new minister.[51]

More intimate relations also existed between Africans and the 1710 immigrants. In 1715 Kocherthal recorded the baptism of Anna Maria, the illegitimate daughter of Maria Catharina Zöller and "Jan, a negro from Martinico."[52] In January 1714 Anna Barbara Asmer, a German widow, married Pieter Christiaan of Madagascar, a slave of Jan van Loon. After Anna Barbara died, Pieter married Elizabeth Brandemoes, another German woman. Justus Falckner traveled up from New York City to perform the ceremony.[53] Kocherthal and his successor Wilhelm Berkenmeyer baptized the Christiaans' children, and Berkenmeyer served as godparent to one of them.[54]

Although the Germans' toleration of mixed-race marriages and of Africans in their churches may have posed a veiled threat to the institution of slavery, the 1710 immigrants never questioned African enslavement. Few of the German immigrants owned slaves during the colonial period, but they were not so impressed by pietist teachings that they tried to prevent anyone from buying slaves, nor was their behavior toward free Africans always exemplary. In fact, Wilhelm Berkenmeyer, the strongly anti-pietist pastor who began serving the Lutheran congregations along the upper Hudson River in the 1730s, owned three slaves.[55] His conscience, like those of his German parishioners, seemed little troubled by his owning Africans while welcoming them into the church as joint members in the family of God.

In other areas the 1710 immigrants, especially those living in the colonial backcountry, seemed more open to experimentation and change. Much to the dismay of their orthodox Lutheran and Reformed pastors, one area of experimentation was religion. Joshua Kocherthal and Johann Haeger, the Lutheran and Reformed pastors who had accompanied the 1710 migration, had learned to cooperate with each other and to serve their respective congregations while minimizing antagonism between them. After Kocherthal died in 1719 and Haeger in 1721, the Germans went many years without regular ministers, and many of the pastors who eventually served them did not come from the German southwest.

Instead of encouraging the cooperative and pietist spirit that had marked the community of Lutheran and Reformed immigrants, the new pastors tried to impose strict adherence to the tenets and practices of their denominations. Wilhelm Berkenmeyer, trained in the orthodox Lutheran city of Altdorf near Nuremberg, ministered to the German communities in upper New York from 1731 to 1751.[56] He expressed dismay at what he saw. Members of the Reformed and Lutheran churches intermarried and showed little interest in the theological points that divided the two denominations. Reporting on his parishioners in Burnetsfield, he wrote, "That except for the family of Rynhard Scheffer, all the families were half [Lutheran, half Reformed]."[57] Their fellow immigrants in Schoharie seemed doomed to damnation, and Berkenmeyer cried when he realized "how far Scoghary still was from our Lutheran Jerusalem."[58] In a sermon to the Schoharie congregation he asked "whether it was not their duty to acknowledge before the face of God, that as long as we [Lutheran and Reformed] are different in doctrine, in ceremonies, in hymns and prayers, yes, even in the 'Our Father,' the holding of a union church service is in fact nothing more than turning the church into a battle place, changing religion into a Spanish or Portuguese bullfight, and making the Pastor either a mute dog or a renegade."[59]

Berkenmeyer's parishioners evidently preferred a mute dog in the pulpit to a long-winded and orthodox Lutheran. Two members of the Lutheran church in Schoharie approached Berkenmeyer before a wedding with special requests. According to Berkenmeyer, "Mr. Kniskern asked me not to have such a long sermon as the one on Sunday, and Mr. Schefer [a Lutheran deacon] asked me not to preach a Lutheran sermon." The men seemed concerned that matters of religion not interrupt a festive occasion. The wedding party must have squirmed in its seats as Berkenmeyer proceeded undeterred, adding to his wedding sermon a pointed reminder of the punishment inflicted on those who turned their backs on God.[60]

The early German settlers grew accustomed to an independence in church affairs unknown in Europe because they often had to run their churches without an ordained minister. Once a pastor did arrive, he had difficulty establishing his authority.[61] This state of affairs clearly threatened a traditional source of community power and made the Germans' seemingly chaotic American settlements appear even more threatening to outsiders. Benjamin Franklin noted the lack of clerical control among Pennsylvania's German settlers, reporting that they seemed "to take an uncommon pleasure in abusing and discharging the Minister on every trivial occasion," so that the German "Clergy have very little Influence over their people."[62]

Berkenmeyer's difficulties in New York were only partly related to his congregations' earlier independence. Members of the Reformed and Lutheran churches had managed to coexist in the German southwest, and most of the 1710 immigrants seemed willing to transfer their traditions of cooperation to America. Even though congregational disputes sometimes split the German communities, personal enmity rather than theological concerns seemed to have sparked the conflicts. Although the pastors who served them often came from orthodox German states with one dominant church, most of the 1710 immigrants moved easily between Lutheran and Reformed. Conrad Weiser was baptized a Lutheran in Württemberg. He and his wife, Anna Feg, who was also raised in the Lutheran Church, were married by a Reformed minister. A Lutheran minister baptized their first child, a Reformed minister baptized their second, and a Lutheran pastor baptized their third.[63]

In 1735 Weiser even allowed himself to be rebaptized, exhibiting a propensity for religious experimentation that extended far beyond simply moving between the Lutheran and Reformed Churches. The man who rebaptized Weiser was Conrad Beissel, a baker from the Palatinate, who had arrived in Pennsylvania in 1720. Beissel led a small religious commune at Ephrata, a dozen miles south of Tulpehocken. Soon his presence was felt in the nearby community of 1710 immigrants.

Beissel had come to Pennsylvania in search of a spiritual home. For several years he moved among various separatist groups, eventually becoming a pastor to the German Baptist Brethren, or Dunkers, at Conestoga. His radical views on marriage and other church issues caused him to part from the Dunkers, and in 1723 Beissel established a celibate community called Ephrata made up of groups of men and women known as the Brotherhood of Angels and the Spiritual Virgins. Married followers joined the commune as Householders.[64]

With its emphasis on celibacy the commune posed a threat to family life and the patriarchal household. Maria Christina Sauer left her family to join Beissel and was "rebaptized into virginity," much to her husband's distress. Other women followed Sauer's example, deserting their husbands and the labors of home and child care to join the Spiritual Virgins.[65] Their devotion to the charismatic Beissel did not ease their toils, however. Beissel's followers faced a harsh regimen at Ephrata, working long hours in communal activities, eating one meal a day, attending midnight worship services, and sleeping only a few hours each night on hard, narrow benches in small, solitary cells.

The 1710 immigrants living at Tulpehocken soon felt the pull of Conrad Beissel's charismatic and mystical personality. Beissel offered an alternative vision of American life that many of the settlers decided to explore. Some of the Tulpehocken settlers may have sought the peace of Ephrata in reaction to the kind of bitter dispute that seemed to follow them wherever they settled. The Lutheran and Reformed settlers of Tulpehocken initially shared a single church but did not have a regular pastor. In 1730 Peter Miller, a Reformed pastor from the Palatinate, arrived to serve the Reformed members of the community. In 1734 the Lutherans hired their own pastor, Caspar Leutbecker, who had strong Moravian connections. Soon a rival Lutheran pastor, Caspar Stoever, arrived in Tulpehocken and denounced Leutbecker and his followers. The Lutheran community split in a fierce struggle for control of the church. When one side locked the other out of the church building, the dispossessed simply cut a new door. Stoever's supporters attacked Leutbecker in his home, and during a winter service a piece of wood that had been hollowed out and filled with gunpowder exploded in the parsonage stove.[66]

In the midst of the so-called "Tulpehocken Confusion," Beissel traveled to the chaotic settlement, seeking new followers. He achieved enormous success. Not only did he win over Conrad Weiser, one of the chief elders in the Lutheran church, but Peter Miller, the Reformed pastor, also agreed to join Beissel's commune. In May 1735 Beissel rebaptized Miller, Weiser, and a number of other Tulpehocken settlers. To make their break with the established churches clear, the new converts burned copies of Luther's Catechism and the Heidelberg Catechism. Miller moved immediately to Ephrata, while Weiser remained at Tulpehocken and served as a spiritual leader to Beissel's followers there.[67]

For the next five years Weiser continued to live in Tulpehocken but traveled frequently to Ephrata and also joined various pilgrimages made by members of the commune. In 1740 he decided to leave his Tulpehocken home and join the Brotherhood of Angels at Ephrata. Although he soon became one of the group's priests, he did not stay long. He grew disenchanted with Beissel's leadership and the mystical power Beissel held over his followers. Ever watchful of overreaching or arbitrary authority, Weiser reported that he and others "were compelled to protest . . . against the domination of conscience, the suppression of innocent minds, against the prevailing pomp and luxury, both in dress and magnificent building."[68]

In 1741 Weiser left Ephrata and returned home. He eventually rejoined the Lutheran church and remained enmeshed in its affairs for the rest of his life. His daughter Anna Maria's marriage in 1745 to Henry Melchior Muhlenberg, the influential leader of the Lutheran Church in colonial America, only increased those ties. But like most other members of the Tulpehocken community, Weiser continued to move easily among the Reformed, Moravian, Quaker, and other sects of the Pennsylvania backcountry.

Weiser and the Tulpehocken settlers also managed to coexist with their Indian neighbors, although coexistence was made easier because the Germans had displaced most of the Delawares who had originally lived in Tulpehocken. In the first half of the eighteenth century the remnants of the original tribes of central Pennsylvania gradually fell under the protection of the Iroquois. Iroquois control over the Indians of Pennsylvania further enhanced relations between the Germans and the Indians. The Tulpehocken Germans had lived among the Iroquois in New York, and Conrad Weiser, one of the leading members of the Tulpehocken community, had a deep understanding of Iroquois language and culture.

James Logan, Pennsylvania's provincial secretary, realized that an Indian policy that emphasized cooperation with the Iroquois would simplify the colony's relations with the other Indians of central Pennsylvania. Therefore the colonial government strove to maintain good relations with the Iroquois and recognized their dominance over the Indians of central Pennsylvania. In return the colony expected the Iroquois to police the Indians under their protection.[69] Logan looked to Weiser, who held the trust of the Iroquois and understood their language, to serve as the colony's chief translator and negotiator. Weiser's respect for the Iroquois and understanding of their culture made him well-suited for the job, and his personal interest in the security of the Tulpehocken settlement ensured his diligent attention to the task.

Altruism rarely shaped relations between Indians and Europeans in British North America. The German settlers, like their British counterparts, dealt with the Indians because they wanted to protect the land where they had settled. But common aims do not always entail common means. When Johann Weiser sent his son to live with the Mohawks at Schoharie, he signaled an approach to Indian relations that differed markedly from that taken by the British authorities in New York City.

Conrad Weiser remained convinced that the security of the German frontier communities depended on a thorough understanding of the culture and language of their Indian neighbors, and he made sure that he was not the last of the Germans to gain such experience. Cultural brokerage became a family business. Just as his father had sent him to live with the Mohawks in 1712, Conrad Weiser sent his sixteen-year-old son, Samuel, to live in the same community in 1751. Weiser's nephew also lived with the Mohawks and learned their language, and both boys later served as Indian interpreters.[70]

The formal negotiations that consumed so much of Conrad Weiser's time did not constitute the only, or even the most important, contacts between the Germans and the Indians. Rather it was the routines of daily life that bound together the Germans and Indians. Mohawks, Mahicans, and remnants of other Indian tribes continued to live near the Germans' Schoharie settlements. One early resident estimated that Indians made up a fourth of Schoharie's residents in 1752, and Iroquois lands surrounded the German communities all along the Mohawk River.[71]

Although few Germans married Indians, their lives touched in other ways.[72] When the Germans first arrived in Schoharie, the Mohawks had provided them with enough food to survive the winter. Forty years later, as many Mohawks took up European styles of farming, the Germans returned the favor by helping to plow the Indians' fields.[73] The Germans also welcomed the Indians into their churches, a practice that stood in marked contrast to their English counterparts, some of whom expressed a concern for Indian souls yet insisted on making the Indians into Englishmen before making them into Christians.[74] Peter Nicholas Sommer, the Lutheran minister at Schoharie, baptized eighty-four Indians. George Michael Weiss, the Reformed minister at Burnetsfield, also baptized many Indians and expressed surprise at how little concern the English showed for the Indians' spiritual welfare.[75] The Indians themselves remarked on the better reception they received at the hands of the Germans. In 1775, when an English minister serving the Iroquois refused to baptize children unless their parents were Christians, the Indians threatened to take their children "to the German Calvinist Minister, or any other at the German Flats, who had offered to Baptize them."[76]

Just as Governor Hunter had misgivings about the Germans' close relations with the Mohawks in Schoharie, colonial officials were wary of German-Iroquois relations along the Mohawk River. The German Flats community had established a lucrative trade with the Iroquois, and members of the western Iroquois nations, including pro-French Oneidas, visited the community regularly. When tensions escalated between the French and British in the mid-eighteenth century, William Johnson, the man responsible for the security of the Mohawk River valley, found his efforts to station British troops at Burnetsfield rebuffed by the Germans, who suggested they could look out for themselves. Their reluctance to accept the soldiers aroused Johnson's suspicions. He wrote that the Germans' attitude "together with some words they now and then drop gives me some Reason to doubt their Fidelity." He suspected that the Germans might even be dealing with the French.[77]

The 1710 Immigrants and the Seven Years' War

By the time the Seven Years' War broke out in America, only one-third of the adults who had led the 1710 immigration were still alive.[78] Some of the old leaders of the immigrant group had died, including Johann Weiser, the most truculent of the early leaders, who died in Tulpehocken in 1746. Yet the differences between the first and second generation of immigrants seem to have been small. Many in the second generation had emigrated along with their parents, and many, like Johann Weiser's son Conrad, were already teenagers when they left the German southwest. They remembered life in Europe, the work in the naval stores camps, and the difficulties of finding land in New York. Because the second generation's experiences were so similar to their parents', they easily absorbed their parents' prejudices and their approaches to life in the colonial backcountry. The 1710 immigrants whom William Johnson dealt with in 1757 did not differ much from the German immigrants Hunter had dealt with forty-five years earlier.

Johnson's suspicions that the Burnetsfield Germans had been negotiating with the French were unfounded, but the Germans did apparently hope to negotiate treaties with the Iroquois independently of the British. In 1756 some of the Burnetsfield Germans evidently approached the Iroquois and suggested an alliance of mutual defense. Some pro-French Iroquois reported to their French allies in Canada that "a Nation which is neither French, nor English, nor Indian, and inhabits the lands round about us . . . has proposed to annex us to itself in order to afford each other mutual help and defence against the English."[79] The Indians understood the traditional rivalry of the French and the English but remained uncertain about where the Germans stood in relation to the three known, and named, powers of eighteenth-century New York. They did not know how to deal with the German request and asked the advice of their French allies.

The Indians' seemingly naive categorization of the Germans actually captured perfectly the Germans' sense of their relationship to the peoples of New York. They were not part of one group or another. They did not share the imperial interests of the British and, despite William Johnson's suspicions to the contrary, had no wish to further the imperial interests of the French. They remembered old stories about French aggression in Europe, and now that they had established themselves in America, the Germans had no desire to replace an English governor with a French one. After forty years in British North America the Germans had not become British Americans, much less French Americans or Native Americans. They conceived of themselves just as the Indians described them and, as such, attempted to negotiate their own alliances, independent of other powers. Just as they had escaped Governor Hunter's control in 1712 and negotiated directly with the Mohawks at Schoharie, the Burnetsfield Germans disregarded the colonial power that ostensibly governed them and made their own bargains with the Indians who lived as their neighbors. The feeble authority of the British government on its imperial periphery made the Germans' defiance possible.

The Germans' western communities seemed particularly isolated from and resentful of English intrusion. Weiser wrote that the backcountry Germans "have no notion of the English government and laws, and are themselves not always satisfied with the administration of Such."[80] John Wernig, the Reformed pastor at Stone Arabia, agreed. In 1752, Wernig, who had not been part of the 1710 migration to New York, described the 1710 immigrants living in Stone Arabia as "fat horses and oxen, which have gone to rich pasture for a long time and then refuse to take the bit or bear the yoke." They did not respect "the noble English freedom." Instead the "liberty, peace, wealth, and abundance which they enjoy cause them to be uncivil, wanton, proud and violent."[81] The Germans in Schoharie also showed little respect for English law and civil order. Johann Christian Gerlach, a 1710 immigrant serving as a judge in Schoharie, made a mockery of the English judicial system. According to Schoharie tradition, Judge Gerlach resolved a particularly difficult case by deciding that "Der blandif an derfendur bot hash reght; zo I dezides . . . der khonshtoplle moosh bay de kosht." ("The plaintiff and the defender are both correct, so I have decided that . . . the constable must pay the cost.")[82]

Indeed, the 1710 immigrants had their own vision of life in colonial America and were little concerned with assimilating to British conventions. Theirs was a vision that centered on a large farm, not because it provided them with the means to ignore the outside world but because it assured them that they could earn their daily bread, an assurance that had evaded them as impoverished peasants in the German southwest. Theirs was a world where people could welcome or ignore religious practices as they saw fit. It was a Christian world, but one that distrusted religious orthodoxy as much as it distrusted any outside pressures toward conformity. It was a world deeply suspicious of petty external authority, whether it be English, Dutch, or French. None seemed much different from the small-minded rulers left behind in the Rhineland. Coming from a corner of Europe where autonomous regions were often minuscule, the 1710 immigrants felt comfortable creating their own small, autonomous communities. These communities could then deal with outside centers of power as they saw fit, including with the Indians, who were as legitimate a power as any of the others around them. Perhaps the German settlers who poured into Pennsylvania starting in the 1720s could afford to be complacent with their large farms and relatively easy prosperity, but the emigrants who left Germany in 1709 had to endure a year-long trek before they even arrived in New York. They then endured a two-year sentence in the naval stores camps and another eight years or more before they procured land of their own. Because they had been the first to emigrate, their vivid dreams of all that America had to offer had not been altered by the experience of other German settlers going before them. It is no wonder that they feared any outside authority standing in their way and insisted on charting their own path in America.

In the mid-eighteenth century, when Benjamin Franklin and other political leaders began writing their attacks on German settlers in the middle colonies, they were not aiming their attacks at the 1710 immigrants. Instead they feared the much larger waves of German settlers who had arrived over the last thirty years. These Germans had initially seemed happy to devote their lives to farming on the colonies' peripheries, but by the 1750s they seemed to want to exert their influence on the political scene. Franklin remembered when the Germans of Pennsylvania "modestly declined intermeddling in our Elections," but noted that "now they come in droves, and carry all before them, except in one or two Counties." Although they behaved "submissively enough at present" he feared their effect on English political institutions. "Not being used to Liberty," he wrote, "they know not how to make a modest use of it."[83]

William Smith echoed Franklin's prejudices. Motivated in part by his anger at the Germans' support of his political enemies, Smith argued that Pennsylvania's German settlers had become "insolent, sullen, and turbulent." He did not trust their fidelity to the English or to Protestantism and feared that the French would woo them to their side "by sending their Jesuitical Emissaries among them, to persuade them over to the Popish Religion." To remove the German threat, Smith proposed prohibiting German newspapers unless English translations accompanied them and forbidding the Germans to vote "till they have a sufficient Knowledge of our Language and Constitution."[84]

Franklin and Smith exaggerated both the possibility of German treachery and the Germans' growing political influence. Still they worried that the changing character of the Pennsylvania German population threatened English interests in colonial America as tensions with France grew. Ironically, it was the 1710 immigrants and their descendants—the people who for the past forty years had exhibited the very characteristics that Franklin and Smith now feared were appearing in the Pennsylvania

Germans—whose vision of American life would be destroyed by the Seven Years' War.

When the war broke out, the German frontier communities seemed convinced that they were immune to its violence. As many British observers, from Robert Hunter to William Johnson, had noted, the German immigrants seemed reluctant to recognize British imperial interests as their own. Since the war pitted French interests against British, not German, interests, the Germans seemed to believe they might be left alone. Certainly their good relations with the Indians prevented attacks from that quarter. Even after the Delaware Indians raided an isolated settlement along the Susquehanna River in October 1755, the Germans living in nearby Tulpehocken believed that their Indian neighbors would leave them in peace. Conrad Weiser, who understood the mood of the Delawares better than most of his countrymen, was not so optimistic: "[T]he people down here seem to be senseless and say the Indians will never come this side Susquehanna River but I fear they will."[85]

The Delawares, whose leader Sassoonan had complained twenty-five years earlier that the Tulpehocken Germans had pushed them from their traditional lands, allied themselves with the French. On November 15, 1755, a party of Delawares led by Pisquetomen, Sassoonan's nephew, attacked the scattered farms of the Tulpehocken settlers.[86] The Indians killed fifteen people and burned the settlers' homes and barns. The Germans abandoned Tulpehocken, finding shelter in Reading and among the Moravians at Bethlehem.[87] Conrad Weiser, the peacemaker, now organized a force of German men to protect the frontier from further Indian attacks. In 1756 he became a lieutenant colonel in the Pennsylvania army.[88]

Despite the attacks in Pennsylvania, the settlers at Burnetsfield still felt secure. The 1710 immigrants' relations with the Mohawks and other Iroquois peoples had always been better than their relations with the Delaware Indians. Even after the French and their Indian allies captured Oswego and Fort Bull, two British outposts in far western New York, the Burnetsfield Germans did not feel threatened.[89] According to Cadwallader Colden, New York's surveyor general, they "obstinately refused to receive any soldiers for their defence." Alluding to the alleged negotiations between the Germans and the Iroquois, Colden wrote that the Germans "trusted to a private Neutrality entered into between the Mohawks and the French Indians, in which the Inhabitants on the Mohawk river were included."[90] The German settlers along the Mohawk apparently envisioned themselves as a sovereign people living independently of both the British and the French. As such, they considered themselves safely removed from the imperial squabbles of the two European powers.

The French and many Indians did not view the situation in the same light. In the fall of 1757 a French and Indian force advanced toward the German settlement at Burnetsfield. Three times a delegation of friendly Oneidas warned the settlers of an imminent attack, but the Germans were so sure of their safety that they heaped scorn on their Indian allies. Canaghquayeeson, an Oneida leader, reported that the Germans "paid not the least regard to what I told them; and laughed at me, slapping their hands on their buttocks."[91]

On November 12, 1757, the Germans covered their buttocks and ran as a party of 260 Indians and ninety Frenchmen attacked their settlement. Although the Germans had received warnings as late as the day before the attack, they had not prepared to defend their families and their homes. A few Germans managed to escape across the river, but at least eight Germans were killed. The remainder, over one hundred people, were taken prisoner and marched off to Canada. The attacking force burned the prosperous town to the ground, destroying over sixty houses and barns. The attackers took away or killed at least five hundred horses and thousands of cattle, sheep, and oxen. The Germans offered little resistance, and the French and Indian force suffered no losses.[92]

The Germans' trust in their Indian allies had not been completely misplaced. The Oneidas later reported that a hundred Indians who had joined the French-led force in Canada turned back when they realized the German settlement was the object of their march.[93] Such limited and indirect support was not enough, however, to save the Germans. The backcountry settlers learned they could no longer live securely in their defenseless communities, isolated from and scornful of the British colonial figures who claimed authority over them. When the Germans in Stone Arabia received news of the Burnetsfield attack, they shipped off their valuables and prepared to flee to the protection of the British army.[94]

After forty-eight years the British at last had some success with their strategy for dealing with the Germans. When the Board of Trade had authorized the settlement of three thousand German emigrants in New York in 1709, it had hoped that the new settlers might provide a defensive buffer for the British colony. The board believed a strategically placed German community could bear the brunt of initial attacks and slow the advance of Britain's French and Indian enemies. In this regard the Burnetsfield Germans succeeded admirably, if unintentionally. Although they ran at the first sight of their attackers, they nevertheless managed to halt the French and Indian advance. Within the prosperous trading village the Germans had stored away a large supply of rum. For several days the French and Indian army remained near the settlement, "frolicking and drunk," before the French commander decided to suspend the campaign and return to Canada for the winter.[95]

Conclusion

In April 1758, when the Indians and the French again attacked the German Flats settlement, the remaining settlers quickly sought refuge in a nearby fort.[1] The events of November 1757 had taught the German farmers that they could no longer trust a "private neutrality" with their Iroquois neighbors. For years the Germans had moved westward to avoid the intrusion of British authority into their lives. Now they fled eastward to escape the deadly incursions of French and Indian soldiers.

The events of the Seven Years' War in America transformed German ideas about their place in the New World. Instead of seeing their freedom threatened by British authority, they realized that the safety of their backcountry farms, and whatever sense of individual freedom that the ownership of land provided, depended on British protection. Rather than threatening German freedom, British power now preserved it. The war forced the Germans to reconsider their relationship with government authority, and they decided to tolerate the intrusion of British troops to ensure the security of their settlements.

The Germans also began to pay greater heed to colonial politics. They could no longer pretend to make treaties of their own. The backcountry settlers finally had to acknowledge that what happened in Philadelphia and New York City could have a profound impact on their individual independence and safety. In the 1760s the Germans throughout the middle colonies began participating actively in assembly elections and elected a few of their own to provincial offices.[2] The 1710 immigrants sometimes still went about politics in their own way. For instance, the settlers living in The Camp and other areas near Robert Livingston Jr. still exhibited the less-than-deferential attitude that had so annoyed his father. He reported in 1761 that the Germans demanded forty shillings a person before providing him their political support.[3] Still, they were at least involved in the political process. Rather than trying to escape America's public life, the descendants of the 1710 immigrants were slowly beginning to integrate themselves into it.

When the Revolutionary War came to the Mohawk Valley, the German settlers did not remain neutral or pretend the conflict would pass them by. They had learned the lessons of the Seven Years' War. They, too, were part of British America, and special arrangements with their Indian neighbors would not shield the Germans from Britain's imperial conflicts. Although some remained loyal to their newly recognized British protectors, most of the descendants of the 1710 immigrants saw a chance to cast off the British authority that their families had resisted since the time of Robert Hunter. They could replace British authority with a more local authority, one that would perhaps be more receptive to the Germans' concerns and maybe less intrusive in their affairs.[4] When the war broke out, the Mohawk Valley Germans quickly organized four battalions to support the rebel cause.[5] Unlike before the Seven Years' War, Benjamin Franklin and other leaders voiced no doubts about German loyalty. America's Palatines were not mistaken for Britain's Hessians.

The Germans' involvement in colonial politics and their support of independence helped them to integrate themselves into the new American, but still distinctly British-American, public culture. The change in their public lives, however, was not limited to a growing involvement in the country's political affairs. The Germans' relations with their Indian and African neighbors also reflected the adoption of prevailing norms of colonial society, norms that made the Germans seem much less dangerous to other European Americans but far more threatening to America's Indians and Africans.

The 1710 immigrants had left the naval stores camps in search of a promised land. Although they framed their quest in religious terms, comparing themselves to the Israelites forced from Egypt, when they entered their Schoharie Canaan they did not attempt to drive its Amalekites and Hittites from the land. Instead they sought only to escape the Egyptians. For forty years they managed to get along with their Iroquois neighbors and, in so doing, kept their British oppressors at a distance.

After the Seven Years' War, the Germans in New York's backcountry no longer relied on good relations with the Indians to ensure the security of their settlements or to distance themselves from British control. The number and power of the Indians declined during the war and continued to diminish as European settlers pushed westward. In 1774 only four hundred Mohawks remained in villages along the Mohawk River and at Schoharie.[6] As the Indians' power declined, the Germans found it easier to ignore them.

For many years Conrad Weiser had helped the Germans and the Iroquois to understand one another. When Weiser died in 1760, his Iroquois friend Seneca George realized the significance of his passing. "We, the seven Nations, and our Cousins are at a great loss," he reported, "and sit in darkness, as well as you, by the death of Conrad Weiser, as since his Death we cannot so well understand one another."[7] The Germans, however, made little effort to replace Weiser. Their survival no longer depended on good relations with the Indians, and they saw no need to send their children to learn the Indians' language and culture. When the Revolutionary War broke out, the Iroquois sided with the British, not the German inhabitants of the New York backcountry. In concert with British and Loyalist troops they destroyed the German settlements at Schoharie, German Flats, and Stone Arabia.[8] Yet the new American army eventually prevailed, and by the end of the war the Iroquois had been driven from the Mohawk Valley.[9]

Weiser's death marked the passing of the generation of 1710 immigrants who had first shaped German society on the colonial frontiers of New York and Pennsylvania.[10] The members of the new generation, made up of people born and raised in America, differed from their immigrant parents and grandparents. They had not experienced the oppressive European order that the 1710 immigrants had sought to escape. The New World was not new to them, and the lack of novelty made it difficult for them to see the possibilities that it had held for earlier generations. Though their private worlds remained distinctly German, they began living public lives that differed little from the lives of the other European settlers around them.

This generational change, coupled with a growing prosperity, also affected the way the Germans viewed themselves in relation to New York's African population. The 1710 immigrants, who imagined that Governor

Hunter was trying to enslave them in the naval stores camps, showed a certain openness to New York's Africans, whose enslavement was real. Early on the Germans accepted Africans in their churches and sometimes as spouses and members of their families, but as the Germans gained greater freedom, they did nothing to secure greater freedom for their African neighbors. Instead, they accepted the growing loss of freedom among the Africans and the institutionalization of African slavery. In 1735 the Lutheran Church in New York began to define more clearly the position of its African members. The church's new constitution still allowed African slaves to join the church but explicitly acknowledged their subject status. Pastors were admonished to ensure that slaves who became members did not intend "to dissolve the tie of obedience."[11]

Few Germans in New York owned slaves in 1735, but that situation also slowly changed. Although many probably had no slaves because they could not afford them, even the relatively prosperous Germans living near Rhinebeck in 1755 owned proportionally far fewer slaves than their Dutch neighbors. As the 1710 immigrants began to die, however, their American-born children and grandchildren began acting more like the Dutch. By 1790 the Dutch and the Germans of Dutchess County owned slaves in almost equal proportion.[12]

Although the descendants of the 1710 immigrants began to integrate themselves more closely into the public life of early America, they remained separate in their private lives. They continued to marry other Germans and to attend German churches. Many learned some English, but German remained their primary language.[13] They also maintained German customs in their everyday work. Unlike the Yankee farmers who joined them in upstate New York during the late eighteenth century, the Germans never manured their fields, rarely rotated their crops, and preferred horses to oxen as draft animals.[14]

Visitors to the German settlements along the Mohawk River noted the difference. They commented on the Germans' barbarous English and their loutish manners. Timothy Dwight, a Connecticut Yankee and the president of Yale, traveled through the Mohawk Valley in 1799. He found the Germans "extremely ignorant" and believed their isolation had deprived them of "all those benefits of knowledge and improvement which are derived from civilized society." They had become so backward that they spoke "their own language . . . with increasing imperfection, and the English they spoke scarcely at all." But the scene that shocked Dwight most of all was ten women dressing flax. He speculated that perhaps he had never been "more struck with the strangeness of any sight."[15]

Just as Magdalene Zee had upset the social conventions of early eighteenth-century New York by making a piss pot of Sheriff Adams, the daughters and granddaughters of the 1710 immigrants continued to challenge conceptions of proper female behavior. In a time when society increasingly sought to limit women's space to the home, German women ignored such boundaries. Although a few non-English observers expressed grudging admiration for the German women's industriousness, the women's field labor offended Dwight's Yankee sensibilities.[16] He compared them unfavorably to the women in New England who were "employed only in and about the house, and in the proper business of the sex."[17]

For almost a century the 1710 immigrants and their descendants had challenged the norms of British American society. As American memories of these stubborn people began to fade, the seemingly bizarre behavior of the German women stood as a final reminder to the new American elite of the contrariness of the 1710 immigrants. Yet this perceived challenge to societal norms was largely superficial, based as it was on outward appearances and not on the underlying reality of farm women's labor. German immigrant men were quick to make this point, noting that just because other women restricted their labors to the house and surrounding farmyard, they did not necessarily work any less hard than German women worked in the fields.[18] Eventually the women's unconventional behavior was no longer noticed. The last Palatine threat disappeared, and the 1710 immigrants largely faded from American memory.[19]

The hard labor of the German women did demonstrate, however, that the easy riches the German emigrants had dreamed of when they left their homes in 1709 had never materialized. The promises of Kocherthal's golden book, which had sustained the Germans in London and for decades in New York, were never fulfilled in the way that the most fiercely independent of the emigrants had hoped. They could not maintain their cantankerous independence in their communities situated between the Iroquois and the British on the New York frontier. The constant disputes between the British and French that had dogged the Germans in the Rhineland and that had helped label them in London finally forced them to throw their lot in with the British authorities they so despised. It was not Kocherthal's golden book that proved prophetic, but the book written by Anton Boehme, the pastor in London who had questioned the Germans' motives for leaving home in the first place. When he titled his book *The Longed for, but Unattained Canaan*, he probably did not realize how close to the mark his description would come.

Although the German immigrants' dream of an easy life in their promised land free from outside interference disappeared with the Seven Years' War, one part of their experience remained permanent: the label they had been given in London. The people who had left their homes as Nassauers, Hessians, and Württembergers had all become Palatines. Although the British generally referred to all German-speaking immigrants in eighteenth-century America as Palatines, other names eventually replaced that label. The German settlers of Pennsylvania became the Pennsylvania Dutch, and other German-speaking immigrants were more commonly, and accurately, referred to as Virginia Germans or Moravians or Salzburgers. Yet through almost three hundred years, the label *Palatine* has remained for the people who first adopted it—the 1709 emigrants and their descendants in New York.[20]

Appendix

DATABASE OF 1709 EMIGRANTS

To glean as much information as possible about a group of people who left few records about their personal lives, I created a database using information from various lists and censuses of the 1709 emigrants and from the extensive genealogical research of Henry Z Jones on the early German families of New York.

Because the British government financed and supplied much of the 1709 German migration, it commissioned detailed censuses to determine who the immigrants were and kept special accounts to track how much aid the immigrants received. The four London censuses compiled by the German pastors Ruperti and Tribekko between May 6 and June 15, 1709, listed 6,519 German migrants.[1] The censuses recorded men's names, ages, occupations, and religions. They also showed whether the men were accompanied by their wives and listed the sexes and ages of any children with them. The censuses provided the same information for widows and single women except that they did not list women's occupations. In New York detailed accounts from the naval stores project, generally known as the Hunter subsistence lists, showed the subsistence paid to 847 families. The Hunter lists, covering the years 1710 through 1712, named the male head of household, or the female head if the male head was no longer living, and the number of family members age ten and older and the number under ten.[2]

Besides the London censuses and the Hunter lists, British and colonial authorities made several other lists of the 1709 emigrants. The commissioners who helped arrange the transport of immigrants from Rotterdam to London wrote five lists showing who sailed, when, and on what ship. The lists gave the name of the male head of household, indicated whether he was married, and listed the number of children in each family, sometimes giving their names.[3] About eleven thousand people appeared on the five lists. In New York the names and ages of the German children apprenticed by Governor Hunter were recorded together, and a register survives of the immigrants who remained in New York City in late 1710 after the other immigrants had moved to the naval stores camps.[4] A census of the families living in the villages on the west side of the Hudson survives, as do several lists of the German men who volunteered to fight in the failed 1711 expedition against Canada.[5] Finally, Ulrich Simmendinger, a 1709 emigrant who returned to the German southwest in 1717, published a list of approximately five hundred immigrant families still in New York. In most cases Simmendinger listed the male and female heads of household and the number of children in each family. He also named the settlement where each family lived.[6]

Recently genealogists interested in the 1709–10 German migration have added to the vast amount of demographic information contained in these lists. The most extensive genealogical research has been directed by Henry Z Jones Jr. For over twenty-five years Jones and his associates have scoured church records and archives in the German southwest, London, New York, New Jersey, and Pennsylvania, collecting data on the 1709 emigrants. Jones's chief accomplishment has been to trace the majority of the 1710 immigrants to New York back to their place of origin in the German southwest.

The various eighteenth-century lists of emigrants compiled in Rotterdam, London, and New York provide valuable information, but none of them names the immigrants' German hometowns. The only source with extensive references to the immigrants' German origins is the church register for Kocherthal's West Camp congregation. Kocherthal listed the German hometowns of people who were married or buried or had children baptized in his church. Jones began his search for the 1709 emigrants in the church records of the German villages listed in Kocherthal's records. From those villages Jones expanded his search to neighboring towns until he and Carla Mittelstaedt-Kubaseck, a German genealogist and Jones's chief assistant, had examined almost all the surviving church records from regions where emigrants were known to have lived.

In 1985 Jones published his two-volume *The Palatine Families of New York*, which included genealogies for almost all 847 families listed in Hunter's subsistence accounts. In 1991 he published *More Palatine Families*, which provided additional information on the 1710 immigrants as well as information on later German immigrants to colonial New York. In 2002, along with Lewis Rohrbach, Jones published the three-volume *Even More Palatine Families*. In all, Jones managed to find references in Europe to over five hundred of the 847 families who settled in the New York naval stores camps.

Jones's genealogies of the 1710 immigrants fill over a thousand pages and contain vast quantities of information on the demographic characteristics and geographic origins of the migrants. Besides attempting to list the villages the immigrants left, Jones provides the dates and places of the baptism and marriage of the immigrants and their children. Whenever possible Jones includes information from the Rotterdam ship lists, the London censuses, the Hunter subsistence lists, and other records pertaining to the immigrants, but his careful research supplements and corrects these lists by providing information on women's ages (which were omitted in most of the eighteenth-century records) and by verifying the ages of men and children using German baptismal records.

Jones organized his books by family, listing the families in the same order they appeared in Hunter's subsistence accounts. If one wants to trace a family tree, Jones's books work splendidly, but if one wants to draw a group portrait of the entire migration rather than a family portrait of one's ancestors, the books' organization works less well. For the purposes of this study it became necessary to extract data from each family's genealogy and to reorganize the information in different categories. With Jones's permission and encouragement, I stripped the demographic and geographic details from his records and entered them into a computer database. Since I was most interested in those immigrants who could be traced from a particular place in Germany to colonial New York, I limited the database to 426 families whose exact origins Jones had confirmed in German parish records and archives.

I first copied the raw data from each of Jones's genealogies onto a data sheet designed for the project. I then entered the information from the data sheet into the computer database. The database consists of sixty-six fields for each family. Individual fields contain the name, birthplace, birth date, and birth order of each head of household as well as religion, date of marriage, and last residence in the German southwest. Other fields include information on family size provided in the Rotterdam lists, London censuses, and Hunter accounts. The database also lists where each family eventually settled and the date of death for adult immigrants. The database deals primarily with the male and female heads of each family. I included less information on immigrant children because I wanted to focus on the people who actually made the decision to emigrate.

Although the main database contains information only on the 1709 emigrants who arrived in New York during the summer of 1710, I also created a much smaller database of 18 families who were sent from London to Ireland or North Carolina rather than to New York. The information in the Irish and North Carolina database was drawn from Jones's *The Palatine Families of Ireland*, 2d ed., and from the meticulous work of Lewis Rohrbach on the North Carolina Palatines included in volume two of Jones and Rohrbach, *Even More Palatine Families*. The German origins of the 18 families in this database along with the 426 families in the New York database are presented in map 2. Of the total of 444 families in the two databases, only five originated in regions outside the area of the map.

Abbreviations

BT Jour.	*Journal of the Commissioners for Trade and Plantations.* 14 vols. London, 1920–38.
CSP Col.	*Calendar of State Papers, Colonial Series. America and the West Indies.* 44 vols. London, 1820–1969.
DHNY	*Documentary History of the State of New York.* 4 vols. Albany, 1850–51.
ERNY	*Ecclesiastical Records of the State of New York.* 8 vols. Albany, 1910–16.
Liv. Dutch letters	Livingston family letters in Dutch, 1680–1726, trans. Adrian J. van der Linde, Livingston Family Papers, Franklin D. Roosevelt Library, Hyde Park, New York.
NYCD	*Documents Relative to the Colonial History of New York.* 15 vols. Albany, 1856–87.
NY Col MSS	New York Colonial Manuscripts, New York State Archives, Albany, New York.
PRO	Public Record Office, London (Kew), England.
SPG	Society for the Propagation of the Gospel.

Notes

INTRODUCTION

1. The forging of a common identity among the 1709 migrants was a gradual process and one in which the labels imposed on the immigrants played an important role. Just as these labels complicated matters for the German-speaking immigrants and the people they encountered, they also challenge historians trying to find a simple term to refer to the immigrants. I have generally opted for the term *Germans*, although, as I hope this book makes clear, I realize the label's shortcomings.

2. For an introduction to the ways that group identities are formed and the importance of real and imagined histories to the process, see the introduction to *The Invention of Ethnicity*, ed. Werner Sollors (New York, 1989); Gerald Sider, *Lumbee Indian Histories: Race, Ethnicity, and Indian Identity in the Southern United States* (Cambridge, 1993), xvii–xviii; and Joane Nagel, "Constructing Ethnicity: Creating and Recreating Ethnic Identity and Culture," *Social Problems* 41 (Feb. 1994): 163–64.

3. See, for example, Don Yoder, "The Pennsylvania Germans: Three Centuries of Identity Crisis," and Stephanie Grauman Wolf, "Hyphenated America: The Creation of an Eighteenth-Century German-American Culture," in Frank Trommler and Joseph McVeigh, eds., *America and the Germans: An Assessment of a Three-Hundred-Year History* (Philadelphia, 1985), 1:44–65 and 1:66–84; William T. Parsons, "Representation of Ethnicity among Colonial Pennsylvania Germans," in *A Mixed Race: Ethnicity in Early America*, Frank Shuffelton, ed. (New York, 1993),

119–41; and Anita Tien, " 'To Enjoy Their Customs': The Cultural Adaptation of Dutch and German Families in the Middle Colonies, 1660–1832" (Ph.D. diss., University of California, Berkeley, 1990). Recently some historians have begun to pay closer attention to the diversity of peasant cultures and experiences in the German southwest. See, in particular, Marianne Wokeck, "German Settlements in the British North American Colonies: A Patchwork of Cultural Assimilation and Persistence," in *In Search of Peace and Prosperity: New German Settlements in Eighteenth-Century Europe and America*, ed. Hartmut Lehmann, Hermann Wellenreuther, and Renate Wilson (University Park, Pa., 2000), 192–99; and Aaron Spencer Fogleman, *Hopeful Journeys: German Immigration, Settlement, and Political Culture in Colonial America, 1717–1775* (Philadelphia, 1996), 18–28, 36–39.

4. Historians of nineteenth-century Germany seem more willing than historians of colonial America to admit that local identities remained strong among the peoples of Germany before the creation of a German state and that even after the creation of Germany, the sense of a common identity evolved slowly. See James Sheehan, *German History, 1770–1866* (Oxford, 1989), 1–7, and Alon Confino, *The Nation as a Local Metaphor: Württemberg, Imperial Germany, and National Memory, 1871–1918* (Chapel Hill, 1997), 13–15. For an approach that makes careful distinctions between cultural and political identities, see Abigail Green, *Fatherlands: State-Building and Nationhood in Nineteenth-Century Germany* (Cambridge, 2001), 1–7.

5. Walter Allen Knittle, *Early Eighteenth-Century Palatine Emigration: A British Government Redemptioner Project to Manufacture Naval Stores* (Philadelphia, 1937). Knittle wrote a detailed and well-researched history, but in it the experience of the German immigrants is often overshadowed by descriptions of British mercantile policy and the operation of the British imperial system.

6. Trommler and McVeigh, eds., *America and the Germans*, vol. 1, *Immigration, Language, Ethnicity* (Philadelphia, 1985), containing revised version of papers presented at the Tricentennial Conference of German-American History, Politics, and Culture held at the University of Pennsylvania, Oct. 3–6, 1983.

7. Marianne Wokeck, *Trade in Strangers: The Beginnings of Mass Migration to North America* (University Park, Pa., 1999), 39–47. By 1790 approximately 280,000 people of German ancestry lived in the United States. Pennsylvania had the most Germans of any state, with around 160,000—38 percent of the state's white population. New York followed, with between 28,000 and 29,000. Just over 9 percent of New York's white population was of German descent in 1790. See Aaron Fogleman, "Migrations to the Thirteen British North American Colonies, 1700–1775: New Estimates," *Journal of Interdisciplinary History* 22 (spring 1992): 701; and Thomas L. Purvis, "The National Origins of New Yorkers in 1790," *New York History* 67 (Apr. 1986): 141.

8. The 1710 immigrants to New York were certainly more representative of later German immigrants than the first settlers in Germantown, Pennsylvania, who despite their small numbers have received far more attention from historians. Germantown had just thirteen families at its founding in 1683 and numbered fewer than 230 people in 1700. Its founders, Quakers descended from recent

Dutch immigrants to the German northwest, did not resemble the majority of later German migrants to colonial America in origin, dialect, or religion. See William I. Hull, *William Penn and the Dutch Quaker Migration to Pennsylvania*, Swarthmore College Monographs on Quaker History, no. 2 (Philadelphia, 1935), 178–79, 189, and Helmut E. Huelsbergen, "The First Thirteen Families: Another Look at the Religious and Ethnic Background of the Emigrants from Crefeld (1683)," *Yearbook of German-American Studies* 18 (1983): 29–40.

9. The primary genealogist of the 1710 migration to New York is Henry Z Jones Jr. He has devoted several decades to the study of these immigrants and has published six extraordinary volumes of genealogical data. See Henry Z Jones Jr., *The Palatine Families of New York*, 2 vols. (Universal City, Calif., 1985), *More Palatine Families* (Universal City, Calif., 1991), and, with Lewis Bunker Rohrbach, *Even More Palatine Families*, 3 vols. (Rockport, Maine, 2002).

CHAPTER 1. "A PARTICULARLY DECEPTIVE SPIRIT"

1. Nancy Wagoner Dixon, *Palatine Roots: The 1710 German Settlement in New York as Experienced by Johann Peter Wagner* (Camden, Maine, 1994), 29–40.
2. Jones, *Palatine Families of New York*, 1:27, 28.
3. Frederick S. Weiser, ed., *Johan Friederich Weisers Buch containing the Autobiography of John Conrad Weiser (1696–1760)* (Hanover, Pa., 1976), 7–11; Paul Wallace, *Conrad Weiser, Friend of Colonist and Mohawk* (Philadelphia, 1945), 3–6.
4. See Frank Diffenderffer, "The German Exodus to England in 1709," *Pennsylvania German Society Proceedings and Addresses* 7 (1897): 266, 411–12; Sanford H. Cobb, *The Story of the Palatines* (New York, 1897), chap. 2; Knittle, *Early Palatine Emigration*, 1–2.
5. Although many genealogists have traced various family lines, Henry Z Jones stands as the premier genealogist of the 1709 migration. His works serve as the basis of the database used for this study. See Jones, *Palatine Families of New York*, *More Palatine Families*, and *The Palatine Families of Ireland*, 2d ed. (Camden, Maine, 1990), and Jones and Rohrbach, *Even More Palatine Families*. A study of German emigrants who married while in London in 1709 confirms Jones's findings on the emigrants' origins. See John Dern, *London Churchbooks and the German Emigration of 1709*, Schriften zur Wanderungsgeschichte der Pfälzer, vol. 26 (Kaiserslautern, 1968).
6. All references to the Palatinate are to the *Kurpfalz*, the eighteenth-century German state known in English as the Electoral Palatinate, the Rhenish Palatinate, the Lower Palatinate, or simply the Palatinate. The situation is even more confusing because several other principalities controlled by different dynasties also made use of the word *Palatinate* or *Pfalz* in their names. These included the Upper Palatinate, a separate eighteenth-century state in what is today northeastern Bavaria, and Pfalz-Zweibrücken, a small principality west of the Kurpfalz (and under the control of the kings of Sweden in the early eighteenth century).
7. Map 2 is based on information for 439 emigrant families whose villages of origin

are known and who eventually settled in New York, North Carolina, or Ireland. Another five families whose origins are known came from villages outside the region shown on the map. Since information in map 2 is based on genealogical data drawn from German church records, it may exaggerate the concentration of emigrants in certain areas. Some pastors kept more detailed and careful records than others, and the church records for some villages have been lost.

8. In the early eighteenth century more of the region was devoted to viticulture than today. Fritz Trautz, *Die pfälzische Auswanderung nach Nordamerika im 18. Jahrhundert* (Heidelberg, 1959), 17. Concerning the introduction of tobacco, see Meinrad Schaab, *Geschichte der Kurpfalz*, vol. 2, *Neuzeit* (Stuttgart, 1992), 226.

9. Alan Mayhew, *Rural Settlement and Farming in Germany* (London, 1973), 88, 89.

10. A few of the migrants came from regions outside the German southwest. Records in London listing marriages between members of the migration show that some came from Schleswig and Schwerin in northern Germany, Dresden in eastern Germany, Bavaria in the southeast, and Alsace in France. See Dern, *London Churchbooks*, 17. Other migrants came from Thuringia and Switzerland. All of these together seem to have represented less than 2 percent of the entire migration, and some of them had probably moved to the German southwest before 1709.

11. Joachim Heinz, *"Bleibe im Lande, und nähre dich redlich!" Zur Geschichte der pfälzischen Auswanderung vom Ende des 17. bis zum Ausgang des 19. Jahrhunderts* (Kaiserslautern, 1989), 35; A. G. Roeber, *Palatines, Liberty, and Property: German Lutherans in Colonial British America* (Baltimore, 1993), 36.

12. Württemberg, which later became an important center of migration to colonial America, played a smaller role in the 1709 emigration, although Johann Conrad Weiser, one of the most influential leaders of the migration, came from the territory.

13. Michael Hughes, *Early Modern Germany, 1477–1806* (Philadelphia, 1992), 109.

14. Schaab, *Geschichte der Kurpfalz*, 2:121.

15. Schaab, *Geschichte der Kurpfalz*, 2:136.

16. Schaab, *Geschichte der Kurpfalz*, 2:150–51; Marc R. Forster, *The Counter-Reformation in the Villages: Religion and Reform in the Bishopric of Speyer, 1560–1720* (Ithaca, 1992), 121, 181.

17. Wolfgang von Hippel, *Auswanderung aus Südwestdeutschland: Studien zur württembergischen Auswanderung und Auswanderungspolitik im 18. und 19. Jahrhundert* (Stuttgart, 1984), 59; Heinz, *Bleibe im Lande*, 21.

18. Karl Zbinden, "Die Pfalz als Ziel und Etappe schweizerischer Auswanderung," in *Pfälzer-Palatines: Beiträge zur pfälzischen Ein- und Auswanderung sowie zur Volkskunde und Mundartforschung der Pfalz und der Zielländer pfälzischer Auswanderer im 18. und 19. Jahrhundert*, ed. Karl Scherer (Kaiserslautern, 1981), 192; Frederick A. Norwood, *Strangers and Exiles: A History of Religious Refugees*, 2 vols. (Nashville, 1969), 2:143; Heinz Schuchmann, *Schweizer Einwanderer im früheren kurpfälzischen Streubesitz des Kraichgaues (1650–1750)*, Schriften zur Wanderungsgeschichte der Pfälzer, vol. 18 (Kaiserslautern, 1963), 3; Schaab, *Geschichte der Kurpfalz*, 2:137.

19. R. Po-chia Hsia, "Between State and Community: Religious and Ethnic Minorities in Early Modern Germany," in *Germania Illustrata: Essays on Early Modern Germany Presented to Gerald Strauss*, ed. Andrew C. Fix and Susan C. Karant-Nunn, Sixteenth Century Essays and Studies, vol. 18 (Kirksville, Mo., 1992), 178–79.

20. Schaab, *Geschichte der Kurpfalz*, 2:161; Norwood, *Strangers and Exiles*, 2:76.

21. Steven Hochstadt, "Migration in Preindustrial Germany," *Central European History* 16 (Sept. 1983): 209.

22. Forster, *Counter-Reformation in the Villages*, 233.

23. Hochstadt, "Migration in Preindustrial Germany," 201.

24. Don Yoder, introduction to Heinrich Rembe, "Emigration Materials from Lambsheim in the Palatinate," *Pennsylvania Folklife* 23 (winter 1973–74): 40–41.

25. Hughes, *Early Modern Germany*, 72.

26. Eda Sagarra, *A Social History of Germany, 1648–1914* (New York, 1977), 108.

27. Forster, *Counter-Reformation in the Villages*, 183.

28. "Wie übel und hart die Evangelischen in Johann Wilhelms Landen bedrückt würden." Quoted in Heinz, *Bleibe im Lande*, 27.

29. Schaab, *Geschichte der Kurpfalz*, 2:157.

30. Schaab, *Geschichte der Kurpfalz*, 2:160; for an extended treatment of the religious situation in the Palatinate during the early modern period, see Meinrad Schaab, "Die Wiederherstellung des Katholizismus in der Kurpfalz im 17. und 18. Jahrhundert," *Zeitschrift für die Geschichte des Oberrheins* 75 (1966): 147–205.

31. Peter C. Erb, "Introduction" in *Pietists: Selected Writings*, ed. Peter C. Erb (New York, 1983), 5.

32. Roeber, *Palatines, Liberty, and Property*, 81.

33. Richard Gawthrop and Gerald Strauss, "Protestantism and Literacy in Early Modern Germany," *Past and Present* 104 (Aug. 1984): 46.

34. Roeber, *Palatines, Liberty, and Property*, 91.

35. John A. Hostetler, "The Plain People: Historical and Modern Perspectives," in *America and the Germans*, 1:112. A good summary of Pietism and the various forms it took in Germany in the late seventeenth and early eighteenth centuries is in Roeber, *Palatines, Liberty, and Property*, chap. 3.

36. In 1777 only seven cities in the Palatinate had more than two thousand people, and only two (Mannheim and Heidelberg) had more than 3,600. Schaab, *Geschichte der Kurpfalz*, 2:223.

37. David Sabean, *Property, Production, and Family in Neckarhausen, 1700–1870* (Cambridge, 1990), 38.

38. Mayhew, *Rural Settlement*, 88, 89.

39. Heinz, *Bleibe im Lande*, 22.

40. A. G. Roeber, "The Origins and Transfer of German-American Concepts of Property and Inheritance," *Perspectives in American History*, n.s., 3 (1987): 126 n. 16; Roeber, *Palatines, Liberty, and Property*, 113. For an account of the economic effects of partible inheritance in the German southwest after 1720 and of how inheritance practices affected migration from the region, see Fogleman, *Hopeful Journeys*, 23–28.

41. Sabean illustrates the process in eighteenth-century Württemberg. See Sabean, *Neckarhausen*, 49.
42. Sabean, *Neckarhausen*, 318–19.
43. Werner Trossbach, " 'Südwestdeutsche Leibeigenschaft' in der Frühen Neu-zeit—eine Bagatelle?" *Geschichte und Gesellschaft* 7 (1981): 82, 83; Kurt Ander-mann, "Leibeigenschaft im pfälzischen Oberrheingebiet während des späten Mittelalters und der frühen Neuzeit," *Zeitschrift für Historische Forschung* 17 (1990): 294, 296, 303; Heinz, *Bleibe im Lande*, 60; Schaab, *Geschichte der Kurpfalz*, 2:225; Jerome Blum, *The End of the Old Order in Rural Europe* (Princeton, 1978), 35–38. Trossbach's and Andermann's articles represent the two sides of the de-bate over the status of serfs in early modern Germany. Andermann argues that the differences between the serfs and the free were in name, not in substance. Trossbach argues that, although serfdom may not have been onerous in the Ger-man southwest, people still perceived it as a real and inferior status.
44. Heinz, *Bleibe im Lande*, 69; Werner Hacker, *Kurpfälzische Auswanderer vom Un-teren Neckar* (Stuttgart, 1983), 27–30; Werner Hacker, *Auswanderungen aus Rheinpfalz und Saarland im 18. Jahrhundert* (Stuttgart, 1987), 83–90. Some of Hacker's findings are summarized in English in Aaron Fogleman, "Review Essay: Progress and Possibilities in Migration Studies: The Contributions of Werner Hacker to the Study of Early German Migration to Pennsylvania," *Penn-sylvania History* 56 (Oct. 1989): 318–29.
45. Roeber, *Palatines, Liberty, and Property*, 31, 34, 46.
46. Gawthrop and Strauss, "Protestantism and Literacy," 38.
47. Gawthrop and Strauss, "Protestantism and Literacy," 43ff.
48. Schaab, *Geschichte der Kurpfalz*, 2:232.
49. Even within religious denominations, significant variations in religious practice existed. See Marc R. Forster, "With and Without Confessionalization: Varieties of Early Modern German Catholicism," *Journal of Early Modern History* 1 (1997): 342.
50. Unless otherwise stated, the demographic information in this section is based on the 444 families who eventually settled in New York, North Carolina, or Ire-land and whose villages of origin are known. Information on occupation and religion is derived primarily from the censuses of the migrants carried out in London. The various sources of demographic information and the database cre-ated from them are described in the appendix.
51. For family size, see Wolfgang von Hippel, *Auswanderung aus Südwestdeutsch-land*, 49. Von Hippel's figures are based on 4,131 emigrants enumerated when boarding ships in Rotterdam to sail to London.
52. Of the adults without spouses, 3.2 percent were widows and 0.7 percent were widowers. The ratio of widows to widowers was not uncommon for early mod-ern Germany. Knodel has shown for eighteenth-century Germany that almost 50 percent of all widowers remarried within two years of losing their wives, while only 20 percent of all widows remarried in the same period. See John Knodel, *Demographic Behavior in the Past: A Study of Fourteen German Village Pop-ulations in the Eighteenth and Nineteenth Centuries* (Cambridge, 1988), 165.

53. The 7 percent figure is from von Hippel, *Auswanderung aus Südwestdeutschland*, 49. Single men made up 13.5 percent of the adult emigrants; single women made up 3.4 percent

54. These figures are drawn from the database of 1709 emigrants described in the appendix. The London censuses of the German emigrants, which cover over 1,600 male heads of household (many of whom never reached New York), reveal an average age of just under thirty-five for adult men.

55. Matheus appears as Marcus Matthes in the London census, PRO CO 388/76:68. Details of his trip to Sweden are in Jones and Rohrbach, *Even More Palatine Families*, 3:1715–16.

56. For the population of major Palatine towns, see Meinrad Schaab, *Geschichte der Kurpfalz*, 2:223.

57. For Frankfurt's population, see Gerald Soliday, *A Community in Conflict: Frankfurt Society in the Seventeenth and Early Eighteenth Centuries* (Hanover, N.H., 1974), 37.

58. Based on information in the London censuses, PRO CO 388/76:56, 64, 68, 69.

59. Apr. 22, 1708, *Journal of the Commissioners for Trade and Plantations, 1704–1708* (London, 1920), 482.

60. Based on information derived from the database of 1709 emigrants (see appendix).

61. PRO CO 388/76:56, 64, 68, 69. The religious diversity of the migrants argues against theories put forth by late nineteenth- and early twentieth-century historians that religious persecution fueled the migration. See Cobb, *Story of the Palatines*, 33, and Albert Faust, *The German Element in the United States*, 2 vols. (Boston, 1909), 1:58–59.

62. Richard K. MacMaster, *Land, Piety, Peoplehood: The Establishment of Mennonite Communities in America, 1683–1790* (Scottdale, Pa., 1985), chap. 2.

63. In this way they differed markedly from the indentured servants who left England in the early eighteenth century, often moving to Virginia and Maryland. David Galenson found that 85 percent of the male and female indentured servants leaving Liverpool from 1697 to 1707 were age twenty-five or younger. The ratio of men to women servants leaving Liverpool was about 2.5:1, again differentiating them from the German men and women who left their homes in 1709 in almost equal numbers. See David W. Galenson, *White Servitude in Colonial America: An Economic Analysis* (Cambridge, 1981), 24, 27.

64. Jon Butler found that almost 50 percent of 761 Huguenot heads of households living in London in 1689 were over fifty-five years of age. Jon Butler, *The Huguenots in America: A Refugee People in New World Society* (Cambridge, Mass., 1983), 29.

65. Forty-seven percent of the men in the database of 1709 emigrants were first-born sons.

66. Claude C. Sturgill, *Marshal Villars and the War of the Spanish Succession* (Lexington, Ky., 1965), 69, 75.

67. Quoted from the Runkel and Selters church records in Jones, *Palatine Families of New York*, 1:iii.

68. Herbert Zielinski, "Klimatische Aspekte Bevölkerungsgeschichtlicher Entwick-lung," in *Historische Demographie als Sozialgeschichte: Giessen und Umgebung vom 17. zum 19. Jahrhundert*, ed. Arthur E. Imhof, 2 vols. (Darmstadt, 1975), 2:949.

69. Wilhelm Abel, *Agricultural Fluctuations in Europe*, trans. Olive Ordisch (New York, 1980), 184; Heinz, *Bleibe im Lande*, 43; Zielinski, "Klimatische Aspekte," 944.

70. Walter Knittle lists seven reasons for the 1709 emigration, including "war dev-astation" and "an extraordinary severe winter." He also includes heavy taxa-tion, religious quarrels, hunger for land and adventure, colonial propaganda, and the cooperation of the British government. Knittle, *Early Palatine Emigration*, 31. A. G. Roeber blames the migration on "war, bad weather, and crop failure in 1709." Roeber, *Palatines, Liberty, and Property*, 8.

71. W. Gregory Monahan, *Year of Sorrows: The Great Famine of 1709 in Lyon* (Colum-bus, Ohio, 1993), 71–153; Walter Rödel, *Mainz und seine Bevölkerung im 17. und 18. Jahrhundert* (Stuttgart, 1985), 241.

72. Such regulations and fees caused many people to leave illegally without in-forming the government. Rulers tried to discourage illegal emigration by seiz-ing property that was left behind, thus ensuring that it did not pass on to rela-tives or heirs remaining in the country.

73. The men's requests, contained in thirty-nine petitions, are in the Hessischen Hauptstadtarchiv, Wiesbaden. Photocopies of the originals are in the Library of Congress, Washington, D.C. The petitions were reprinted in Julius Goebel, ed., "Briefe Deutscher Auswanderer aus dem Jahre 1709," *Jahrbuch der Deutsch-Amerikanischen Historischen Gesellschaft von Illinois* (1912): 124–89.

74. "Mein brod anders zu suchen." Petition of Johann Conrath Petter, Goebel, "Briefe," 130–31.

75. "Diesen schlechten Zeitten" and "diesen armen Zeitten," Goebel, "Briefe," 171, 176.

76. "Bey denen in die Viele Jahr getroffenen schlechten Zeitten und Kriegstrube-len," Goebel, "Briefe," 175.

77. Goebel, "Briefe," 139–40, 151.

78. Rüdiger Renzing, *Pfälzer in Irland: Studien zur Geschichte deutscher Auswander-erkolonien des frühen 18. Jahrhunderts* (Kaiserslautern, 1989), 22.

79. Wokeck, *Trade in Strangers*, 150–52; Aaron Fogleman, "Contributions of Werner Hacker," 323.

80. "So bin Ich willens, mit andern armen leuten mich nach der Carolinischen insul mich zu fügen, mein glück da zu verbessern," Goebel, "Briefe," 138.

81. Examples of such comments can be found in the reports on the petitions of Hen-rich Müller and his brothers, Daniel Focht, Daniel Reubel, Jörg Schmitt, and Henrich Peter. Goebel, "Briefe," 145, 151, 156, 158, 160.

82. Among those denied on such grounds were Henrich Gast, Jost Steubing, Philips Weber, and Wilhelm Cunze. Goebel, "Briefe," 161–62.

83. Heinz, *Bleibe im Lande*, 3.

84. Lowell C. Bennion, "Flight from the Reich: A Geographic Exposition of South-west German Emigration, 1683–1815" (Ph.D. diss., Syracuse University, 1973), 169–70.

85. Hans Fenske, "International Migration: Germany in the Eighteenth Century," *Central European History* 13 (Dec. 1980): 344, 346.

86. Mack Walker, *The Salzburg Transaction: Expulsion and Redemption in Eighteenth-Century Germany* (Ithaca, 1992), 74.

87. Julius Friederich Sachse, "The Fatherland: Showing the Part It Bore in the Discovery, Exploration, and Development of the Western Continent," *Pennsylvania German Society Proceedings and Addresses* 7 (1897): 187.

88. Daniel Falckner, *Curieuse Nachricht von Pennsylvania* (Frankfurt and Leipzig, 1702), trans. and ed. by Julius Friederich Sachse as *Daniel Falckner's Curieuse Nachricht von Pennsylvania* (Philadelphia, 1905).

89. "Woran in America Mangel sey? Vornehmlich an Menschen, und Handwerckern, der übrige Mangel würde leicht zu ersetzen seyn." Sachse, ed., *Daniel Falckner's Curieuse Nachricht*, 206–7.

90. *The Journals of the House of Commons* 17 (Apr. 14, 1711): 597.

91. Joshua Kocherthal, *Ausführlich und Umständlicher Bericht von der berühmten Landschafft Carolina, in dem Engelländischen America gelegen* (Frankfurt and Leipzig, 1707 and 1709). Reprinted under the same title but with a foreword and introduction (Neustadt an der Weinstrasse, 1983).

92. Today copies of the book are harder to find. The second edition can be found at the Library Company of Philadelphia and in the Harold Jantz Collection at Duke University. The third edition is also at Duke University. The Library of Congress and the University of Illinois haves copies of the fourth edition. At least two copies of the fourth edition are also in Germany—one at the university library in Göttingen and one in the city library of Mainz.

93. Julius Goebel, ed., "Neue Dokumente zur Geschichte der Massenauswanderung im Jahre 1709," *Jahrbuch der Deutsch-Amerikanischen Historischen Gesellschaft von Illinois* (1913): 185. The emigrant did not specifically say that the English envoy was distributing Kocherthal's book, but his description of the literature, along with our knowledge of the place and year of the book's publication, certainly points to Kocherthal's book.

94. Anton Boehme, *Das verlangte, nicht erlangte Canaan* (Frankfurt and Leipzig, 1711). The book, which describes the emigrants' suffering in England and condemns their foolish desire for an easier life in America, was written by the German court chaplain in London.

95. Kocherthal was a pseudonym for Joshua Harrsch. For more information on his origins, see Heinz Schuchmann, "Der 1708 nach Amerika ausgewanderte Pfarrer Josua Kocherthal hiess ursprünglich Josua Harrsch," *Mitteilungen zur Wanderungsgeschichte der Pfälzer* 6 (Nov. 1967): 121–28.

96. Introduction to the 1983 reprint edition of Joshua Kocherthal, *Ausführlich und Umständlicher Bericht* (Neustadt an der Weinstrasse, 1983), iii. Kocherthal briefly mentions his trip to London in a postscript to the second edition of his book. See Kocherthal, *Bericht*, 2d ed. (1709), 38–39.

97. Although no other accounts of Carolina seem to have appeared in German before Kocherthal's in 1706, several English accounts of the colony had been published. Four such reports are published in Alexander S. Salley Jr., ed., *Narratives*

of Early Carolina, 1650–1708 (New York, 1911). Jack Greene summarizes the typical contents of English-language promotional literature in Greene, *The Intellectual Construction of America: Exceptionalism and Identity from 1492 to 1800* (Chapel Hill, 1993), 68–78.

98. Even though the number of books printed in early modern Germany increased tremendously with the advent of the printing press, literacy rates remained low. Many people heard books rather than read them, and authors wrote their pamphlets bearing this in mind. See R.W. Scribner, *Popular Culture and Popular Movements in Reformation Germany* (London, 1987), 50, 54, and *For the Sake of Simple Folk: Popular Propaganda for the German Reformation* (Cambridge, 1981), 1–3. Scribner writes about sixteenth-century Germany, but literacy rates had not increased substantially by the early eighteenth century. See Gawthrop and Strauss, "Protestantism and Literacy," 43, 50–55.

99. For an extended account of the 1708 migration, see Knittle, *Early Palatine Emigration*, chap. 2.

100. The second edition also appeared in early 1709. It does not seem to have differed from the first edition except that it included a report, which was already out-of-date, that Kocherthal was in Holland with a small group of migrants. This was the group that arrived in London in 1708.

101. "Ja selbst in Virginia siehet man, dass einer, wann er nur so ziemlich, und nicht eben so sonderbar fleissig seyn will, bey 3000. Pfund Tobacco und 20. Pfund Barrels Korn jährlich erbauen kan." Kocherthal, *Bericht*, 4th ed. (1709), 70.

102. Kocherthal, *Bericht*, 2d ed., 24; 4th ed., 28.

103. More than likely the author of the letter was Joshua Kocherthal, but this cannot be proven. The author describes his family as including his wife and three children, a description that fits Kocherthal's family, which included three daughters.

104. Kocherthal, *Bericht*, 4th ed. (1709), 77–80.

105. The questions and the responses are in the Staatsarchiv Wiesbaden, Nassau-Weilburg Abt. 150, no. 4493. Photocopies of the original document are in the Library of Congress, Washington, D.C. The document was also transcribed in Goebel, "Neue Dokumente," 181–201. The document records the men's responses to the following questions: What is your name, age, and religion? Where were you born? How long have you been married and how many children do you have? What made you decide to apply to leave and who gave you the idea? Did someone advise you to do it? Who? What do you actually know about the so-called new Island? Who told you this and under what circumstances? Where and when did this happen? Who made the application? Where will you get the means to make the journey?

106. "... ob er schon tag und nacht auff seinem Zimmerhandwerk arbeitete, so wolte es ihm doch die Nahrung nicht gewinnen machen." Goebel, "Neue Dokumente," 187.

107. "... wollte er von Hertzen gern hir bleiben." Goebel, "Neue Dokumente," 192.

108. "Man habe hin und wieder im Land davon geredt." Goebel, "Neue Dokumente," 185.

109. Robert Darnton elaborates on this theme in *The Forbidden Best-Sellers of Pre-Revolutionary France* (New York, 1995), 217.

110. "Dass die Königen von Engelland den leuthen das brod geben wolte, bis sie dasselbige erziehen konten." Goebel, "Neue Dokumente," 189.

111. "Wüste weiter nichts alss wass aus dem Buch ihm daraus vorgelesen worden." Goebel, "Neue Dokumente," 189. Hermann Wellenreuther also notes the hazy notions of the emigrants about life in America; see "Image and Counterimage, Tradition and Expectation: The German Immigrants in English Colonial Society in Pennsylvania, 1700–1765," in *America and the Germans: An Assessment of a Three-Hundred-Year History*, ed. Frank Trommler and Joseph McVeigh, 2 vols. (Philadelphia, 1985), 1:87.

112. ". . . dass man in einem Jahr so viel ziehen und Erndten könte, umb 2 Jahr davon zu leben, wann arbeiten wolte." Goebel, "Neue Dokumente," 186. Kocherthal had written that the fertility of the land in South Carolina was such that one could harvest two crops of corn in a year. "Die Früchte belangend, so geräht vor allem das Indianische Korn wol, so dass, wo man will, solches in einem Jahr 2 mal kan eingeerndtet werden." Kocherthal, *Bericht*, 12. Falckner made a similar claim, writing that the America's climate and the land's fertility caused plants to grow quickly and allowed a second harvest. Sachse, ed., *Falckner's Curieuse Nachricht*, 103.

113. Wilhelm Yoland's wife and children arrived in New York, but he apparently died along the way. None of the other petitioners appeared on lists of emigrants in New York or North Carolina.

114. Goebel, "Briefe," 169, 174.

115. Anton Boehme, a German pastor in London and a close observer of the migration, made such arguments in his book criticizing the 1709 emigration. See Boehme, *Das verlangte, nicht erlangte Canaan*, chap. 2.

116. George Fenwick Jones, *The Georgia Dutch: From the Rhine and Danube to the Savannah, 1733–1783* (Athens, Ga., 1992), 24. The quote is from Psalms 37:3. Luther translated the verse as "Hoffe auf den Herrn, und thue Gutes; bleibe im Lande, und nähre dich redlich!" The connotation of the last half of Luther's translation differs from the King James version of the same verse—"so shalt thou dwell in the land, and verily thou shalt be fed"—which might not have served the purposes of the German princes as well.

117. Quoted in Jones, *Palatine Families of New York*, 1:vii.

CHAPTER 2. "THE POOR PALATINE REFUGEES"

1. W. Gregory Monahan, *Year of Sorrows*, 73.

2. Historians often report that the trip down the Rhine was a slow one of four to six weeks, basing their assertions on Gottlieb Mittelberger's account from the mid-eighteenth century. Mittelberger blamed the slow progress on the numerous customhouses along the river that required boats to stop for inspection. Although he began his journey somewhat farther north than Mittelberger, Hans Stauffer, a Mennonite emigrant who traveled the Rhine in late 1709, needed only seventeen days to travel from Mainz to Holland, and less than two weeks

to travel from Neuwied—a center of the 1709 emigration—to the Dutch border. Strong head winds, rather than customhouses, caused most of the delays. See Gottlieb Mittelberger, *Journey to Pennsylvania*, ed. and trans. Oscar Handlin and John Clive (Cambridge, Mass., 1960), 11, and Jones, *Palatine Families of New York*, 1:ix–x.

3. Letter of Dayrolle, Mar. 29/Apr. 9, 1709, PRO 84/232:91.

4. French report dated May 14, 1709 (NS), from Leiden. Goebel, "Neue Dokumente," 198–99.

5. Resolutions and Proceedings of the Burgomasters of Rotterdam, Apr. 22 and 29, 1709 (NS), Historical Society of Pennsylvania, Dutch West Indies, box 3, folder 9; Knittle, *Early Palatine Emigration*, 52.

6. "Decree of the Elector Palatine," Library of Congress, Foreign Copying Project, Germany, box 2545 (microfilm); PRO SP 84/232:124; *Post-Man*, London, May 7–10, 1709.

7. Order from Hesse-Darmstadt dated May 1, 1709 (NS), Marion Dexter Learned, *Guide to the Manuscript Materials Relating to American History in the German State Archives* (Washington, D.C., 1912), 171; Nassau-Idstein report dated June 12, 1709 (NS), Goebel, "Neue Dokumente," 195; Nassau-Weilburg decree dated May 24, 1709 (NS), Goebel, "Neue Dokumente," 183–84; Nassau-Dillenburg decree dated June 25, 1709 (NS), Goebel, "Briefe Deutscher Auswanderer," 136; Württemberg decree dated June 25, 1709 (NS), Württembergisches Staatsarchiv, Stuttgart, Generalrescripts Bd. 2, s. 647, microfilm copy in Manuscript Collection, Library of Congress, Washington, D.C.; Sayn decree dated June 13, 1709 (NS), Staatsarchiv Koblenz, Abt. 30, Nr. 34.

8. British Library, Add. MSS 4743:109.

9. Secretary of State Henry Boyle to Dayrolle, Apr. 20, 1709, British Library, Add. MSS 15866:166; Dayrolle letter of May 6, 1709, PRO SP 84/232:124.

10. Unsigned letter dated Apr. 28, 1709, PRO SP 34/10:235.

11. The 1598 description is from John Stow's *A Survey of Modern London* and is quoted in Norman G. Brett-James, *The Growth of Stuart London* (London, 1935), 33. The second description is from 1684 and is quoted in M. Dorothy George, *London Life in the XVIIIth Century* (New York, 1925), 66.

12. L'Hermitage to Heinsius, July 12, 1709 (NS), in *De Briefwisseling van Anthonie Heinsius 1702–1720*, ed. A. J. Veenendahl, 10 vols. (The Hague, the Netherlands, 1976–89), 9:42 (hereafter, *Heinsius Correspondence*); PRO SP 34/10:235; Richard S. and Mary Maples Dunn, ed., *The Papers of William Penn*, 5 vols. (Philadelphia, 1981–86), 4:647. Penn left Pennsylvania in 1701 and lived in England for the rest of his life.

13. Daniel L. Brunner, "The Role of Halle Pietists (c.1700–c.1740), with Special Reference to the S.P.C.K.," (Ph.D. diss., Oxford University, 1988), 72.

14. Brunner, "Role of the Halle Pietists," 64.

15. The Board of Trade had been created in 1696 to oversee colonial policy. By 1709 it had lost some of its influence and was clearly subordinate to the secretary of state for the Southern Department, but it still remained the most important government advisory group on colonial affairs. See I. K. Steele, *Politics of Colonial Policy: The Board of Trade in Colonial Administration 1696–1720* (Oxford, 1968), 109.

16. PRO CO 388/76:56, 56i.
17. PRO CO 388/76:56ii.
18. Minutes of meetings, May 20, 23, and 24, 1709, PRO CO 388/76:60.
19. PRO SP 34/10:237; British Library, Add. MSS 61649:72.
20. PRO CO 388/76:54; British Library, Add. MSS 61652:139.
21. E. A. Wrigley and R. S. Schofield, *The Population History of England, 1541–1871: A Reconstruction* (Cambridge, Mass., 1981), 175, 179.
22. Daniel Statt, *Foreigners and Englishmen: The Controversy over Immigration and Population, 1660–1760* (Newark, Del., 1995), 48–49.
23. Quoted in Statt, *Foreigners and Englishmen*, 49.
24. Daniel Statt, "The Birthright of an Englishman: The Practice of Naturalization and Denization of Immigrants under the Later Stuarts and Early Hanoverians," *Proceedings of the Huguenot Society of Great Britain and Ireland* 25 (1989): 63. A similar process known as denization also allowed aliens to become British subjects, but denizens could not inherit property or pass it on to children born before denization had been granted. Denization was bestowed by letters patent from the Crown, naturalization by an act of Parliament.
25. Geoffrey Holmes, *British Politics in the Age of Anne*, rev. ed. (London, 1987), 69.
26. Statt, *Foreigners and Englishmen*, 101.
27. Statt, "Birthright of an Englishman," 69; H. T. Dickinson, "The Poor Palatines and the Parties," *English Historical Review* 82 (July 1967): 464.
28. PRO CO 388/76:58.
29. Knittle, *Early Palatine Emigration*, 53–54; PRO T.1/119:6–11.
30. PRO T.1/119:1.
31. PRO SP 34/10:237–38.
32. PRO T.1/119:19–26, 68–72.
33. Dayrolle to Boyle, June 3/11, 1709, PRO 84/232:138.
34. PRO CO 388/76:64, 68, 69.
35. Queen Anne to the Elector Palatine, Feb. 20, 1704, in Beatrice Curtis Brown, ed., *The Letters and Diplomatic Instructions of Queen Anne* (London, 1935), 114–15.
36. William Shaw, ed., *Calendar of Treasury Books*, 1709, vol. 23, pt. 2 (London, 1949), 172, 202, 226.
37. *Post Boy*, June 14–16, 1709.
38. PRO SP 34/10:237–38; British Library, Add. MSS 61649:72 and 61652:155.
39. British Library, Add. MSS 61649:40; Narcissus Luttrell, *A Brief Historical Relation of State Affairs*, 6 vols. (Oxford, 1857), 6:455; L'Hermitage to Heinsius, July 1/12, 1709, *Heinsius Correspondence*, 9:42.
40. A decade later Defoe wrote that "Black-Heath, both for beauty of situation, and an excellent air, is not out-done by any spot of ground so near the river and so near land in England." Daniel Defoe, *A Tour through the Whole Island of Great Britain* (London, 1724–26), reprint, abridged, ed. Pat Rogers (New York, 1971), 114.
41. PRO T.1/119:130, 132.
42. Queen's order from the Court of St. James, June 16, 1709, printed in *The State of the Palatines for Fifty Years Past to This Present Time* (London, 1709), 8–9. The Guildhall Library, London, has an original copy of the order: Proc. 25.17.

43. *London Gazette*, July 5–7, 1709.

44. *BT Jour.* (1708–14), 39. Daniel Defoe later argued he had personally presented the plan to Godolphin. See Defoe, *A Tour through England and Wales Divided into Circuits or Journies* (London, 1724–26; reprint in 2 vols., London, 1927), 1:200.

45. PRO CO 388/76:58, 65i.

46. PRO CO 388/76:66ii, 67; *BT Jour.* (1708–14), 47.

47. *BT Jour.* (1708–14), 47.

48. British Library, Add. MSS 61649:70, 74.

49. A copy of the letter sent to Chester, dated June 29, 1709, is in the Cheshire Record Office, Mayor's Letter Book 1674–1715, ML4:634.

50. British Library, Add. MSS 61652:178b; 61611:85.

51. *BT Jour.* (1708–14), 60.

52. *London Gazette*, July 2–5, 1709; St. Paul's Cathedral, destroyed in the Great Fire of 1666, was rebuilt from 1675 to 1710.

53. *London Gazette*, July 19–21, 1709, and July 28–30, 1709.

54. *London Gazette*, July 14–16, 1709.

55. PRO T.1/119:68–72, 79–82, 132.

56. Letter of June 8, 1709 (NS), PRO SP 84/232:138.

57. Letter of June 14, 1709 (NS), PRO SP 84/232:268.

58. Boyle to Dayrolle, June 24, 1709, British Library, Add. MSS 15866:176.

59. Dayrolle report of July 1, 1709 (NS), PRO SP 84/232:168.

60. Knittle, *Early Palatine Emigration*, 59–60.

61. British Library, Add. MSS 61534:171.

62. Resolutions and Proceedings of the Burgomasters of Rotterdam, Aug. 24, 1709 (NS), and Resolutions of States General of the United Netherlands, Sept. 16, 1709 (NS), Historical Society of Pennsylvania, Dutch West Indies collection, box 3, folder 9.

63. Knittle, *Early Palatine Emigration*, 62–63. Dayrolle was unsure who had printed the fliers, but they were the work of the Carolina proprietors who, wanting to ensure the success of their proposal, had sent copies to Rotterdam to encourage further German migration. See Vincent Hollis Todd, "Baron Christoph von Graffenried's New Bern Adventures" (Ph.D. diss., University of Illinois, 1912), 43.

64. Historical Manuscripts Commission, *14th Report, Appendix, Part IV, MSS of Lord Kenyon*, 442–43, and *15th Report, Appendix, Part IV, MSS of Duke of Portland*, 527.

65. L'Hermitage to Heinsius, July 8/19, 1709, in *Heinsius Correspondence*, 9:74; *The State of the Palatines for Fifty Years Past to this Present Time* (London, 1709), 10.

66. Luttrell recorded on Sept. 29 that eighteen men enlisted in Lord Hayes's regiment. Luttrell, *Brief Historical Relation*, 6:494. Writing two years later, Boehme said 322 men joined the military. Boehme, *Das verlangte, nicht erlangte Canaan* (Frankfurt and Leipzig, 1711), chap. 6, translated by Frank Diffenderffer in "German Exodus to England," appendix F, 399.

67. Many of the listmasters' names appear on a petition to the Society for the Propagation of the Gospel asking for a German pastor to accompany the migrants to America. Society for the Propagation of the Gospel minutes, vol. 9, no. 162.

68. Luttrell, *Brief Historical Relation*, 6:464; Brunner, "Role of Halle Pietists," 74. The

Lambeth Palace Library has a copy of the Sermon on the Mount, which was also printed for the Germans in a side-by-side translation. *Our Savior's Sermon on the Mount . . . Oder Die Bergpredigt Christi* (London, 1710).

69. Dern, *London Churchbooks and the German Emigration*, 14.

70. R. Palmer to Ralph Verney, Aug. 17, 1709, Historical Manuscripts Commission, *7th Report, Appendix, Verney MSS*, 507.

71. L'Hermitage to Heinsius, July 8/19, 1709, *Heinsius Correspondence*, 9:73; *History of the Reign of Queen Anne, Digested into Annals, Year the Eighth* (London, 1710), 167.

72. Undated journal attributed to Johan George Smidt in William V. H. Barker, *Early Families of Herkimer County, New York* (Baltimore, 1986), 326.

73. Sunderland to the Board of Trade, May 3, 1709, PRO CO 388/76:54.

74. *BT Jour.* (1708–14), 32, 33, 37, 38, 40, 46.

75. E. B. O'Callaghan, ed., *Ecclesiastical Records of the State of New York*, 8 vols. (Albany, 1910–16), 3:1738; Defoe, *A Review of the State of the British Nation* 6 (June 2, 1709): 103–4.

76. Paula R. Backscheider, *Daniel Defoe, His Life* (Baltimore, 1989), 254.

77. *Review* 6 (June 23, 1709): 137; (June 30, 1709): 150; (July 2, 1709): 154.

78. *Review* 6 (Aug. 6, 1709): 216.

79. Daniel Defoe, *A Brief History of the Poor Palatine Refugees* (London, 1709; reprint, Augustan Reprint Society, Los Angeles, 1964). Defoe wrote the book in the form of a long letter to an anonymous correspondent.

80. Defoe, *Brief History*, 1.

81. Defoe, *Brief History*, 2, 3.

82. Defoe, *Brief History*, 4–8.

83. *Review* 6 (Aug. 6, 1709): 216.

84. Bernard Cottret, *The Huguenots in England: Immigration and Settlement c. 1550–1700*, trans. Peregrine and Adriana Stevenson (Cambridge, 1991), 2.

85. David Underdown, *Fire from Heaven: Life in an English Town in the Seventeenth Century* (New Haven, 1992), 126, 170.

86. Richard Parker, *An Account of the Present Condition of the Protestants in the Palatinate* (London, 1699), reprinted in *ERNY*, 3:1453–59.

87. *Review* 6 (June 2, 1709): 103.

CHAPTER 3. "A PARCEL OF VAGABONDS"

1. "The Most humble Petition of Five hundred & Twelve, miserably by war distressed and ruined German Protestants from the Palatinate," British Library, Add. MSS 61649:66.

2. "The State of the Poor Palatines," reprinted in *The History of the Reign of Queen Anne, Year the Eighth* (London, 1710), appendix, 34–35.

3. Peter Sahlins expands on the notions of "us" and "them" and how they help shape people's perceptions of who they are in the introduction to his book *Boundaries: The Making of France and Spain in the Pyrenees* (Berkeley, 1989). On the

role of anti-French and anti-Catholic attitudes in the development of eighteenth-century British identity, see Linda Colley, *Britons: Forging the Nation, 1707–1837* (New Haven, 1992), chap. 1.

4. Colley, *Britons*, 19.

5. "State of the Poor Palatines," *History of the Reign of Queen Anne, Year the Eighth*, appendix, 34.

6. "State of the Poor Palatines," *History of the Reign of Queen Anne, Year the Eighth*, appendix, 34, 35.

7. Dickinson, "Poor Palatines and the Parties," 471; L'Hermitage to Heinsius, Aug. 19/30, 1709, *Heinsius Correspondence*, 9:209. Dickinson reports that the duchess of Marlborough contributed £1,000; L'Hermitage's reference may be an inflated account of her generosity.

8. Cottret, *Huguenots in England*, 222.

9. *Bishop Burnet's History of My Own Time: with the Suppressed Passages of the First Volume, and Notes by the Earls of Dartmouth and Hardwicke, and Speaker Onslow, hitherto Unpublished*, 6 vols. (Oxford, 1823), 5:425.

10. Quoted in Dickinson, "Poor Palatines and the Parties," 473.

11. Defoe, *Brief History*, 11, 12.

12. Defoe, *Brief History*, 14, 15.

13. *The Palatines' Catechism or a True Description of Their Camps at Black Heath and Camberwell: In a pleasant Dialogue between an English Tradesman and a High-Dutchman* (London, 1709), reprinted in *ERNY*, 3:1818.

14. Board of Trade to Sunderland, June 1, 1709, in W. N. Sainsbury, ed., *Calendar of State Papers, Colonial Series: America and the West Indies*, 44 vols. (London, 1820–1969), vol. *1708–1709*, 322.

15. Herbert Davis, ed., *The Prose Works of Jonathan Swift*, vol. 7, *The History of the Four Last Years of the Queen* (Oxford, 1951; original written in 1713 and first published in 1758), 94–95. Swift, a political moderate but a staunch supporter of the established Church, supported Robert Harley and the Tory government that replaced the Whigs in 1710. See A. L. Rowse, *Jonathan Swift* (New York, 1975), 52, 65–66.

16. *A Short and Easy Way for the Palatines to Learn English (Oder Eine kurze Anleitung zur Englischen Sprach: Zum Nutz der armen Pfälzer)* (London, 1710).

17. Floyer to Lady Dartmouth, Aug. 23, 1709, Historical Manuscripts Commission, *15th Report, Appendix, Dartmouth MSS*, 3:146. It is not clear how the Germans to whom Floyer referred reached Litchfield, a small town about sixty miles west of London.

18. Joseph Addison, *Spectator* (July 30, 1711). Quoted in Katie Trumpener, "The Time of the Gypsies: A 'People without History' in the Narratives of the West," *Critical Inquiry* 18 (summer 1992): 850 n. 9. Trumpener's article presents a careful analysis of the presentation of Gypsies in western literature.

19. There is at least one indication that the Britons saw the Germans in the same light and ascribed to them mysterious powers. A rumor concerning the fertility of the German women spread across the Atlantic. In March 1710 a Boston newspaper reporting on the German camps outside London claimed that the

German women "seldom fail of two at a birth." *Boston News-Letter,* Mar. 6–13, 1710.

20. L'Hermitage to Heinsius, June 21/July 2, 1709, *Heinsius Correspondence,* 9:5.
21. Robert Kenyon to his sister-in-law, Aug. 2, 1709, *Historical Manuscripts Commission Reports,* 14th Report, appendix, part IV, 442–43.
22. Defoe, *Brief History,* 23.
23. Undated letter of the bishop of Norwich to the clergy of his diocese, *History of the Reign of Queen Anne, Year the Eighth,* appendix, 55.
24. *Palatines' Catechism* reprinted in *ERNY,* 3:1817–20.
25. *A View of the Queen's and Kingdom's Enemies in the Case of the Poor Palatines* (London, [1711]).
26. Boehme, *Das verlangte, nicht erlangte Canaan,* chap. 6, trans. in Diffenderffer, "The German Exodus to England," 401.
27. *Canary-Birds Naturaliz'd in Utopia: A Canto* (London, 1709), 30.
28. British Library, Add. MSS 61611:87.
29. L'Hermitage to Heinsius, July 5/16, 1709, *Heinsius Correspondence,* 9:58.
30. L'Hermitage to Heinsius, July 15/26, 1709, *Heinsius Correspondence,* 9:97.
31. Boehme, *Das verlangte, nicht erlangte Canaan,* chap. 6, trans. in Diffenderffer, "The German Exodus to England," 395.
32. C. E. Doble, ed., *Remarks and Collections of Thomas Hearne,* 11 vols. (Oxford, 1885–1921), 2:239–40.
33. The petition is in *State of the Palatines,* 6–7.
34. *Palatines' Catechism,* reprinted in *ERNY,* 3:1820.
35. For an examination of the ways real or imagined histories can shape group identity and of how people produce their own histories to help gain control of their present, see Sider, *Lumbee Indian Histories,* xvii–xviii, and Nagel, "Constructing Ethnicity," 163–64.
36. *London Gazette,* July 19–21, 1709.
37. Resolution of the Irish Parliament, Aug. 23, 1709. Quoted in Renzing, *Pfälzer in Irland,* 53.
38. British Library, Add. MSS 61638:127.
39. Minutes of the Commission for the Palatines, July 28, 1709, PRO T.1/119:91.
40. Minutes of the Commission for the Palatines, July 30, 1709, PRO T.1/119:92.
41. *London Gazette,* Aug. 6–9, 1709; L'Hermitage to Heinsius, Aug. 2/13, 1709, *Heinsius Correspondence,* 9:157; Minutes of the Commission for the Palatines, July 28, 1709, PRO T.1/119:91.
42. Report of the Commission for the Palatines in Ireland, Feb. 15, 1711, British Library, Add. MSS 35933:18.
43. Report of the Commission for the Palatines in Ireland, Feb. 15, 1711, British Library, Add. MSS 35933:12, 13, 19. The most complete history of the Germans in Ireland is Rüdiger Renzing's *Pfälzer in Irland.* For accounts in English, see Patrick J. O'Connor, *People Make Places: The Story of the Irish Palatines* (Coolanoran, Ireland, 1989), and Jones, *Palatine Families of Ireland.*
44. *London Gazette,* July 14–16, 1709.
45. Vincent H. Todd and Julius Goebel, *Christoph von Graffenried's Account of the*

Founding of New Bern (Raleigh, 1920), 45; Knittle, *Early Palatine Emigration,* 98–101.

46. "De Graffenried's Contract for the Palatines," in *The Colonial Records of North Carolina,* vol. 1, *1662 to 1712,* ed. William L. Saunders (Raleigh, 1886), 986–89.
47. British Library, Add. MSS, 22202:130.
48. "De Graffenried's Manuscript," reprinted in *Colonial Records of North Carolina,* 905–86. Quote is from p. 908.
49. For a more complete account of the New Bern settlement, see Todd and Goebel, *Christoph von Graffenried's Account,* and Knittle, *Early Palatine Emigration,* 104–10.
50. "Order of Council for Naturalizing and Sending Certain Palatines to New York," in E. B. O'Callaghan, ed., *Documentary History of the State of New York,* 4 vols. (Albany, 1850–51), 3:541.
51. Board of Trade to the Lord High Treasurers, Aug. 30, 1709, *CSP Col.* (1708–9), 452–55.
52. A few Germans did apparently settle in Jamaica in 1710. Narcissus Luttrell noted in his journal on Aug. 3, 1710, that the "Palatines sent to Jamaica have arrived according to letters from there." Luttrell, *A Brief Historical Relation,* 6:613. For the St. Christopher's plan, see *CSP Col.* (1710–11), 96; for the Scilly Islands, see PRO SP 34/11:59; British Library, Add. MSS 61649:92, 94, 96, 110, 112, and Diffenderffer, "German Exodus to England," 315, 397; for Barbados, see Knittle, *Early Palatine Emigration,* 77.
53. Boyle to the secretary of war, Apr. 17, 1709, PRO SP 44/107:267.
54. List of Germans sent back to Holland, PRO T.1/119:136–53; *London Gazette,* Sept. 15–17, 1709.
55. Ulrich Simmendinger, *Warhaffte und glaubwurdige Verzeichnüss . . .* (Reuttlingen, Germany, circa 1717), trans. Herman F. Vesper and reprinted as *Simmendinger's Register* (Baltimore, 1962), 8.
56. PRO SP 84/232:242.
57. PRO SP 84/232:260.
58. British Library, Add. MSS 61534:177, 15866:193; L'Hermitage to Heinsius, Oct. 21/Nov. 1, 1709, *Heinsius Correspondence,* 9:396.
59. British Library, Add. MSS 61534:175, 15866:192.
60. British Library, Add. MSS 61652:188, 194b; 61649:102, 112.
61. In a request presented to the SPG on May 16, the Germans asked for a pastor "if they should be sent to New York or any other of Her Majesties Plantations." SPG correspondence, 8:92.
62. *CSP Col.* (1708–9), 455–56.
63. *CSP Col.* (1708–9), 456.
64. Ibid.
65. Steele, *Politics of Colonial Policy,* 121.
66. Sunderland to the president of the Council of New York, Nov. 10, 1709, British Library, Add. MSS 61647:152.
67. Joseph J. Malone, *Pine Trees and Politics: The Naval Stores and Forest Policy in Colonial New England, 1691–1775* (Seattle, 1964), 6–7, chap. 1; Robert Greenhalgh Albion, *Forests and Sea Power: The Timber Problem of the Royal Navy, 1652–1862*

(Cambridge, Mass., 1926), 238–46; Justin Williams, "English Mercantilism and Carolina Naval Stores, 1705–1776," *Journal of Southern History* 1 (May 1935): 172.

68. Hunter to the Board of Trade, Nov. 30 and Dec. 1, 1709, in E. B. O'Callaghan, ed., *Documents Relative to the Colonial History of New York*, 15 vols. (Albany, 1856–87), 5:112–14.

69. British Library, Add. MSS 61599:84–90; "Report of the Board of Trade on the Plans for Settling the Palatines," Dec. 5, 1709, *NYCD*, 5:117–20.

70. British Library, Add. MSS 61645:86; Joseph Redington, ed., *Calendar of Treasury Papers*, 6 vols. (London, 1869–89), vol. *1708–1714*, 149; Weiser, *Autobiography*, 13.

71. Letter from the attorney general to the Board of Trade, Dec. 21, 1709, PRO CO 5/1049:144; Board of Trade to Sunderland, Dec. 23, 1709, *CSP Col.* (1708–9), 563.

72. James du Pré, who was one of the commissaries for the project, reported that the contract "was finally executed at Plymouth the beginning of April 1710." Du Pré's copy of the contract showed that it had been witnessed by him and two German migrants, Jean Cast and Godfriedt de Wulffen, who spoke French and perhaps some English, and who served as translators and intermediaries for the Germans in New York. There is no indication that any of the other Germans signed the document. Harleian MSS 7021:281, 284–85.

73. For the story of the Indians' visit to London, see Richmond P. Bond, *Queen Anne's American Kings* (Oxford, 1952). In a letter dated April 2, 1710, Hunter mentioned seeing the ship with the Indians on board, but he did not write anything about their reaction to the Germans. Hunter to Sunderland, British Library, Add. MSS 61645:111.

74. Some reports indicate the convoy set sail on April 10, but Hunter sent at least one letter from Plymouth dated April 20. British Library, Add. MSS 61645:129; Harleian MSS 7021:280; Knittle, *Early Palatine Emigration*, 146.

75. Memorial of Alex. Cairnes, one of the commissioners for the Palatines, Dec. 19, 1710, PRO SP 34/14:31.

76. John Seams to Lord Dartmouth, secretary of state, Jan. 15, 1710/11, PRO SP 34/28:143.

77. Henry Z Jones Jr. and John Dern, "Palatine Emigrants Returning in 1710" in *Pfälzer-Palatines*, ed. Scherer, 54. One shipload of about two hundred Germans returned as late as 1717. Henry Z Jones and Lewis Rohrbach, *Even More Palatine Families*, 2:1632.

78. Diary of Ralph Thoresby, June 15, 1712, in Joseph Hunter, ed., *The Diary of Ralph Thoresby, F. R. S.*, 2 vols. (London, 1830), 2:120.

79. For an analysis of the role the Naturalization Act played in the debate between the Tories and the Whigs over the German immigrants, see Dickinson, "Poor Palatines and the Parties," 464–85. According to Daniel Statt, almost all the people naturalized under the 1709 act had French surnames. Statt, "Birthright of an Englishman," 70.

80. Letter dated Oct. 14, 1709, quoted and translated by Daniel L. Brunner, "Role of Halle Pietists," 76.

81. Boehme, *Das verlangte, nicht erlangte Canaan*, 5.

82. Tribbeko's sermon is included in Boehme's *Das verlangte, nicht erlangte Canaan* as

chapter 7. The quotations are from a translation by Henry Eyster Jacobs included in Jacobs, "The German Migration to America 1709–1740," *Pennsylvania German Society Proceedings and Addresses* 8 (1898): 76–79.

CHAPTER 4. "A DEPLORABLE SICKLY CONDITION"

1. "Second Immigration of the Palatines," *DHNY*, 3:551; Hunter to the Board of Trade, July 24, 1710, *DHNY*, 3:559; Harleian MSS 7021:280. Incomplete ledger entered at the back of deed book, vol. 13 (1736–39), New York State Archives.
2. "Petition of Thomas Benson," *DHNY*, 3:558. Voyages from Britain and northern Europe to British North America typically lasted from eight to thirteen weeks. See John Duffy, "The Passage to the Colonies," *Mississippi Valley Historical Review* 38 (June 1951): 22–23, 27, 31.
3. "A Memorial Representing the Materials There Are for Raising Naval Stores," Harleian MSS 7021:281; *Calendar of Council Minutes of New York, 1668–1783* (Albany, 1902), 236; Council Minutes MSS, New York State Archives, 10:496.
4. *Minutes of the Common Council of the City of New York, 1675–1776* (New York, 1905), 2:408–9.
5. "Second Immigration of the Palatines," *DHNY*, 3:552. Nutten Island is present-day Governor's Island, just south of Manhattan.
6. Hunter to Board of Trade, June 16, 1710, *NYCD*, 5:165; du Pré to Board of Trade, Dec. 14, 1711, PRO CO 5/1050:33.
7. J. F. Haeger to the SPG, July 25, 1710, *ERNY*, 3:1863.
8. "Petition of Peter Willemse Romers," *DHNY*, 3:568. An archaeological dig in 1994 on the northern end of the island uncovered what may have been the graves of some of the Germans who had died there almost three hundred years earlier. *New York Times*, June 4, 1994, sec. 1, p. 23.
9. "A Memorial . . . for Raising Naval Stores," Harleian MSS 7021:280; Knittle, *Early Palatine Emigration*, 143, 147.
10. "A Memorial . . . for Raising Naval Stores," Harleian MSS 7021:281; Hunter to the Board of Trade, July 24, 1710, *DHNY*, 3:559.
11. "An Estimate of the Sums of Money that will be needfull for Compleating the Settlement of the Palatins," Harleian MSS 7021:286.
12. *BT Jour.* (1708–14), 226. This figure, though large, could have been much higher if the convoy's passage had not gone so smoothly. Their fellow migrants who left London for North Carolina in January 1710 suffered a mortality rate of over 50 percent when the ships were blown off course, leading to a 13-week voyage. See Jones and Rohrbach, *Even More Palatine Families*, 2:819. A group of German immigrants who left England for Philadelphia in 1739 lost 75 percent of its members to disease during the voyage. Bad weather or poor winds could dangerously extend voyages to the point that disease and starvation exacted horrible tolls. See Duffy, "Passage to the Colonies," 27, 31.
13. "Account of the charge of Subsisting the Palatin's," *DHNY*, 3:668.

14. Petition of Johannes Wilhelm Schefs, agent for the Palatines, to the Board of Trade, Nov. 1, 1720, *NYCD*, 5:575.
15. Du Pré to the Board of Trade, *NYCD*, 5:289.
16. "Order for Apprenticing the Palatine Children," *DHNY*, 3:553.
17. "Names of the Palatine Children Apprenticed by Gov. Hunter, 1710–1714," *DHNY*, 3:566–67.
18. "The Condition Grievances and Oppressions of the Germans," 1720, *DHNY*, 3:707–8.
19. This paragraph and the following are based on information in the Lutheran church records kept by Kocherthal at West Camp, New York. See Christian Krahmer, trans., "The Kocherthal Records," *Olde Ulster* 3 (Feb. 1907): 51.
20. Rapid remarriage was typical of early modern Germany. John Knodel has shown that in eighteenth-century German villages 40 percent of men remarried within one year of the death of their spouses and 50 percent within two years. Fifteen percent of women remarried within one year and 20 percent within two. See Knodel, *Demographic Behavior in the Past*, 165, 183. Since the total number of Palatine widows and widowers is unknown, comparing figures for the New York Palatines to Knodel's figures is impossible. Yet it seems probable that in the German villages, the support of extended families and neighbors made rapid remarriage less imperative than it was for the Palatines in New York.
21. She wrote, in part, "I have learned that the princely house of Nassau has died out, except Nassau-Ditz. I would like to find out from you . . . who rules over the principality, and whether things are still as rough as they were then." Quoted in Jones, *Palatine Families of New York*, 2:662.
22. Some of the ships' listmasters had also served as listmasters in the German camps around London.
23. Haeger to SPG, Oct. 28, 1710, *ERNY*, 3:1872.
24. "List of the Palatins Remaining at New York, 1710," *DHNY*, 3:562; *BT Jour.* (1708–14), 226; du Pré to Board of Trade, *NYCD*, 5:289.
25. "Accompt of wood Cutt at Morisania," NY Col MSS 54:76; Jean Cast to Hunter, *NYCD*, 5:215. The manor was located in what is today the south Bronx.
26. Minutes of the SPG, Dec. 1709, *ERNY*, 3:1817.
27. Haeger to the SPG, July 25, 1710, *ERNY*, 3:1862. Justus Falckner's career reflects the informal cooperation between Swedish, Dutch, and German Lutherans in North America. He came from Saxony and had studied with Franke at Halle. He joined his brother Daniel, the author of *Curieuse Nachricht von Pennsylvania*, in Pennsylvania in 1700. There Justus was ordained under the authority of the Swedish Lutheran Church but was sent to New York to serve its Dutch Lutheran congregation. He had to learn Dutch in order to preach to his new congregation, which was administered by the Lutheran Consistory in Amsterdam. See Harry Julius Kreider, *Lutheranism in Colonial New York* (New York, 1942), 30–32.
28. Haeger to SPG, July 25, 1710, *ERNY*, 3:1862.
29. Ibid.
30. Haeger to SPG, Oct. 28, 1710, *ERNY*, 3:1872.
31. Kocherthal to SPG, Nov. 15, 1710, SPG letter books, 14:218. Since Kocherthal

was not an official missionary of the SPG, the society refused his request for money. Chamberlayne to Kocherthal, May 24, 1711, SPG letter books, 14:244.

32. The Huguenots in England, whose pastors often received support from the Anglican Church, also resisted pressure to adopt such seemingly Catholic conventions as kneeling and using the sign of the cross. See Butler, *Huguenots in America*, 36–37.

33. "Propositions made by the Maquas Indians owners of the Land called Skohere," New-York Historical Society, Misc. MSS Indians, folder 3; Hunter to Board of Trade, July 24, 1710, and [Oct. 3, 1710], *NYCD*, 5:167, 171; Mary Lou Lustig, *Robert Hunter, 1666–1734: New York's Augustan Statesman* (Syracuse, 1983), 67–68.

34. Hunter to Board of Trade, July 24, 1710, *NYCD*, 5:167; Knittle, *Early Palatine Emigration*, 153.

35. Hunter to Board of Trade, Oct. 3, 1710, *DHNY*, 3:560.

36. Lustig, *Hunter*, 69. For an extended discussion of Hunter's negotiations to secure land for the naval stores project see Knittle, *Early Palatine Emigration*, 138–40, 149–58.

37. "Deed of the Land Now Constituting . . . Germantown," *DHNY*, 3:644–51. Although Robert Livingston was the sole owner of the land, the negotiations took into consideration Alida Livingston's interest in the land. She signed the deed along with her husband. Before the deal was concluded, she was questioned privately without her husband being present to ensure that she willingly agreed to the transaction. This procedure was customary in New York but not required by law. See Marylynn Salmon, *Women and the Law of Property in Early America* (Chapel Hill, 1986), 18, 28.

38. Perry, Keill, and du Pré to Board of Trade, *NYCD*, 5:291.

39. "Deed of Land," *DHNY*, 3:649.

40. "Contract with R. Livingston to Victual the Palatines," *DHNY*, 3:653–55.

41. Lawrence H. Leder, *Robert Livingston 1654–1728 and the Politics of Colonial New York* (Chapel Hill, 1961), 213. Lord Cornbury, New York's governor from 1702 to 1708, lamented that Hunter "at his first arrival in his Government fell into so ill hands." He believed that Livingston sold the land only so he could land a generous contract to victual the Germans. See *NYCD*, 5:196. Settling the Germans near the manor no doubt spurred the development of the Livingston's lands and helped cement a mutually beneficial political alliance between Hunter and Livingston. Yet Governor Hunter was the naval stores project's most ardent supporter, investing large amounts of time and money in the scheme; it is unlikely that he would have jeopardized its success simply to gain the favor of Livingston.

42. "Deed of Land," *DHNY*, 3:651.

CHAPTER 5. "THEY WILL NOT LISTEN TO TAR MAKING"

1. Hunter to Board of Trade, Nov. 14, 1710, *DHNY*, 3:655; "Acct. of the Subsistence of the Palatines," *DHNY*, 3:657.

2. East Camp was in the vicinity of present-day Germantown. The area occupied by the villages on the west bank of the Hudson is still known as West Camp.
3. J. Bridger to Board of Trade, Nov. 13, 1710, *NYCD*, 5:176; *BT Jour.* (1708–14), 226.
4. "An estimate of the things necessary for the settlement of the Palatins," NY Col MSS 54:98a.
5. Report of E. Harley, auditor, to Board of Trade, Mar. 31, 1724, including a description of the naval stores project, PRO CO 5/1085:67(i). Cast had also served as a commissary to the Germans while they were still in London. How he received his appointment is unclear, but his ability to speak French and German obviously made him valuable to those in charge of administering the German immigrants.
6. PRO CO 5/1085:67(i). Although the villagers were to choose their leaders, on at least one occasion Hunter appears to have attempted to impose a listmaster on a village. See Cast to Hunter, Mar. 17, 1711, *NYCD*, 5:212.
7. "Estimate of things necessary for the Settlement of the Palatines together the Yearly Salaries to Officers & other Incidents, November 1710," *DHNY*, 3:561.
8. Cast to Hunter, Mar. 17 and 27, 1711, *NYCD*, 5:212, 215.
9. Wallace, *Weiser*, 4.
10. The village listmasters in 1711 were Johann Peter Kneskern at Hunterstown; Johann Conrad Weiser at Queensbury; Hartmann Windecker at Annsbury; Johann Christopher Fuchs at Haysbury; Johann Gerlach at Elizabethtown; Jacob Manck at Georgetown; and Philipp Peter Grauberger at Newtown. See "Meeting of the Commis'y," July 5, 1711, NY Col MSS 55:100(3). Fuchs's election may have been influenced by the large number of people from his home village living together in Haysbury. Information on the listmasters' backgrounds is drawn from Jones, *Palatine Families of New York* and *More Palatine Families*.
11. Report of E. Harley, auditor, to Board of Trade, Mar. 31, 1724, PRO CO 5/1085:67(i).
12. Hunter to Board of Trade, Oct. 3, 1710(?), *NYCD*, 5:171; *B.T. Jour.* (1708–14), 227; Hunter to Board of Trade, Nov. 14, 1710, *CSP Col.* (1710–11), 261.
13. "An Estimate of the things that are necessary for . . . the Palatins" and "An Estimate of the Sums of Money that will be needfull for . . . the Palatins," Harleian MSS 7021:287, 288.
14. "An Estimate of the Sums of Money," Harleian MSS 7021:288.
15. "Account of cloathing, Shoes, Stockins, Hats, & Soop for the Palatens," NY Col MSS 54:120.
16. Hunter to Board of Trade, May 7, 1711, *NYCD*, 5:211.
17. Hunter to Board of Trade, May 7, 1711, *NYCD*, 5:211, 214.
18. William W. Hagen, "Seventeenth-Century Crisis in Brandenburg: The Thirty Years' War, the Destabilization of Serfdom, and the Rise of Absolutism," *American Historical Review* 94 (Apr. 1989): 315.
19. David Sabean describes the many forms of peasant resistance in the German southwest during the early modern period. See David Warren Sabean, *Power in the Blood: Popular Culture and Village Discourse in Early Modern Germany* (Cambridge, 1984). A. G. Roeber notes a strong sense of what he terms "negative" lib-

erty—the desire to be free from constraint and outside interference—among the peasants of the German southwest. See Roeber, *Palatines, Liberty, and Property*, 2, 9–13.

20. James Scott, in his studies of peasant and slave societies, emphasizes the risks of open defiance by oppressed people and shows how these risks alter forms of public resistance. See James Scott, *Domination and the Arts of Resistance* (New Haven, 1990), chap. 2. It should be noted, however, that the German immigrants did not face some of the traditional constraints on peasant resistance. Eric Wolf argues that the isolation of peasant work, the weight of such work, the possibility of subsistence production on peasant holdings, and support networks based on kinship ties all keep peasants from uniting to resist threats to their survival. See Eric R. Wolf, "On Peasant Rebellions," *International Social Science Journal* 21 (1969): 286. The German immigrants had left behind their lands, and many of their kinship networks had been destroyed. In some ways they had less to lose than those who remained behind in Europe.

21. Sherry Ortner discusses the important ways that the internal politics of subordinated communities affect resistance. See Sherry B. Ortner, "Resistance and the Problem of Ethnographic Refusal," *Comparative Studies in Society and History* 37 (Jan. 1995): 176–80. For an exploration of factional conflict among peasants in early modern Germany, see David Martin Luebke, "Peasants and Communities in Early Modern Central Europe," *Central European History* 25 (1992): 281–301. Eugene Genovese's study of slave society explores the varied forms of resistance and accommodation adopted by people sharing common goals and facing a common oppressor. See Eugene Genovese, *Roll, Jordan, Roll: The World the Slaves Made* (New York, 1974), book 4.

22. Hunter to Board of Trade, May 7, 1711, *NYCD*, 5:211.

23. Ibid.

24. Cast to Hunter, Mar. 27, 1711, *NYCD*, 5:214.

25. Cast to Hunter, Mar. 17, 1711, *NYCD*, 5:212.

26. Cast to Hunter, Mar. 27, 1711, *NYCD*, 5:215.

27. Ibid.

28. Ibid.

29. Cast described the gathering in a letter to Hunter, Mar. 27, 1711, *NYCD*, 5:214.

30. "Palatines subsisted at New York," *DHNY*, 3:568; report of E. Harley, auditor, to Board of Trade, Mar. 31, 1724, PRO CO 5/1085:67(i).

31. Hunter to Board of Trade, May 7, 1711, *NYCD*, 5:210, and *DHNY*, 3:661; George Clarke to Robert Livingston, Apr. 6, 1711, Livingston Family Papers, Franklin Roosevelt Library, Hyde Park, N.Y., General Correspondence.

32. *DHNY*, 3:660.

33. For a series of maps illustrating the territorial backgrounds of each of the villages, see Philip Otterness, "The New York Naval Stores Project and the Transformation of the Poor Palatines, 1710–1712," *New York History* 75 (Apr. 1994): 145.

34. "Memorandum of the Sorts & Quantities of Seeds to be Provided for the Palatins," NY Col MSS 54:101a. The Germans also received seeds for beans, radishes, lettuce, mustard, spinach, parsnips, parsley, and potatoes.

35. Cast to Hunter, Mar. 17, 1711, *NYCD*, 5:213; Kenneth W. Keller, "From the Rhineland to the Virginia Frontier: Flax Production as a Commercial Enterprise," *Virginia Magazine of History and Biography* 98 (July 1990): 488.
36. *BT Jour.* (1708–14), 226.
37. Cast to Hunter, May 1, 1711, *DHNY*, 3:659.
38. Cast to Hunter, May 1, 1711, *DHNY*, 3:659–60.
39. Cast to Hunter, Mar. 27, 1711, *NYCD*, 5:214.
40. Except where noted, the account in the following paragraphs of the Germans' rebellion in May 1711 is based on a report from George Clarke to the Board of Trade, May 30, 1711, *NYCD*, 5:238–41.
41. *BT Jour.* (1718–22), 195; Clarke to Board of Trade, May 30, 1711, *NYCD*, 5:239.
42. Clarke to Board of Trade, May 30, 1711, *NYCD*, 5:239.
43. Copies of the English version still exist. Harleian MSS 7021:284–85; *NYCD*, 5:121.
44. "The Condition . . . of the Germans, 1720," *DHNY*, 3:708.
45. Clarke to Board of Trade, May 30, 1711, *NYCD*, 5:240.
46. Clarke to Board of Trade, May 31, 1711, *NYCD*, 5:249–50.
47. Clarke to Board of Trade, May 31, 1711, *NYCD*, 5:250.
48. Hunter to Board of Trade, Jan. 1, 1711/12, *NYCD*, 5:301.
49. Clarke to Board of Trade, May 30, 1711, *NYCD*, 5:241.
50. Board of Trade to Bridger, Feb. 19, 1711, *CSP Col.* (1710–11), 369.
51. C. Whitworth, ambassador to Russia, to Board of Trade, 1/12 Apr. 1712, PRO CO 5/1050:40.
52. Pine trees maintain a pressure of around 180 pounds per square inch within the gum duct system. The gum duct system is separate from the sap system, which carries water from the roots to the tree's branches and needles. Robert D. McReynolds, "Development of Gum Naval Stores in the United States of America," Naval Stores and Timber Production Laboratory, Olustee, Fla., Nov. 1, 1977.
53. William Falconer, *An Universal Dictionary of the Marine* (London, 1780), reprinted as *Falconer's Marine Dictionary (1780)* (New York, 1970), 215, 290.
54. Turpentine was not produced in any significant amounts in America until the nineteenth century. C. Dorsey Dyer, "History of the Gum Naval Stores Industry," *AT-FA Journal* 25 (Jan. 1963):7–8. Gum naval stores are still produced in Florida and Georgia, but they have been largely supplanted by petroleum-based products. For more information on naval stores production, including nineteenth-century illustrations of the process, see Michael Williams, *Americans and Their Forests: A Historical Geography* (Cambridge, 1989), 83–90. Johann David Schoepf, a German-speaking traveler to America in the 1780s, described pitch and tar production in North Carolina in *Travels in the Confederation [1783–1784]*, trans. Alfred E. Morrison (Philadelphia, 1911), 2:140–43.
55. Certification by Sackett of the Palatines' work, NY Col MSS 55:21d.
56. Clarke to Board of Trade, June 7, 1711, *NYCD*, 5:250. Clarke claimed the men on the east side of the river were preparing 15,000 trees a day. He seems to have exaggerated to impress the Board of Trade. Other reports contend that over the life of the project 70,000 to 100,000 trees were stripped of bark. Each tree had to be

barked several times over a two-year period, but it is unlikely that 15,000 were barked in a day. In 1750, the German pastor, Henry Muhlenberg, visited the site where the Germans had worked making tar and pitch. He described it as being located "six or seven miles" from the German settlements on the Hudson and said the area was known as "Tar Busch." Theodore G. Tappert and John W. Doberstein, ed. and trans., *The Journals of Henry Melchior Muhlenberg*, 3 vols. (Philadelphia, 1942–58), 1:250.

57. A few men also gathered pine knots when the grass grew so tall that the children had difficulty finding the knots ("Court over the Palatines," *DHNY*, 3:671), but Hunter credited the children for most of the tar that was eventually produced. Hunter to Board of Trade, June 23, 1712, *NYCD*, 5:342.

58. "Method of Preparing Tar in Muscovy," PRO CO 5/1050:40(i).

59. Roeber, *Palatines, Liberty, and Property*, 31. Charcoal burners received no more respect in America. See Williams, *Americans and Their Forests*, 106.

60. For an analysis of German attitudes about the forest, see H. Fischer, " 'Draussen vom Walde . . . ' Die Einstellung zum Wald im Wandel der Geschichte," *Mensch und Tier* (Wintersemester 1992/93 bis 1994/95): 119–35. For the various, often negative, conceptions of the forest in early America, see James H. Merrell, *Into the American Woods: Negotiators on the Pennsylvania Frontier* (New York, 1999), 24–27.

61. There are many examples, but *Hansel and Gretel* and *Little Red Riding Hood* illustrate the point. See Ruth B. Bottigheimer, *Grimms' Bad Girls and Bold Boys: The Moral and Social Vision of the Tales* (New Haven, 1987). She writes, "The forest embodies and expresses noncommunity and thus harbors egregious creatures like witches . . . murderers and robbers . . . dwarves and wolves" (p. 102). For a discussion of fairy tales and how they reflect the way peasants in early modern Germany viewed the world, see Peter K. Taylor, *Indentured to Liberty: Peasant Life and the Hessian Military State, 1688–1815* (Ithaca, 1994), 232–39.

62. "Court over the Palatines," *DHNY*, 3:669.

63. "Court over the Palatines," *DHNY*, 3:669, 672.

64. "Court over the Palatines," *DHNY*, 3:669.

65. "Court over the Palatines," *DHNY*, 3:670; Cast to Hunter, July 13, 1711, *DHNY*, 3:673.

66. The Germans' actions are typical of the low-profile forms of resistance that James Scott finds are common to serfs and slaves. Scott, *Domination*, 198.

67. Dickinson, "Poor Palatines and the Parties," 482.

68. Board of Trade to Hunter, June 29, 1711, *NYCD*, 5:251.

69. Robert to Alida Livingston, Aug. 5, 1711, Liv. Dutch letters.

70. Robert to Alida Livingston, July 21, 1711, Liv. Dutch letters.

71. Alida to Robert Livingston, July 17, 1711, in Linda Biemer, ed., "Business Letters of Alida Schulyer Livingston, 1680–1726," *New York History* 63 (Apr. 1982): 197.

72. Lustig, *Hunter*, 92 (91–96 summarizes the campaign).

73. Hunter to Secretary St. John, Sept. 12, 1711, *NYCD*, 5:253.

74. Hunter to Cast, July 10, 1711, NY Col MSS 55:112.

75. Lists of the German volunteers from Annsbury, Haysbury, Queensbury, and Hunterstown are in the NY Col MSS 55:144–46.
76. Haeger to SPG, July 12, 1712, *ERNY*, 3:1961.
77. Alida to Robert Livingston, Aug. 7, 1711, Livingston Family Papers, General Correspondence, translated from the Dutch, translator not named.
78. Lustig, *Hunter*, 94.
79. Hunter to Board of Trade, Jan. 1, 1711/12, *NYCD*, 5:301.
80. "The Condition . . . of the Germans, 1720," *DHNY*, 3:709.
81. Robert to Alida Livingston, Sept. 8, 1711, Liv. Dutch letters.
82. Hunter to Board of Trade, Jan. 1, 1711/12, *NYCD*, 5:302.
83. Alida to Robert Livingston, Sept. 29, 1711, Livingston Family Papers, General Correspondence, translated from the Dutch, translator not named.
84. Hunter to Capt. Mathews, Dec. 24, 1711, NY Col MSS 57:36.
85. Hunter to Alexander Strahen, Jan. 1, 1711/12, *CSP Col.* (1712–14), 70–71.
86. "Governor Hunter's Scheme for Imploying the Palatines the Ensuing Summer," Mar. 31, 1712, *DHNY*, 3:678–79.
87. The Commissioners of the Palatines to Col. Ingoldsby, May 2, 1712, *DHNY*, 3:682.
88. "Arrival of Troops at Livingston Manor," *DHNY*, 3:682.
89. Hunter to Board of Trade, Oct. 31, 1712, *CSP Col.* (1712–14), 83.
90. Hunter to Board of Trade, June 23, 1712, *NYCD*, 5:342.
91. "Account. R. Livingston of incidental charges for the Palatines," NY Col MSS 57:124b.
92. Haeger to SPG, July 12, 1712, *ERNY*, 3:1962.
93. Robert to Alida Livingston, May 15, 1712, Liv. Dutch letters.
94. Hunter to Livingston, July 30, 1712, *DHNY*, 3:682–83.
95. Livingston to R. Smith, Apr. 2, 1712, *DHNY*, 3:679. Ironically the bridge that caused the ice jam was probably the same bridge between the German settlements and the pine woods that Hunter had earlier bragged was "the best Bridge in all North America." Hunter to Board of Trade, *NYCD*, 5:264.
96. Robert to Alida Livingston, Nov. 12, 1771, Liv. Dutch letters.
97. Robert to Alida Livingston, Aug. 22, 1712, Liv. Dutch letters.
98. Hunter to Cast, Sept. 6, 1712, *DHNY*, 3:683.

CHAPTER 6. "THE PROMIS'D LAND"

1. Robert to Alida Livingston, Nov. 8, 1712, Livingston Family Papers, General Correspondence.
2. Hunter to Cast, Sept. 6, 1712, *DHNY*, 3:684.
3. Ibid.
4. Haeger to SPG, July 6, 1713, *ERNY*, 3:2001.
5. Few accounts describe the movement of Palatines to these areas, but in late 1712 and in 1713 the names of Palatines from the naval stores camps begin showing up in the local records of New Jersey. See Norman C. Wittwer Jr., *The Faithful and*

the Bold: The Story of the First Service of the Zion Evangelical Lutheran Church, Old-wick, New Jersey (Oldwick, N.J., 1984), 22.

6. Shirley W. Dunn, *The Mohicans and Their Land, 1609–1730* (Fleischmanns, N.Y., 1994), 56–57.

7. T. J. Brasser, "Mahican," in William C. Sturtevant, gen. ed., *Handbook of North American Indians*, vol. 15, *The Northeast*, ed. Bruce G. Trigger (Washington, D.C., 1978), 198; Daniel Richter, *The Ordeal of the Longhouse: The Peoples of the Iroquois League in the Era of European Colonization* (Chapel Hill, 1992), 54–56. Epidemic disease may also have played an important role in the displacement of the Mahicans. See Matthew Dennis, *Cultivating a Landscape of Peace: Iroquois-European Encounters in Seventeenth-Century America* (Ithaca, 1993), 132.

8. Richter, *Ordeal of the Longhouse*, 59.

9. Francis Jennings, *The Ambiguous Iroquois Empire* (New York, 1984), 131–32, 176–77, 202.

10. James Axtell, *The Invasion Within: The Contest of Cultures in Colonial North America* (New York, 1985), 257–59.

11. Richter, *Ordeal of the Longhouse*, 227; Bond, *Queen Anne's American Kings*, 1–2. The Germans later claimed that the Indians offered the Schoharie lands to the British Crown for the German refugees they supposedly saw languishing in London's parks. The Germans seem to have transformed a possible sighting of the four Indians when their ships crossed paths near Plymouth in April 1710 into this tale of Indian generosity toward them. The records of the Indians' meetings in London do not mention the Germans.

12. Hunter to the Board of Trade, Oct. 31, 1712, *NYCD*, 5:349; Richter, *Ordeal of the Longhouse*, 230.

13. William N. Fenton and Elisabeth Tooker, "Mohawk," in Sturtevant, ed., *Handbook of North American Indians*, vol. 15, *Northeast*, 474; Wallace, *Weiser*, 18, 25.

14. The term *Wilden* is closely tied to the earlier German phrase *wilder Mann*, which, according to one historian, evoked images of "a hairy, naked, club-wielding child of nature who existed halfway between humanity and nature." The term *savage* had the same connotation in the sixteenth century. Robert F. Berkhofer Jr., *The White Man's Indian: Images of the American Indian from Columbus to the Present* (New York, 1978), 13.

15. Falckner, *Curieuse Nachricht*, 112–13, 122–23.

16. Kocherthal, *Bericht*, 20.

17. "In vollkommener Freundschafft und guten Vernehmen." Kocherthal, *Bericht*, 57–58.

18. Karen Ordahl Kupperman, *Settling with the Indians: The Meeting of English and Indian Cultures in America, 1580–1640* (Totowa, N.J., 1980), 39, 46, 55, 112. Kupperman provides an excellent analysis of how early English writers portrayed the Indians.

19. Kupperman, *Settling with the Indians*, 121.

20. Haeger to SPG, Aug. 15, 1711, *ERNY*, 3:1886.

21. Brasser, "Mahican," 205. The so-called River Indians were the surviving remnants of the tribes whose homelands had once been along the Hudson River.

22. "Proposalls made by the Sachims of the five Nations," Aug. 26, 1711, *NYCD*, 5:272.

23. Kupperman argues that such attacks, beginning with the Virginia massacre of 1622, had an important effect on English attitudes toward the Indians. The English became more respectful, more fearful, and less trusting of the Indians. Although they did not yet have the power to do it and, in fact, remained to some degree dependent on the Indians, the English began speaking of driving the Indians from the land in order to ensure their own survival. See Kupperman, *Settling with the Indians*, 176–83.

24. Hunter to the Board of Trade, Oct. 31, 1712, *CSP Col.* (1712–14), 82; Weiser, *Autobiography*, 17; "Condition . . . of the Germans," *DHNY*, 3:709–10.

25. "Condition . . . of the Germans," *DHNY*, 3:710.

26. Hunter to the Board of Trade, Oct. 31, 1712, *CSP Col.* (1712–14), 82; "Condition . . . of the Germans," *DHNY*, 3:710.

27. Frank E. Lichtenthaeler, "Storm Blown Seed of Schoharie," *The Pennsylvania German Folklore Society* 9 (1944): 35.

28. Weiser, *Autobiography*, 21. Father and son shared the same name. When it is not clear to whom I am referring from the context, I refer to the older Weiser as Johann Conrad and to his son as Conrad.

29. Donna Merwick, *Possessing Albany, 1630–1710: The Dutch and English Experiences* (Cambridge, 1990), 277, 291.

30. Thomas Burke, *Mohawk Frontier: The Dutch Community of Schenectady, New York, 1660–1710* (Ithaca, 1991), 213.

31. Dennis, *Cultivating a Landscape of Peace*, 131.

32. Merwick, *Possessing Albany*, 204, 259, 294.

33. Jennings, *Ambiguous Iroquois Empire*, 193.

34. Weiser, *Autobiography*, 19, 21.

35. "Condition . . . of the Germans," *DHNY*, 3:711.

36. "Condition . . . of the Germans," *DHNY*, 3:712.

37. As Richard White points out, such "creative, and often expedient misunderstandings" were not uncommon in places where such dissimilar cultures came in contact. Richard White, *The Middle Ground: Indians, Empires, and Republics in the Great Lakes Region, 1650–1815* (Cambridge, 1991), x.

38. "Condition . . . of the Germans," *DHNY*, 3:710.

39. J. Munsell, ed., *Annals of Albany*, 10 vols. (Albany, 1850–59), 7:236–37.

40. Hunter to Cast, Oct. 17, 1712, *DHNY*, 3:685.

41. Hunter to the Board of Trade, Oct. 31, 1712, *NYCD*, 5:347.

42. Weiser, *Autobiography*, 27; Lichtenthaeler, "Storm Blown Seed," 37.

43. Weiser, *Autobiography*, 27.

44. John M. Brown, *Brief Sketch of the First Settlement of the County of Schoharie by the Germans* (Schoharie, 1823), 19.

45. "Condition . . . of the Germans," *DHNY*, 3:710.

46. Brown, *Brief Sketch*, 11.

47. Knittle, *Early Palatine Emigration*, 200–201.

48. Brown, *Brief Sketch*, 11–12. Brown, a grandson of one of the German immigrants,

believed that Bayard's offer was legitimate and that the Germans had been foolish to reject it.

49. E. B. O'Callaghan, comp., *Calendar of N.Y. Colonial Manuscripts, Indorsed Land Papers, 1643–1803* (reprint, Harrison, N.Y., 1987), 110.

50. Knittle, *Early Palatine Emigration*, 201–2. Like the better-known Nine Partners, who controlled a large stretch of land along the Hudson, the Seven Partners represented just one of the many coalitions of powerful land speculators operating in New York.

51. Edith M. Fox, *Land Speculation in the Mohawk Country* (Ithaca, 1949), 11.

52. "Condition . . . of the Germans," *DHNY*, 3:711.

53. Ibid.

54. "Condition . . . of the Germans," *DHNY*, 3:712.

55. O'Callaghan, *Calendar of Indorsed Land Papers*, 109.

56. "Condition . . . of the Germans," *DHNY*, 3:711.

57. Vrooman to Hunter, June 9, 1715, NY Col MSS 60:3a.

58. Vrooman to Hunter, July 9, 1715, *DHNY*, 3:687.

59. Vrooman to Hunter, July 9, 1715, *DHNY*, 3:688.

60. "Warrant to arrest Conrad Weiser, July 22, 1715," *DHNY*, 3:688. For the way the term *skulking* was used in unflattering descriptions of Indian behavior, see Patrick M. Malone, *The Skulking Way of War: Technology and Tactics among the New England Indians* (Lanham, Md., 1991; reprint, Baltimore, 1993), 31, 115, 117. Malone notes that New England Indians were not the only ones accused of skulking. In 1665 colonists chastised five captured Mohawks for fighting "in a secret, skulking manner . . . and so killing people in a base and ignoble manner" (31).

61. Hunter to the Board of Trade, July 25, 1715, *NYCD*, 5:418.

62. "Condition . . . of the Germans," *DHNY*, 3:711.

63. The story remains a favorite of the German settlers' twenty-first-century descendants.

64. Brown, *Brief Sketch*, 12–13.

65. Ibid. Magdalene Zee was married and had at least five children living with her in 1715. She and her husband, Johannes, appeared frequently in various censuses of the Germans. They had emigrated from near Oppenheim on the Rhine. See Jones, *Palatine Families of New York*, 2:1126–29.

66. Jeptha R. Simms, *History of Schoharie County and Border Wars of New York* (Albany, 1845), 70.

67. *Oxford English Dictionary*, 2d ed., s.v. *skimmington*; Natalie Zemon Davis, *Society and Culture in Early Modern France* (Stanford, 1975), 140; David Underdown, *Revel, Riot, and Rebellion: Popular Politics and Culture in England, 1603–1660* (Oxford, 1985), 100–102; Bruce Thomas Boehrer, "*Epicoene*, Charivari, Skimmington," *English Studies* (1994): 18. For a comprehensive study of skimmingtons and other forms of "rough music" in early America, see William Pencak, Matthew Dennis, and Simon P. Newman, eds., *Riot and Revelry in Early America* (University Park, Pa., 2002).

68. Underdown, *Revel, Riot, and Rebellion*, 108, 110. Scott, *Domination*, 172–75.

69. Brown, *Brief Sketch*, 13. Brown originally sent his manuscript to New York Gov-

ernor DeWitt Clinton, who had solicited a history of the region. After reading Brown's vivid account of Magdalene Zee's attack on Adams, Clinton allegedly asked Brown to rewrite the episode. Brown refused and decided to print the Schoharie history at his own expense. See Friedrich Kapp, *Geschichte der Deutschen im Staate New York* (New York, 1867), 380 n. 106.

70. Scribner, *Popular Culture*, 116; E. P. Thompson, "The Moral Economy of the English Crowd in the Eighteenth Century," *Past and Present* 50 (Feb. 1971): 115; Davis, *Society and Culture*, 145–47; Joy Wiltenburg, *Disorderly Women and Female Power in the Street Literature of Early Modern England and Germany* (Charlottesville, Va., 1992).

71. Wiltenburg, *Disorderly Women*, 184.

72. Davis, *Society and Culture*, 147.

73. Davis, *Society and Culture*, 146. Differences in levels of accountability of men and women began to narrow throughout western Europe after the Reformation. Governments became less tolerant of unruly women, and women were especially vulnerable to prosecution for gender-linked crimes such as witchcraft and infanticide. See Wiltenburg, *Disorderly Women*, 16, and Merry Wiesner, "Frail, Weak, and Helpless: Women's Legal Position in Theory and Reality," in *Regnum, Religio et Ratio: Essays Presented to Robert M. Kingdon*, ed. Jerome Friedman, vol. 7 of Sixteenth Century Essays and Studies (Kirksville, Mo., 1987), 169.

74. Brown, *Brief Sketch*, 13.

75. "The Condition . . . of the Germans," *DHNY*, 3:713. Perhaps the arrested woman was Magdalene Zee; the petition did not give a name or a reason for the arrest.

76. Hunter to the Board of Trade, Oct. 10, 1715, *NYCD*, 5:449.

77. "Condition . . . of the Germans," *DHNY*, 3:712.

78. "The Condition, Grievances and Oppressions of the Germans," *DHNY*, 3:707–14. A summary of the petition that makes more explicit the Germans' demands is "Petition of the New-York Palatines to the Lords of Trade," *NYCD*, 5:553–55.

79. "Condition . . . of the Germans," *DHNY*, 3:712.

80. Ibid.

81. "Condition . . . of the Germans," *DHNY*, 3:713.

82. Ibid.

83. Ibid.

84. Hunter to the Board of Trade, July 7, 1718, *NYCD*, 5:510.

85. Weiser, *Autobiography*, 39.

86. Ibid.

87. Weiser, *Autobiography*, 39–41.

88. *BT Jour.* (1718–22), July 21, 1718, 188.

89. "Condition . . . of the Germans," *DHNY*, 3:708.

90. Weiser, *Autobiography*, 17.

91. "Condition . . . of the Germans," *DHNY*, 3:710.

92. "Petition of the New-York Palatines to the Lords of Trade, August 2, 1720," *NYCD*, 5:553–55.

93. *BT Jour.* (1718–22), Aug. 9, 1720, 195.

94. *BT Jour.* (1718–22), Sept. 1, 1720, 205.

95. *BT Jour.* (1718–22), Sept. 6, 1720, 207.

96. Weiser, *Autobiography*, 47.

CHAPTER 7. "A NATION WHICH IS NEITHER FRENCH,
NOR ENGLISH, NOR INDIAN"

1. Another group of 1710 immigrants—the children apprenticed on their arrival in New York—followed a third path. Despite the hardships these children faced, a few established themselves more quickly and more successfully than their fellow immigrants. John Peter Zenger served an apprenticeship with the New York printer William Bradford and by 1720, while many of the Germans struggled for land in Schoharie, he had established himself as a printer in Maryland. He returned to New York in 1726 and began printing the *New York Weekly Journal* in 1733. See Stanley Nider Katz, introduction to *A Brief Narrative of the Case and Trial of John Peter Zenger* [by James Alexander], ed. Katz, 2d ed. (Cambridge, Mass., 1972), 8.

2. By 1728 over fifty German families lived on Livingston's manor. Ruth Piwonka, *A Portrait of Livingston Manor, 1686–1850* (Clermont, N.Y., 1986), 34.

3. Sung Bok Kim, *Landlord and Tenant in Colonial New York: Manorial Society, 1664–1775* (Chapel Hill, 1978), 243.

4. Cadwallader Colden to Burnet, Aug. 26, 1724, and "Report in Favor of Issuing Letters Patent to the Palatines in Germantown," *DHNY*, 3:723, 725; Robert to Alida Livingston, May 29, 1724, June 8, 1724, and May 27, 1726, Liv. Dutch letters.

5. Philip L. White, *The Beekmans of New York in Politics and Commerce, 1647–1877* (New York, 1965), 162.

6. Records of Ulster County, N.Y., liber BB, 386; deed books of Ulster County, N.Y., trustees' records of the corporation of Kingston, book 1st, part B, 116–17; E. M. Ruttenber and L. H. Clark, comps., *History of Orange County, New York* (Philadelphia, 1881), 371, 372; "A list of the Freeholders within the County of Ulster, 1728," *DHNY*, 3:969–72.

7. Wittwer, *Faithful and the Bold*, 22.

8. Henry Z Jones Jr., Ralph Connor, and Klaus Wust, *German Origins of Jost Hite, Virginia Pioneer, 1685–1761* (Edinburg, Va., 1979), 15. The 1710 immigrants who moved to Pennsylvania were joined by several of the Germans who had been part of Kocherthal's original emigrant group of 1708, which had originally settled near Quassaic Creek in the vicinity of present-day Newburgh. See Ruttenber and Clark, comps., *History of Orange County*, 249.

9. Theobald Gerlach, Anna Catharina Gerlach, and Carl Erhardt moved to the Shenandoah Valley from Stone Arabia, a German village in the Mohawk River valley founded in 1723. Michael Brack also settled in the valley. See Jones, *Palatine Families of New York*, 1:215, 277, and *More Palatine Families*, 322, and Jones, Connor, and Wust, *Jost Hite*, 22.

10. Jones, Connor, and Wust, *Jost Hite*, 21; Warren R. Hofstra, "Land Policy and Settlement in the Northern Shenandoah Valley," in *Appalachian Frontiers: Settlement, Society and Development in the Preindustrial Era*, ed. Robert D. Mitchell (Lexington, 1991), 108. The Hites settled south of present-day Winchester.

11. "Number of Palatine Families remaining in the Province of New-York, Anno 1718," *NYCD*, 5:515.

12. Deposition of Godfrey Fidler, Oct. 6, 1726, Penn-Physick Papers. Quoted in Charles Berwind Montgomery, "Notes on the Tulpehocken Lands," *Historical Review of Berks County* 1 (July 1936): 42–43. The town of Reading, a dozen miles east of the Tulpehocken settlement, was not settled until 1733.

13. Weiser, *Autobiography*, 49. For a discussion of the route the Germans followed, see Lichtenthaeler, "Storm Blown Seed," 66–77.

14. Fidler deposition in Montgomery, "Notes on the Tulpehocken Lands," 42.

15. *Minutes of the Provincial Council of Pennsylvania*, vol. 3 (Philadelphia, 1852), 322; Francis Jennings, "Incident at Tulpehocken," *Pennsylvania History* 35 (Oct. 1968): 342, 352, and "Brother Miquon: Good Lord!" in *The World of William Penn*, ed. Richard S. Dunn and Mary Maples Dunn (Philadelphia, 1986), 208–9.

16. Lichtenthaeler, "Storm Blown Seed," 94.

17. Weiser, *Autobiography*, 52. Weiser married Anna Eva Feg, another of the 1709 emigrants, in 1720.

18. Board of Trade to Burnet, Nov. 29, 1720, *NYCD*, 5:581–82.

19. Burnet to Board of Trade, Oct. 16, 1721, *NYCD*, 5:634.

20. Burnet to Board of Trade, Nov. 21, 1722, *NYCD*, 5:656.

21. The village was later renamed Herkimer, exchanging its gubernatorial namesake for that of Nicholas Herkimer, a Revolutionary War hero and an early German settler in the region. The area across the Mohawk River from Herkimer is still called German Flats.

22. New York State Archives, New York Patent Book, 9:140.

23. A map of the Burnetsfield patent showing the individual lots and their owners is included in a recent history of Herkimer County. See Herkimer County Historical Society, *Herkimer County at 200* (Herkimer, N.Y., 1992), 36.

24. Robert Kuhn McGregor, "Cultural Adaptation in Colonial New York: The Palatine Germans of the Mohawk Valley," *New York History* 69 (Jan. 1988): 11–13.

25. This statement is not meant to imply that peasants in western Europe divided land in a tradition-bound, inefficient, and irrational manner—an assertion refuted by Donald McCloskey in his studies of English open field patterns. The point is that the 1710 German immigrants quickly adapted ways of distributing land in America that had not been part of their experience in the German southwest. For McCloskey's argument, see Donald N. McCloskey, "The Prudent Peasant: New Findings on Open Fields," *Journal of Economic History* 51 (June 1991): 343–55, and "English Open Fields as Behavior toward Risk," *Research in Economic History* (fall 1976): 124–70.

26. Stone Arabia remains a farming community without a central village. Two eighteenth-century churches—one Lutheran, the other Reformed—stand at a coun-

try crossroad marking the community's center a few miles north of the towns of Palatine Bridge and Canajoharie.

27. Dixon, *Palatine Roots*, 195–97. The Fuchs, Nellis, Wormuth, and Bellinger families all purchased land from Harrison.

28. Wallace, *Weiser*, 34.

29. O'Callaghan, *Indorsed Land Papers*, 171–73, 195–96.

30. John Dern, ed., *The Albany Protocol: Wilhelm Christoph Berkenmeyer's Chronicle of Lutheran Affairs in New York Colony, 1731–1750* (Camden, Maine, 1992), 98 n. 56.

31. Charles Gehring, *Agriculture and the Revolution in the Mohawk Valley* (St. Johnsville, N.Y., n.d.), 3; Timothy J. Shannon, *Indians and Colonists at the Crossroads of Empire* (Ithaca, 2000), 48, 235.

32. Jones, *More Palatine Families*, i–iii; New York Council minutes, Oct. 27, 1722, *DHNY*, 3:715.

33. Jones, *More Palatine Families*, vii. Mark Häberlein has noted the same trend among German immigrants to colonial Pennsylvania. Immigrants from Baden tended to settle among Badeners, marry Badeners, and choose Badeners as godparents for their children. See Mark Häberlein, *Vom Oberrhein zum Susquehanna* (Stuttgart, 1993), 132, 141–43.

34. Krahmer, "Kocherthal Records."

35. Hofstra, "Land Policy and Settlement," 112.

36. An examination of 1710 migrants who settled in or near New York City and Hackensack reveals that in fourteen of seventeen marriages involving children of immigrants, the spouses were both Germans. The other three marriages appear to have been to Dutch or French members of the Reformed Church. Based on information drawn from the database of 1709 emigrants (see appendix).

37. "Translation of the Journal of Peter Nicholas Sommer," in Royden Vosburgh, ed., *Records of St. Paul's Evangelical Lutheran Church* (New York, 1914), 284, 287–89.

38. Franklin and Smith wrote these descriptions in the 1750s, when they feared that the Pennsylvania Germans were becoming less complacent and no longer simply satisfied with a large farm. They suspected that the Germans might aid their political enemies or even the French. Benjamin Franklin, "Observations Concerning the Increase of Mankind," in Leonard W. Labaree, ed., *The Papers of Benjamin Franklin*, vol. 4, *July 1, 1750, through June 30, 1753* (New Haven, 1961), 234; [William Smith], *A Brief State of the Province of Pennsylvania* (London, 1755), 30.

39. Lustig, *Robert Hunter*, 155.

40. Clarke to auditor general Horatio Walpole, Nov. 22, 1722, *DHNY*, 3:717.

41. Lustig, *Robert Hunter*, 166. Robert Livingston claimed that Hunter had twenty-five signatures by September 1722, but George Clarke reported he still needed more in November. See Robert to Alida Livingston, Sept. 9, 1722, Liv. Dutch letters, and Clarke to Walpole, Nov. 22, 1722, *DHNY*, 3:717.

42. All these terms are contained in one vitriolic letter. Robert to Alida Livingston, May 31, 1713, Liv. Dutch letters.

43. Robert to Alida Livingston, May 29, 1724, Liv. Dutch letters.

44. Burnet to Board of Trade, Nov. 21, 1722, *NYCD*, 5:656.

45. Joyce D. Goodfriend, *Before the Melting Pot: Society and Culture in Colonial New York City, 1664–1730* (Princeton, 1992), 115.

46. Kenneth Scott, "The Slave Insurrection in New York in 1712," *New-York Historical Society Quarterly* 45 (Jan. 1961): 47–52, 58–59, 67, 71.

47. Kreider, *Lutheranism in Colonial New York*, 55; Goodfriend, *Before the Melting Pot*, 126.

48. Wittwer, *Faithful and the Bold*, 24–25.

49. Roeber, *Palatines, Liberty, and Property*, 173, 207.

50. Wittwer, *Faithful and the Bold*, 1.

51. Graham Russell Hodges, *Root and Branch: African Americans in New York and East Jersey, 1613–1863* (Chapel Hill, 1999), 86–88; Wittwer, *Faithful and the Bold*, 7, 11, 41.

52. Krahmer, "Kocherthal Records," 253.

53. Dern, *Albany Protocol*, 545.

54. Dern, *Albany Protocol*, 545–46.

55. Graham Russell Hodges, "The Pastor and the Prostitute: Sexual Power among African Americans and Germans in Colonial New York," in Martha Hodes, ed., *Sex, Love, Race: Crossing Boundaries in North American History* (New York, 1999), 65. Hodges's article indicates that Berkenmeyer may have done more than just own slaves. It describes a case in which one of Berkenmeyer's slaves accused him of fathering her child.

56. Dern, *Albany Protocol*, xxii.

57. Dern, *Albany Protocol*, 92.

58. Dern, *Albany Protocol*, 101.

59. Dern, *Albany Protocol*, 218. The reference to the "Our Father" is to the difference between how Reformed and Lutherans began the Lord's Prayer. The Lutherans began with *Vater Unser*, the Reformed with *Unser Vater*.

60. Dern, *Albany Protocol*, 197.

61. Patricia U. Bonomi, *Under the Cope of Heaven: Religion, Society, and Politics in Colonial America* (New York, 1986), 78.

62. Franklin to Peter Collinson, May 9, 1753, *Papers of Benjamin Franklin*, 4:484.

63. Weiser, *Autobiography*, 52. The German settlers often had no pastors living in their communities and had to rely on infrequent visits by itinerant ministers. The settlers often used whichever pastor arrived first to perform baptisms and marriages, but settlers who held firm to their denominational convictions could either wait until a pastor of their own faith arrived or travel to a community served by such a pastor. Apparently few of the Germans felt denominational concerns were worth the bother.

64. E. G. Alderfer, *The Ephrata Commune: An Early American Counterculture* (Pittsburgh, 1985), chap. 4.

65. Alderfer, *Ephrata Commune*, 46, 47.

66. J. Taylor Hamilton, "The Confusion at Tulpehocken," *Transactions of the Moravian Historical Society* 4 (1895): 250, 251; Wallace, *Weiser*, 55–57.

67. Charles H. Glatfelter, *Pastors and People: German Lutheran and Reformed Churches*

in the Pennsylvania Field, 1717–1793, vol. 2, *The History* (Breinigsville, Pa., 1981), 95; Wallace, *Weiser*, 59–61.

68. Quoted in Alderfer, *Ephrata Commune*, 97.

69. Paul Wallace, "Conrad Weiser: Holder of the Heavens," *Historic Pennsylvania Leaflet*, no. 27 (1965): 2; Wallace, *Weiser*, 44. For how the agreement benefited the Iroquois, see Fred Anderson, *Crucible of War: The Seven Years' War and the Fate of Empire in British North America, 1754–1766* (New York, 2000), 16.

70. Wallace, *Weiser*, 330–31; Nancy L. Hagedorn, " 'A Friend to Go between Them': The Interpreter as Cultural Broker during Anglo-Iroquois Councils, 1740–70," *Ethnohistory* 35 (winter 1988): 74. In contrast to Weiser, New York's superintendent of Indian affairs, William Johnson, never lived as a full-fledged member of an Indian community and never became fluent in one of the Iroquois dialects used in negotiations. See Hagedorn, "A Friend to Go between Them," 76 n. 17.

71. Brown, *Brief Sketch*, 4.

72. Genealogical records suggest that two Burnetsfield families intermarried with the Iroquois. See Herkimer County Hist. Soc., *Herkimer County at 200*, viii.

73. William Johnson's Indian Transactions, Mar. 5, 1756, *NYCD*, 7:92.

74. For an analysis of the attitudes of English missionaries to the Indians, see Michael Zuckerman, "Identity in British America: Unease in Eden," in Nicholas Canny and Anthony Pagden, eds., *Colonial Identity in the Atlantic World, 1500–1800* (Princeton, 1987), 147–49, and James Axtell, *The European and the Indian: Essays in the Ethnohistory of Colonial North America* (New York, 1981), 44, 68.

75. Kreider, *Lutheranism in Colonial New York*, 56; Weiss to the Classis of Amsterdam, July 14, 1741, *ERNY*, 4:2760.

76. Meeting of Col. Guy Johnson with the Six Nations, Jan. 27, 1775, *NYCD*, 8:541.

77. Johnson to James Abercromby, Apr. 13, 1757, and Johnson to John Butler, May 18, 1757, James Sullivan, ed., *The Papers of Sir William Johnson*, 14 vols. (Albany, 1921–65), 9:676, 725.

78. Of the heads of households who survived the high mortality of the first two years in New York and whose date of death is known, 36 percent died before 1740, 30 percent died in the 1740s, and 34 percent lived until 1750 or beyond. Database of 1709 emigrants (see appendix).

79. "Conferences between M. de Vaudreuil and the Indians," *NYCD*, 10:513.

80. Quoted in Sally Schwartz, *"A Mixed Multitude": The Struggle for Toleration in Colonial Pennsylvania* (New York, 1987), 237.

81. John Aemilius Wernig to his patron, Sept. 14, 1752, *ERNY*, 5:3285.

82. Simms, *History of Schoharie County*, 87. The anecdote may refer to Johann Gerlach's son Elias rather than to the older immigrant. See Jones, *Palatine Families of New York*, 1:278.

83. Franklin to Peter Collinson, May 9, 1753, *Papers of Benjamin Franklin*, 4:484. Franklin expressed similar misgivings about the Germans in other writings in the early 1750s. See Franklin to James Parker, Mar. 20, 1750/51, and "Observations concerning the Increase of Mankind, Peopling of Countries &c," (1751), *Papers of Benjamin Franklin*, 4:120–21, 234.

84. [Smith, William], *A Brief State of the Province of Pennsylvania (London, 1755)*, 28,

30, 40, 42. For a description of the political situation that inspired Smith's pamphlet, see Alan Tully, *Forming American Politics: Ideals, Interests, and Institutions in Colonial New York and Pennsylvania* (Baltimore, 1994), 110–16.

85. Quoted in Wallace, *Weiser*, 396.
86. Jennings, "Incident at Tulpehocken," 354.
87. Wallace, *Weiser*, 417, 427.
88. Wallace, *Weiser*, 417.
89. Johnson to James Abercromby, Apr. 13, 1757, *William Johnson Papers*, 676. The marquis de Montcalm captured the two British forts in late 1756.
90. Colden to Peter Collinson, Dec. 31, 1757, "The Letters and Papers of Cadwallader Colden," *Collections of the New-York Historical Society*, 8 vols. (New York, 1918–34), 5:212–13.
91. Narrative of Canaghquayeeson, Nov. 30, 1757, *DHNY*, 1:520–22.
92. Various Indian accounts of the attack are found in *William Johnson Papers*, 9:855–63. Official French accounts are in *DHNY*, 1:515–20.
93. George Croghan to the earl of Loudoun, Nov. 20, 1757, *William Johnson Papers*, 9:658.
94. William Johnson to James Abercromby, Dec. 5, 1757, *William Johnson Papers*, 2:759.
95. Canaghquayeeson's report to George Croghan, *William Johnson Papers*, 9:862.

CONCLUSION

1. "Extract of a Letter from Albany," May 13, 1758, *DHNY*, 1:522.
2. Roeber, "Origins," 277–79; Roeber, *Palatines, Liberty, and Property*, 292; Tully, *Forming American Politics*, 196–98.
3. Tully, *Forming American Politics*, 345.
4. A. G. Roeber suggests the backcountry German communities remained attached to their negative definition of liberty—one that defined liberty as the freedom from outside interference—even after the events of the Seven Years' War. During the Revolution they lent their allegiance to the force that seemed least likely to interfere in their affairs. See Roeber, *Palatines, Liberty, and Property*, 307–8.
5. Faust, *German Element in the United States*, 1:306.
6. Report to Governor Tyron, June 1774, *NYCD*, 8:451–52.
7. Quoted in Wallace, *Weiser*, 574.
8. Barbara Graymont, *The Iroquois in the American Revolution* (Syracuse, 1972), 179, 237–38; Isabel Thompson Kelsay, *Joseph Brant 1743–1807: Man of Two Worlds* (Syracuse, 1984), 226, 296–97.
9. Fenton and Tooker, "Mohawk," in Sturtevant, ed., *Handbook of North American Indians*, vol. 15, *Northeast*, 475–76.
10. By 1760 all but one of the listmasters who had served as the 1710 immigrants' earliest leaders had died. Christopher Fuchs, the last surviving listmaster, died at age eighty-three in 1767. Jones, *Palatine Families of New York*, 1:260.
11. Kreider, *Lutheranism in Colonial New York*, 56.

12. William P. McDermott, "Slaves and Slaveowners in Dutchess County," *Afro-Americans in New York Life and History* 19 (1995): 29–30.

13. Anita Tien demonstrates that these "traditions of the heart" were the least vulnerable to assimilation and that they were the principal markers of ethnicity among the Germans of colonial America. Tien, " 'To Enjoy Their Customs,' " chapters 1 and 4.

14. David Maldwyn Ellis, *Landlords and Farmers in the Hudson-Mohawk Region, 1790–1850* (Ithaca, 1946), 96. To a degree, the Germans' farming techniques reflected the richer, less rocky soil of the Mohawk River valley. Manuring the fields was less necessary than in New England, and horses could easily pull plows through the loamy soil.

15. Timothy Dwight, *Travels in New England and New York*, 4 vols. (New Haven, 1821; reprint, Cambridge, Mass., 1969), 3:122.

16. Crèvecoeur viewed them favorably, at least in comparison with their Scotch counterparts. "The Scotch are frugal and laborious, but their wives cannot work so hard as German women, who on the contrary vie with their husbands, and often share with them the most severe toils of the field, which they understand better." J. Hector St. John de Crèvecoeur, *Letters from an American Farmer* (London, 1782; reprint, New York, 1981), 58. The female descendants of the 1709 emigrants who were sent to Ireland rather than to New York elicited similar notice. An early historian of Limerick wrote of its German settlers: "The women are very industrious, and perform many things which the Irish women could never be prevailed on to do. Besides their domestic employments, and the care of children, they reap the corn, plough the ground, and assist the men in every thing." Elizabeth A. Kessel, "Germans in the Making of Frederick County, Maryland," in Mitchell, ed., *Appalachian Frontiers*, 104 n. 52. Kessel quotes John Ferrar, *The History of Limerick, Ecclesiastical, Civil, and Military from the Earliest Records to the Year 1787* (Limerick, 1787).

17. Dwight, *Travels*, 3:142. Thomas Jefferson also found the activities of the German women unnatural. African women may have worked in the fields around Monticello, but English women certainly did not. Even in seventeenth-century Virginia, when labor was often in short supply, European women rarely labored in the fields. Jefferson had noticed the peculiar habits of the Germans in America, and, when traveling through the Rhineland in 1788, he realized that their customs originated in the German southwest. Like Dwight, he was disturbed by the activities of German women. From Mainz he wrote, "The women do everything here. They dig the earth, plough, saw, cut, and split wood, row, tow the batteaux &c." A few days later, reflecting on what he had seen, he wrote that women "are formed by nature for attention and not for hard labour." Julian P. Boyd, ed., *The Papers of Thomas Jefferson*, vol. 13, *March to 7 October 1788* (Princeton, 1956), 18, 27–28.

18. Parsons, "Representation of Ethnicity," 125.

19. Some of the traits of the 1710 immigrants may have survived in the immigrants' descendants. It was, after all, a descendant of Valentin Bresseler, one of the first Palatine emigrants of 1709, who stood American music on its head starting in

the 1950s. His Anglicized name and Southern birth obscured his distant New York Palatine roots, but Elvis Presley seems to have retained some of the rebelliousness and independent spirit of his ancestors.

20. So strong remains the Palatine identity in New York that when a descendant of the 1710 immigrants wrote a genealogical study in 1994 that carefully and with meticulous detail pinpointed her family's origins in Hesse, she still called the book *Palatine Roots*.

APPENDIX

1. PRO CO 388/76:64, 68, 69.
2. The lists are in PRO CO 5/1231, and the ledger based on the lists is in PRO CO 5/1230.
3. PRO T.1/119:6–10, 19–26, 58–65, 68–72, 79–82.
4. "Names of the Palatine Children Apprenticed by Gov. Hunter, 1710–1714," *DHNY*, 3:566–67; "List of the Palatins Remaining at New York, 1710," *DHNY*, 3:562–63.
5. "Statement of heads of Palaten famileys and number of Persons in both Towns on the west side of Hudsons River. Winter, 1710," *DHNY*, 3:569–70. Lists of German volunteers from Annsbury, Haysbury, Queensbury, and Hunterstown are in the NY Col MSS, 55:144–46.
6. Ulrich Simmendinger, *Warhaffte und glaubwurdige Verzeichnüss* (Reutilingen, Germany, circa 1717; trans. by Herman F. Vesper as *Simmendinger's Register*, Baltimore, 1962).

Bibliography

Manuscript Sources

British Library, London

Blenheim Papers, Additional MSS 61534–61653
Additional MSS 4743, 15866, 17677DDD, 21132, 22202, 28055, 35584, 35933

Cheshire Record Office, Chester

Mayor's Letter Book, 1674–1715

Franklin D. Roosevelt Library, Hyde Park, N.Y.

Livingston Family Papers
Robert Livingston, General Correspondence, 1667–1728
Livingston family letters in Dutch, 1680–1726, trans. Adrian J. van der Linde

Guildhall Library, London

A Brief for the Relief, Subsistence, and Settlement of the Poor Distressed Palatines
Parish records, City of London

Historical Society of Pennsylvania, Philadelphia

Dutch West Indies Company, "Copies of Dutch documents at Rotterdam and The Hague relating to early German immigration, 1709"

Lambeth Palace Library, London

Fulham Papers, American
Lambeth Papers

Library of Congress, Manuscript Division, Washington, D.C.

Microfilm copies of manuscripts dealing with the 1709 emigration from the Württembergisches Staatsarchiv, the Hessischen Haupstadtarchiv, and the Staatsarchiv Wiesbaden
Transcriptions of Public Record Office, Colonial Papers, America and West Indies, Original Correspondence, PRO CO 5
Copy of Harleian MS 7021

New-York Historical Society, New York City

Colden papers
Misc. Willett
Misc. MSS Indians

New York State Archives, Albany

New York Colonial Council manuscripts
Deed Book, vol. 13 (1736–1739)
New York Patent Book

Public Record Office, London

CO 388	Board of Trade Papers, Original Correspondence
SP 34	State Papers Domestic, Anne
SP 44/107	Boyle Letter Books
SP 84	State Papers Foreign, Holland
T.1	Treasury Board Papers

Society for the Propagation of the Gospel, London

SPG minutes, correspondence, and letter books (microfilm copies viewed at the Billy Graham Center Archives, Wheaton College, Wheaton, Illinois)

Other Manuscripts

Deed books of Ulster County, N.Y., Trustees' Records of the Corporation of Kingston

Decree of the Count of Sayn, June 13, 1709, Staatsarchiv Koblenz, Germany

Published Primary Sources—Official

Annals of Albany. Ed. J. Munsell. 10 vols. Albany, 1850–59.
Calendar of Council Minutes of New York, 1688–1783. Ed. Berthold Fernow. Albany, 1902.
Calendar of N.Y. Colonial Manuscripts, Indorsed Land Papers, 1643–1803. Comp. E. B. O'Callaghan. Reprint, Harrison, N.Y., 1987.
Calendar of State Papers, Colonial Series. America and the West Indies. Ed. W. N. Sainsbury et al. 44 vols. London, 1860–1969.
Calendar of Treasury Books. Ed. William Shaw. 32 vols. London, 1904–62.
Calendar of Treasury Papers. Ed. Joseph Redington. 6 vols. London, 1860–89.
Colonial Records of North Carolina. Ed. William L. Saunders. 30 vols. Raleigh, 1886–1914.
Documentary History of the State of New York. Ed. E. B. O'Callaghan. 4 vols. Albany, 1850–51.
Documents Relative to the Colonial History of New York. Ed. E. B. O'Callaghan. 15 vols. Albany, 1856–87.
Ecclesiastical Records of the State of New York. Ed. Hugh Hastings. 8 vols. Albany, 1901–16.
Historical Manuscripts Commission Reports. London, 1870–.
Journal of the Commissioners for Trade and Plantations. 14 vols. London, 1920–38.
Journals of the House of Commons. London, 1803–.
Messages from the Governors. Ed. Charles Z. Lincoln. Albany, 1909.
Minutes of the Common Council of the City of New York, 1675–1776. Ed. Herbert L. Osgood. 8 vols. New York, 1905.
Minutes of the Provincial Council of Pennsylvania. Ed. Samuel Hazard. 10 vols. Philadelphia, 1851–52.

Published Primary Sources—Unofficial

Biemer, Linda, ed. "Business Letters of Alida Schuyler Livingston, 1680–1726." *New York History* 63 (Apr. 1982): 183–207.
Boehme, Anton. *Das verlangte, nicht erlangte Canaan*. Frankfurt and Leipzig, 1711.
Boyd, Julian P., ed. *The Papers of Thomas Jefferson*. Vol. 13, *March to 7 October 1788*. Princeton, 1956.
Brown, Beatrice Curtis, ed. *The Letters and Diplomatic Instructions of Queen Anne*. London, 1935.

Brown, John M. *Brief Sketch of the First Settlement of the County of Schoharie by the Germans.* Schoharie, N.Y., 1823.

Burnet, Gilbert. *Bishop Burnet's History of His Own Time: with the Suppressed Passages of the First Volume, and Notes by the Earls of Dartmouth and Hardwicke, and Speaker Onslow, hitherto Unpublished.* 6 vols. Oxford, 1823.

Canary-Birds Naturaliz'd in Utopia: A Canto. London, 1709.

Crèvecoeur, J. Hector St. John de. *Letters from an American Farmer.* London, 1782. Reprint, New York, 1981.

Defoe, Daniel. *A Brief History of the Poor Palatine Refugees.* London, 1709. Reprint, Los Angeles, 1964.

——. *A Tour through England and Wales Divided into Circuits or Journies.* London, 1724–26. Reprint in 2 vols., London, 1927.

——. *A Tour through the Whole Island of Great Britain.* 1724–26. Abridged and edited by Pat Rogers. New York, 1971.

Dern, John P., ed. *The Albany Protocol: Wilhelm Christoph Berkenmeyer's Chronicle of Lutheran Affairs in New York Colony, 1731–1750.* Camden, Maine, 1992.

Doble, C. E., ed. *Remarks and Collections of Thomas Hearne.* 11 vols. Oxford, 1885–1921.

Dunn, Richard S., and Mary Maples Dunn, eds. *The Papers of William Penn.* 5 vols. Philadelphia, 1981–86.

Dwight, Timothy. *Travels in New England and New York.* 4 vols. New Haven, 1821. Reprint, Cambridge, Mass., 1969.

Falckner, Daniel. *Curieuse Nachricht von Pennsylvania.* Frankfurt and Leipzig, 1702. Trans. and ed. by Julius Friederich Sachse as *Daniel Falckner's Curieuse Nachricht von Pennsylvania.* Philadelphia, 1905.

Falconer, William. *An Universal Dictionary of the Marine.* London, 1780. Reprint, *Falconer's Marine Dictionary (1780).* New York, 1970.

Ferrar, John. *The History of Limerick, Ecclesiastical, Civil, and Military from the Earliest Records to the year 1787.* Limerick, 1787.

Goebel, Julius, ed. "Briefe Deutscher Aswanderer aus dem Jahre 1709." *Jahrbuch der Deutsch-Amerikanischen Historischen Gesellschaft von Illinois* (1912): 124–89.

——, ed. "Neue Dokumente zur Geschichte der Massenauswanderung im Jahre 1709." *Jahrbuch der Deutsch-Amerikanischen Historischen Gesellschaft von Illinois* (1913): 181–201.

History of the Reign of Queen Anne, Digested into Annals, Year the Eighth. London, 1710.

Hunter, Joseph, ed. *The Diary of Ralph Thoresby, F.R.S.* 2 vols. London, 1830.

Kocherthal, Joshua. *Ausführlich und Umständlicher Bericht von der berühmten Landschafft Carolina, in dem Engelländischen America gelegen.* Frankfurt, 1709. Reprinted with new introduction, Neustadt an der Weinstrasse, 1983.

Krahmer, Christian, trans. "The Kocherthal Records." *Olde Ulster* 3 and 4 (1907 and 1908).

Labaree, Leonard W., ed. *The Papers of Benjamin Franklin.* Vol. 4, *July 1, 1750, through June 30, 1753.* New Haven, 1961.

Learned, Marion Dexter. *Guide to the Manuscript Materials Relating to American History in the German State Archives.* Washington, D.C., 1912.

"The Letters and Papers of Cadwallader Colden." *Collections of the New-York Historical Society.* 8 vols. New York, 1918–34.

Luttrell, Narcissus. *A Brief Historical Relation of State Affairs.* 6 vols. Oxford, 1857.

Mittelberger, Gottlieb. *Journey to Pennsylvania.* Ed. and trans. Oscar Handlin and John Clive. Cambridge, Mass., 1960.

Our Savior's Sermon on the Mount, According to St. Matthew the V, VI, and VIII, Chapter. Both English and High Dutch, for the Use of the Palatines, Oder Die Bergpredigt Christi . . . . London, 1710.

The Palatines' Catechism or a True Description of Their Camps at Black Heath and Camberwell. In a Pleasant Dialogue between an English Tradesman and a High-Dutchman. London, 1709.

Parker, Richard. *An Account of the Present Condition of the Protestants in the Palatinate.* London, 1699.

Roque, John. *An Exact Survey of the Citys of London Westminster the Borough of Southwark and the Country near Ten Miles Round.* London, 1746.

Salley, Alexander S., Jr., ed. *Narratives of Early Carolina, 1650–1708.* New York, 1911.

Schoepf, Johann David. *Travels in the Confederation [1783–1874].* Trans. Alfred E. Morrison. Philadelphia, 1911.

A Short and Easy Way for the Palatines to Learn English. Oder eine kurze Anleitung zur Englischen Sprach. Zum Nutz der armen Pfälzer. London, 1710.

Simmendinger, Ulrich. *Warhaffte und glaubwurdige Verzeichniiss . . . .* Reutlingen, Germany, circa 1717. Trans. by Herman F. Vesper as *Simmendinger's Register.* Baltimore, 1962.

Simms, Jeptha R. *History of Schoharie County and Border Wars of New York.* Albany, 1845.

[Smith, William]. *A Brief State of the Province of Pennsylvania.* London, 1755.

The State of the Palatines for Fifty Years Past to This Present Time. London, 1709.

Sullivan, James, ed. *The Papers of Sir William Johnson.* 14 vols. Albany, 1921–65.

Swift, Jonathan. *The History of the Four Last Years of the Queen.* Reprinted in *The Prose Works of Jonathan Swift.* Ed. Herbert Davis. Vol. 7. Oxford, 1951.

Tappert, Theodore G., and John W. Doberstein, ed. and trans. *The Journals of Henry Melchior Muhlenberg.* 3 vols. Philadelphia, 1942–58.

Veenendal, A. J., ed. *De briefwisseling van Anthonie Heinsius 1702–1720.* 10 vols. The Hague, 1976–89.

A View of the Queen and Kingdom's Enemies in the Case of the Poor Palatines. London, [1711].

Zeiller, Martin. *Topographia Palatinatus Rheni et Vicinarum Regionum.* Frankfurt, 1645.

Secondary Sources

Abel, Wilhelm. *Agricultural Fluctuations in Europe.* Trans. Olive Ordisch. New York, 1980.

Albion, Robert Greenhalgh. *Forests and Sea Power: The Timber Problem of the Royal Navy, 1652–1862.* Cambridge, Mass., 1927.

Alderfer, E. G. *The Ephrata Commune: An Early American Counterculture*. Pittsburgh, 1985.

Andermann, Kurt. "Leibeigenschaft im pfälzischen Oberrheingebiet während des späten Mittelalters und der frühen Neuzeit." *Zeitschrift für Historische Forschung* 17 (1990): 281–303.

Anderson, Fred. *Crucible of War: The Seven Years' War and the Fate of Empire in British North America, 1754–1766*. New York, 2000.

Aretin, Karl Otmar von. "Der deutsche Südwesten in der lezten Phase des Reiches— 1648 bis 1806." In *Stukturwandel im Pfälzischen Raum vom Ancien Regime bis zum Vormärz*, ed. Friederich Ludwig Wagner, 11–18. Speyer, 1982.

Axtell, James. *The European and the Indian: Essays in the Ethnohistory of Colonial North America*. New York, 1981.

——. *The Invasion Within: The Contest of Cultures in Colonial North America*. New York, 1985.

Backscheider, Paula R. *Daniel Defoe, His Life*. Baltimore, 1989.

Barker, William V. H. *Early Families of Herkimer County, New York*. Baltimore, 1986.

Bennion, Lowell C. "Flight from the Reich: A Geographic Exposition of Southwest German Emigration, 1683–1815." Ph.D. diss., Syracuse University, 1973.

Berkhofer, Robert F., Jr. *The White Man's Indian: Images of the American Indian from Columbus to the Present*. New York, 1978.

Blum, Jerome. *The End of the Old Order in Rural Europe*. Princeton, 1978.

Boehrer, Bruce Thomas. "*Epicoene*, Charivari, Skimmington." *English Studies* (1994): 17–33.

Bond, Richmond P. *Queen Anne's American Kings*. Oxford, 1952.

Bonomi, Patricia. *Under the Cope of Heaven: Religion, Society, and Politics in Colonial America*. New York, 1986.

Bottigheimer, Ruth B. *Grimms' Bad Girls and Bold Boys: The Moral and Social Vision of the Tales*. New Haven, 1987.

Brett-James, Norman G. *The Growth of Stuart London*. London, 1935.

Brunner, Daniel L. "The Role of Halle Pietists (c. 1700–c. 1740), with Special Reference to the S.P.C.K." Ph.D. diss., Oxford University, 1988.

Burke, Thomas. *Mohawk Frontier: The Dutch Community of Schenectady, New York, 1660–1710*. Ithaca, 1991.

Butler, Jon. *The Huguenots in America: A Refugee People in New World Society*. Cambridge, Mass., 1983.

Cobb, Sanford H. *The Story of the Palatines*. New York, 1897.

Colley, Linda. *Britons: Forging the Nation, 1707–1837*. New Haven, 1992.

Cottret, Bernard. *The Huguenots in England: Immigration and Settlement c. 1550–1700*. Trans. Peregrine Stevenson and Adriana Stevenson. Cambridge, 1991.

Darnton, Robert. *The Forbidden Best-Sellers of Pre-Revolutionary France*. New York, 1995.

Davis, Natalie Zemon. *Society and Culture in Early Modern France*. Stanford, 1975.

Dennis, Matthew. *Cultivating a Landscape of Peace: Iroquois-European Encounters in Seventeenth-Century America*. Ithaca, 1993.

Dern, John. *London Churchbooks and the German Emigration of 1709.* Schriften zur Wanderungsgeschichte der Pfälzer, vol. 26. Kaiserslautern, 1968.

Dickinson, H. T. "The Poor Palatines and the Parties." *English Historical Review* 82 (July 1967): 464–85.

Diffenderffer, Frank. "The German Exodus to England in 1709." *Pennsylvania German Society Proceedings and Addresses* 7 (1897): 257–413.

Dixon, Nancy Wagoner. *Palatine Roots: The 1710 German Settlement in New York as Experienced by Johann Peter Wagner.* Camden, Maine, 1994.

Duffy, John. "The Passage to the Colonies." *Mississippi Valley Historical Review* 38 (June 1951): 21–38.

Dunn, Shirley W. *The Mohicans and Their Land, 1609–1730.* Fleischmanns, N.Y., 1994.

Dyer, C. Dorsey. "History of the Gum Naval Stores Industry." *The AT-FA Journal* 25 (Jan. 1963): 5–8.

Ellis, David Maldwyn. *Landlords and Farmers in the Hudson-Mohawk Region, 1790–1850.* Ithaca, 1946.

Erb, Peter C., ed. *Pietists: Selected Writings.* New York, 1983.

Faust, Albert. *The German Element in the United States,* 2 vols. Boston, 1909.

Fenske, Hans. "International Migration: Germany in the Eighteenth Century." *Central European History* 13 (Dec. 1980): 332–47.

Fischer, H. "'Draussen vom Walde . . .' Die Einstellung zum Wald im Wandel der Geschichte." *Mensch und Tier* (Wintersemester 1992/93 bis 1994/95): 119–35.

Fogleman, Aaron. "Review Essay: Progress and Possibilities in Migration Studies: The Contributions of Werner Hacker to the Study of Early German Migration to Pennsylvania." *Pennsylvania History* 56 (Oct. 1989): 318–29.

——. "Hopeful Journeys: German Immigration and Settlement in Greater Pennsylvania, 1717–1775." Ph.D. diss., University of Michigan, 1991.

——. "Migrations to the Thirteen British North American Colonies, 1700–1775: New Estimates." *Journal of Interdisciplinary History* 22 (spring 1992): 691–709.

——. *Hopeful Journeys: German Immigration, Settlement, and Political Culture in Colonial America, 1717–1775.* Philadelphia, 1996.

Forster, Marc R. *The Counter-Reformation in the Villages: Religion and Reform in the Bishopric of Speyer, 1560–1720.* Ithaca, 1992.

——. "With and Without Confessionalization: Varieties of Early Modern German Catholicism." *Journal of Early Modern History* 1 (1997): 315–43.

Fox, Edith M. *Land Speculation in the Mohawk Country.* Ithaca, 1949.

Galenson, David W. *White Servitude in Colonial America: An Economic Analysis.* Cambridge, 1981.

Gawthrop, Richard, and Gerald Strauss. "Protestantism and Literacy in Early Modern Germany." *Past and Present* 104 (Aug. 1984): 31–55.

Gehring, Charles. *Agriculture and the American Revolution in the Mohawk Valley.* St. Johnsville, N.Y., n.d.

Genovese, Eugene D. *Roll, Jordan, Roll: The World the Slaves Made.* New York, 1974.

George, M. Dorothy. *London Life in the XVIIIth Century.* New York, 1925.

Glatfelter, Charles H. *Pastors and People: German Lutheran and Reformed Churches in the Pennsylvania Field, 1713–1793.* 2 vols. Breinigsville, Pa., 1980–81.

Goodfriend, Joyce D. *Before the Melting Pot: Society and Culture in Colonial New York City, 1664–1730*. Princeton, 1992.

Graymont, Barbara. *The Iroquois in the American Revolution*. Syracuse, 1972.

Green, Abigail. *Fatherlands: State-Building and Nationhood in Nineteenth-Century Germany*. Cambridge, 2001.

Greene, Jack P. *The Intellectual Construction of America: Exceptionalism and Identity from 1492 to 1800*. Chapel Hill, 1993.

Häberlein, Mark. *Vom Oberrhein zum Susquehanna*. Stuttgart, 1993.

Hacker, Werner. *Kurpfälzische Auswanderer vom Unteren Neckar*. Stuttgart, 1983.

——. *Auswanderung aus Rheinpfalz und Saarland im 18. Jahrhundert*. Stuttgart, 1987.

Hagedorn, Nancy L. "'A Friend to Go between Them': The Interpreter as Cultural Broker during Anglo-Iroquois Councils, 1740–70." *Ethnohistory* 35 (winter 1988): 60–80.

Hagen, William W. "Seventeenth-Century Crisis in Brandenburg: The Thirty Years' War, the Destabilization of Serfdom, and the Rise of Absolutism." *American Historical Review* 94 (Apr. 1989): 302–35.

Hamilton, J. Taylor. "The Confusion at Tulpehocken." *Transactions of the Moravian Historical Society* 4 (1895): 237–73.

Heinz, Joachim. *"Bleibe im Lande, und nähre dich redlich!" Zur Geschichte der pfälzischen Auswanderung vom ende des 17. bis zum Ausgang des 19. Jahrhunderts*. Kaiserslautern, 1989.

Herkimer County Historical Society. *Herkimer County at 200*. Herkimer, N.Y., 1992.

Hippel, Wolfgang von. *Auswanderung aus Südwestdeutschland: Studien zur württembergischen Auswanderung und Auswanderungspolitik im 18. und 19. Jahrhundert*. Stuttgart, 1984.

Hochstadt, Steven. "Migration in Preindustrial Germany." *Central European History* 16 (Sept. 1983): 195–224.

Hodges, Graham Russell. *Root and Branch: African Americans in New York and East Jersey, 1613–1863*. Chapel Hill, 1999.

——. "The Pastor and the Prostitute: Sexual Power among African Americans and Germans in Colonial New York." In *Sex, Love, Race: Crossing Boundaries in North American History*, ed. Martha Hodes. New York, 1999.

Hofstra, Warren. "Land Policy and Settlement in the Northern Shenandoah Valley." In *Appalachian Frontiers: Settlement, Society and Development in the Preindustrial Era*, ed. Robert D. Mitchell, 105–26. Lexington, 1991.

Holmes, Geoffrey. *British Politics in the Age of Anne*. Rev. ed. London, 1987.

Hostetler, John A. "The Plain People: Historical and Modern Perspectives." In *America and the Germans: An Assessment of a Three-Hundred-Year History*, 2 vols., ed. Frank Trommler and Joseph McVeigh, 1:106–17. Philadelphia, 1985.

Hsia, R. Po-chia. "Between State and Community: Religious and Ethnic Minorities in Early Modern Germany." In *Germania Illustrata: Essays on Early Modern Germany Presented to Geral Strauss*, ed. Andrew C. Fix and Susan C. Karant-Nunn, 169–80. Sixteenth Century Essays and Studies, vol. 18. Kirksville, Mo., 1992.

Huelsbergen, Helmut E. "The First Thirteen Families: Another Look at the Religious and Ethnic Background of the Emigrants from Crefeld (1683)." *Yearbook of German-American Studies* 18 (1983): 29–40.

Hughes, Michael. *Early Modern Germany, 1477–1806*. Philadelphia, 1992.

Hull, William I. *William Penn and the Dutch Quaker Migration to Pennsylvania*. Swarthmore College Monographs on Quaker History, no. 2. Philadelphia, 1935.

Jacobs, Henry Eyster. "The German Migration to America 1709–1740." *Pennsylvania German Society Proceedings and Addresses* 8 (1898): 31–150.

Jennings, Francis. "Incident at Tulpehocken." *Pennsylvania History* 35 (Oct. 1968): 335–55.

——. *The Ambiguous Iroquois Empire*. New York, 1984.

——. "Brother Miquon: Good Lord!" In *The World of William Penn*, ed. Richard S. Dunn and Mary Maples Dunn, 195–214. Philadelphia, 1986.

Jones, Henry Z, Jr. *The Palatine Families of New York*. 2 vols. Universal City, Calif., 1985.

——. *The Palatine Families of Ireland*. 2d ed. Camden, Maine, 1990.

——. *More Palatine Families*. Universal City, Calif., 1991.

Jones, Henry Z, Jr., and Lewis Bunker Rohrbach. *Even More Palatine Families*. 3 vols. Rockport, Maine, 2002.

Jones, Henry Z, Jr., and John Dern. "Palatine Emigrants Returning in 1710." In *Pfälzer-Palatines: Beiträge zur pfälzischen Ein- und Auswanderung sowie zur Volkskunde und Mundartforschung im 18. und 19. Jahrhundert*, ed. Karl Scherer, 53–78. Kaiserslautern, 1981.

Jones, Henry Z, Jr., Ralph Connor, and Klaus Wust. *German Origins of Jost Hite, Virginia Pioneer, 1685–1761*. Edinburg, Va., 1979.

Jones, George Fenwick. *The Georgia Dutch: From the Rhine and Danube to the Savannah, 1733–1783*. Athens, Ga., 1992.

Kapp, Friedrich. *Geschichte der Deutschen im Staate New York*. New York, 1867.

Keller, Kenneth W. "From the Rhineland to the Virginia Frontier: Flax Production as a Commercial Enterprise." *Virginia Magazine of History and Biography* 98 (July 1990): 487–511.

Kelsay, Isabel Thompson. *Joseph Brant 1743–1807: Man of Two Worlds*. Syracuse, 1984.

Kessel, Elizabeth A. "Germans in the Making of Frederick County, Maryland." In *Appalachian Frontiers: Settlement, Society and Development in the Preindustrial Era*, ed. Robert D. Mitchell, 87–104. Lexington, 1991.

Kierner, Cynthia. *Traders and Gentlefolk: The Livingstons of New York, 1675–1790*. Ithaca, 1992.

Kim, Sung Bok. *Landlord and Tenant in Colonial New York: Manorial Society, 1664–1775*. Chapel Hill, 1978.

Knittle, Walter Allen. *Early Eighteenth-Century Palatine Emigration: A British Government Redemptioner Project to Manufacture Naval Stores*. Philadelphia, 1937.

Knodel, John. *Demographic Behavior in the Past: A Study of Fourteen German Village Populations in the Eighteenth and Nineteenth Centuries*. Cambridge, 1988.

Kreider, Harry Julius. *Lutheranism in Colonial New York*. New York, 1942.

Kupperman, Karen Ordahl. *Settling with the Indians: The Meeting of English and Indian Cultures in America, 1580–1640*. Totowa, N.J., 1980.

Leder, Lawrence H. *Robert Livingston 1654–1728 and the Politics of Colonial New York*. Chapel Hill, 1961.

Lichtenthaeler, Frank E. "Storm Blown Seed of Schoharie." *The Pennsylvania German Folklore Society* 9 (1944): 3–105.

Luebke, David Martin. "Factions and Communities in Early Modern Central Europe." *Central European History* 25 (1992): 281–301.

Lustig, Mary Lou. *Robert Hunter, 1666–1734: New York's Augustan Statesman*. Syracuse, 1983.

———. "The Real Livingstons." *Reviews in American History* 22 (1994): 26–31.

MacMaster, Richard K. *Land, Piety, Peoplehood: The Establishment of Mennonite Communities in America, 1683–1790*. Scottdale, Pa., 1985.

Malone, Joseph J. *Pine Trees and Politics: The Naval Stores and Forest Policy in Colonial New England, 1691–1775*. Seattle, 1964.

Malone, Patrick M. *The Skulking Way of War: Technology and Tactics among the New England Indians*. Lanham, Md., 1991. Reprint, Baltimore, 1993.

Mayhew, Alan. *Rural Settlment and Farming in Germany*. London, 1973.

McCloskey, Donald N. "English Open Fields as Behavior toward Risk." *Research in Economic History* 1 (fall 1976): 124–70.

———. "The Prudent Peasant: New Findings on Open Fields." *Journal of Economic History* 51 (June 1991): 343–55.

McDermott, William P. "Slaves and Slaveowners in Dutchess County." *Afro-Americans in New York Life and History* 19 (1995): 17–41.

McGregor, Robert Kuhn. "Cultural Adaptation in Colonial New York: The Palatine Germans of the Mohawk Valley." *New York History* 69 (Jan. 1988): 5–34.

McReynolds, Robert D. "Development of Gum Naval Stores in the United States of America." Naval Stores and Timber Production Laboratory, Olustee, Fla., Nov. 1977.

Merrell, James H. *Into the American Woods: Negotiators on the Pennsylvania Frontier*. New York, 1999.

Merwick, Donna. *Possessing Albany, 1630–1710: The Dutch and English Experiences*. Cambridge, 1990.

Monahan, W. Gregory. *Year of Sorrows: The Great Famine of 1709 in Lyon*. Columbus, Ohio, 1993.

Montgomery, Charles Berwind. "Notes on the Tulpehocken Lands." *Historical Review of Berks County* 1 (July 1936): 42–44.

Nagel, Joane. "Constructing Ethnicity: Creating and Recreating Ethnic Identity and Culture." *Social Problems* 41 (Feb. 1994): 152–76.

Norwood, Frederick A. *Strangers and Exiles: A History of Religious Refugees*. 2 vols. Nashville, 1969.

O'Connor, Patrick J. *People Make Places: The Story of the Irish Palatines*. Coolanoran, Ireland, 1989.

Ortner, Sherry B. "Resistance and the Problem of Ethnographic Refusal." *Comparative Studies in Society and History* 37 (Jan. 1995): 173–93.

Otterness, Philip. "The New York Naval Stores Project and the Transformation of the Poor Palatines, 1710–1712." *New York History* 75 (Apr. 1994): 133–56.

———. "The 1709 Palatine Migration and the Formation of German Immigrant

Identity in London and New York." *Explorations in Early American Culture*, a supplement to *Pennsylvania History* 66 (1999): 8–23.

Parsons, William T. "Representation of Ethnicity among Colonial Pennsylvania Germans." In *A Mixed Race: Ethnicity in Early America*, ed. Frank Shuffelton, 119–41. New York, 1993.

Pencack, William, Matthew Dennis, and Simon P. Newman, eds. *Riot and Revelry in Early America*. University Park, Pa., 2002.

Piwonka, Ruth. *A Portrait of Livingston Manor, 1686–1850*. Clermont, N.Y., 1986.

Purvis, Thomas L. "The National Origins of New Yorkers in 1790." *New York History* 67 (Apr. 1986): 133–53.

Renzing, Rüdiger. *Pfälzer in Irland: Studien zur Geschichte deutscher Auswandererkolonien des frühen 18. Jahrhunderts*. Kaiserslautern, 1989.

Richter, Daniel. *The Ordeal of the Longhouse: The Peoples of the Iroquois League in the Era of European Colonization*. Chapel Hill, 1992.

Rödel, Walter. *Mainz und seine Bevölkerung im 17. und 18. Jahrhundert*. Stuttgart, 1985.

Roeber, A. G. "The Origins and Transfer of German-American Concepts of Property and Inheritance." *Perspectives in American History*, n.s., 3 (1987): 115–71.

——. *Palatines, Liberty, and Property: German Lutherans in Colonial British America*. Baltimore, 1993.

Rowse, A. L. *Jonathan Swift*. New York, 1975.

Ruttenber, E. M., and L. H. Clark, comps. *History of Orange County, New York*. Philadelphia, 1881.

Sabean, David. *Power in the Blood: Popular Culture and Village Discourse in Early Modern Germany*. Cambridge, 1984.

——. *Property, Production, and Family in Neckarhausen, 1700–1870*. Cambridge, 1990.

Sachse, Julius Friederich. "The Fatherland: Showing the Part It Bore in the Discovery, Exploration, and Development of the Western Continent." *Pennsylvania German Society Proceedings and Addresses* 7 (1897): 33–256.

Sagarra, Eda. *A Social History of Germany, 1648–1914*. New York, 1977.

Sahlins, Peter. *Boundaries: The Making of France and Spain in the Pyrenees*. Berkeley, 1989.

Salmon, Marylynn. *Women and the Law of Property in Early America*. Chapel Hill, 1986.

Schaab, Meinrad. "Die Wiederherstellung des Katholizismus in der Kurpfalz im 17. und 18. Jahrhundert." *Zeitschrift für die Geschichte des Oberrheins* 75 (1966): 147–205.

——. *Geschichte der Kurpfalz*. Vol. 2, *Neuzeit*. Stuttgart, 1992.

Scherer, Karl, ed. *Pfälzer-Palatines: Beiträge zur pfälzischen Ein- und Auswanderung sowie zur Volkskunde und Mundartforschung im 18. und 19. Jahrhundert*. Kaiserslautern, 1981.

Schuchmann, Heinz. *Schweizer Einwanderer im früheren kurpfälzischen Streubesitz des Kraichgaues (1650–1750)*. Schriften zur Wanderungsgeschichte der Pfälzer, vol. 18. Kaiserslautern, 1963.

——. "Der 1708 nach Amerika ausgewanderte Pfarrer Josua Kocherthal hiess ursprünglich Josua Harrsch." *Mitteilungen zur Wanderungsgeschichte der Pfälzer* 6 (Nov. 1967): 121–28.

Schwartz, Sally. *"A Mixed Multitude": The Struggle for Toleration in Colonial Pennsylvania.* New York, 1987.

Scott, James. *Domination and the Arts of Resistance,* New Haven, 1990.

Scott, Kenneth. "The Slave Insurrection in New York in 1712." *New-York Historical Society Quarterly* 45 (Jan. 1961): 43–74.

Scribner, R. W. *For the Sake of Simple Folk: Popular Propaganda for the German Reformation.* Cambridge, 1981.

———. *Popular Culture and Popular Movements in Reformation Germany.* London, 1987.

Shannon, Timothy J. *Indians and Colonists at the Crossroads of Empire: The Albany Congress of 1754.* Ithaca, 2000.

Sider, Gerald. *Lumbee Indian Histories: Race, Ethnicity, and Indian Identity in the Southern United States.* Cambridge, 1993.

Soliday, Gerald. *A Community in Conflict: Frankfurt Society in the Seventeenth and Early Eighteenth Centuries.* Hanover, N.H., 1974.

Sollors, Werner, ed. *The Invention of Ethnicity.* New York, 1989.

Statt, Daniel. "The Birthright of an Englishman: the Practice of Naturalization and Denization of Immigrants under the Later Stuarts and Early Hanoverians." *Proceedings of the Huguenot Society of Great Britain and Ireland* 25 (1989): 61–74.

———. *Foreigners and Englishmen: The Controversy over Immigration and Population, 1660–1760.* Newark, Del., 1995.

Steele, I. K. *Politics of Colonial Policy: The Board of Trade in Colonial Administration, 1696–1720.* Oxford, 1968.

Sturgill, Claude C. *Marshal Villars and the War of the Spanish Succession.* Lexington, Ky., 1965.

Sturtevant, William C., ed. *Handbook of North American Indians.* Vol. 15, *Northeast,* ed. Bruce G. Trigger. Washington, D.C., 1978.

Taylor, Peter K. *Indentured to Liberty: Peasant Life and the Hessian Military State, 1688–1815.* Ithaca, 1994.

Thompson, E. P. "The Moral Economy of the English Crowd in the Eighteenth Century." *Past and Present* 50 (Feb. 1971): 76–136.

Tien, Anita. " 'To Enjoy Their Customs': The Cultural Adaptation of Dutch and German Families in the Middle Colonies, 1660–1832." Ph.D. diss., University of California, Berkeley, 1990.

Todd, Vincent Hollis. "Baron Christoph von Graffenried's New Bern Adventures." Ph.D. diss., University of Illinois, 1912.

Todd, Vincent Hollis, and Julius Goebel. *Christoph von Graffenried's Account of the Founding of New Bern.* Raleigh, 1920.

Trautz, Fritz. *Die pfälzische Auswanderung nach Nordamerika im 18. Jahrhundert.* Heidelberg, 1959.

Trommler, Frank, and Joseph McVeigh, eds. *America and the Germans: An Assessment of a Three-Hundred-Year History.* Vol. 1, *Immigration, Language, Ethnicity.* Philadelphia, 1985.

Trossbach, Werner. " 'Südwestdeutsche Leibeigenschaft' in der Frühen Neuzeit— eine Bagatelle?" *Geschichte und Gesellschaft* 7 (1981): 69–90.

Trumpener, Katie. "The Time of the Gypsies: A 'People without History' in the Narratives of the West." *Critical Inquiry* 18 (summer 1992): 843–84.

Tully, Alan. *Forming American Politics: Ideals, Interests, and Institutions in Colonial New York and Pennsylvania.* Baltimore, 1994.

Underdown, David. *Revel, Riot, and Rebellion: Popular Politics and Culture in England, 1603–1660.* Oxford, 1985.

——. *Fire from Heaven: Life in an English Town in the Seventeenth Century.* New Haven, 1992.

Walker, Mack. *The Salzburg Transaction: Expulsion and Redemption in Eighteenth-Century Germany.* Ithaca, 1992.

Wallace, Paul. *Conrad Weiser, Friend of Colonist and Mohawk.* Philadelphia, 1945.

——. "Conrad Weiser: Holder of the Heavens." *Historic Pennsylvania Leaflet* 27 (1965).

Weiser, Frederick S., ed. *Johan Friederich Weisers Buch containing the Autobiography of John Conrad Weiser (1696–1760).* Hanover, Pa., 1976.

Wellenreuther, Hermann. "Image and Counterimage, Tradition and Expectation: The German Immigrants in English Colonial Society in Pennsylvania, 1700–1765." In *America and the Germans: An Assessment of a Three-Hundred-Year History,* ed. Frank Trommler and Joseph McVeigh, 1:85–105. Philadelphia, 1985.

White, Philip L. *The Beekmans of New York in Politics and Commerce 1647–1877.* New York, 1956.

White, Richard. *The Middle Ground: Indians, Empires, and Republics in the Great Lakes Region, 1650–1815.* Cambridge, 1991.

Wiesner, Merry. "Frail, Weak, and Helpless: Women's Legal Position in Theory and Reality." In *Regnum, Religio et Ratio: Essays Presented to Robert M. Kingdon,* ed. Jerome Friedman, vol. 7 of Sixteenth Century Essays and Studies, 161–69. Kirksville, Mo., 1987.

Williams, Justin. "English Mercantilism and Carolina Naval Stores, 1705–1776." *Journal of Southern History* 1 (May 1935): 169–85.

Williams, Michael. *Americans and Their Forests: A Historical Geography.* Cambridge, 1989.

Wiltenburg, Joy. *Disorderly Women and Female Power in the Street Literature of Early Modern England and Germany.* Charlottesville, Va., 1992.

Wittwer, Norman C., Jr. *The Faithful and the Bold: The Story of the First Service of the Zion Evangelical Lutheran Church, Oldwick, New Jersey.* Oldwick, N.J., 1984.

Wokeck, Marianne. "The Flow and the Composition of German Immigration to Philadelphia, 1727–1775." *Pennsylvania Magazine of History and Biography* 105 (July 1981): 249–78.

——. *Trade in Strangers: The Beginnings of Mass Migration to North America.* University Park, Pa., 1999.

——. "German Settlements in the British North American Colonies: A Patchwork of Cultural Assimilation and Persistence." In *In Search of Peace and Prosperity: New German Settlements in Eighteen-Century Europe and America,* eds. Hartmut

Lehmann, Hermann Wellenreuther, and Renate Wilson, 191–216. University Park, Pa., 2000.

Wolf, Eric R. "On Peasant Rebellions." *International Social Science Journal* 21 (1969): 286–93.

Wolf, Stephanie Grauman. "Hyphenated America: The Creation of an Eighteenth-Century German-American Culture." In *America and the Germans: An Assessment of a Three-Hundred-Year History*, ed. Frank Trommler and Joseph McVeigh, 1:66–84. Philadelphia, 1985.

Wrigley, E. A., and R. S. Schofield. *The Population History of England, 1541–1871: A Reconstruction*. Cambridge, Mass., 1981.

Yoder, Don. Introduction to "Emigration Materials from Lambsheim in the Palatinate," by Heinrich Rembe. *Pennsylvania Folklife* 23 (winter 1973–74): 40–48.

——. "The Pennsylvania Germans: Three Centuries of Identity Crisis." In *America and the Germans: An Assessment of a Three-Hundred-Year History*, ed. Frank Trommler and Joseph McVeigh, 1:44–65. Phildelphia, 1985.

Zbinden, Karl. "Die Pfalz als Ziel und Etappe schweizerischer Auswanderung." In *Pfälzer-Palatines: Beiträge zur pfälzischen Ein- und Auswanderung sowie zur Volkskunde und Mundartforschung im 18. und 19. Jahrhundert*, ed. Karl Scherer, 177–206. Kaiserslautern, 1981.

Zielinski, Herbert. "Klimatische Aspekte Bevölkerungsgeschichtlicher Entwicklung." In *Historische Demographie als Sozialgeschichte: Giessen und Umgebung vom 17. zum 19. Jahrhundert*, 2 vols., ed. Arthur E. Imhof, 2:919–1015. Darmstadt, 1975.

Zuckerman, Michael. "Identity in British America: Unease in Eden." In *Colonial Identity in the Atlantic World, 1500–1800*, ed. Nicholas Canny and Anthony Pagden, 115–57. Princeton, 1987.

Index

German migrants of 1709 *(continued)*
  in Mohawk Valley, 141–45, 155–56, 158–60
  in New York City, 78–81, 83–86
  number of, 2, 8, 40, 45, 47, 50, 97
  occupations, 20–21, 40
  in Pennsylvania, 139–41, 151–52, 158
  proposals to settle in Britain, 49, 53, 66
  proposals to settle outside Britain, 49, 66–69, 71–74
  religious affiliation, 21, 40, 44–45, 59, 62, 149–52
  resistance to naval stores project, 92–96, 98–102, 104, 106
  in Schoharie Valley, 123–33, 136
  settling in naval stores camps, 89–92, 97–99
  and Seven Years' War, 154–61
  and slavery, 147–49, 163–64
  splits among, 102, 111, 137, 145
  territorial origins, 8–12
  view of life in America, 4, 34, 82, 93, 96, 106, 121, 156–57, 161
  See also Catholics; identity of German migrants; Lutherans; Reformed church members; Weilburg petitioners; women, German
German migration of 1708, 30, 55
German migration of 1709
  beginning of, 37–39
  British efforts to stop, 50–51
  causes of, 21–27
  direction of, 24–25
  and promotional literature, 25–30
  See also German migrants of 1709
"Germans," use of term, 173 n1
Germantown, N.Y., 138
Germany. *See* Holy Roman Empire
Godolphin, Sydney, 41
"golden book," 25–27, 136, 165. *See also Ausführlich und Umständlicher Bericht*
Graffenried, Christoph von, 68
Grauberger, Philipp Peter, 195 n10

Guinee, Aree van, 148
Guinee, Jora van, 148
guns, 92, 100, 102
Gypsies, 61–62

Hackensack, N.J., 114, 138, 145
Haeger, Johann Friedrich, 84–86, 107–8, 110, 114, 118, 149
Hanau-Münzenberg, 13
Harrison, Francis, 143
Hartman, Adam, 34
Hartmannsdorf, N.Y., 124, 141
Haysbury, N.Y., 89, 97
Hearne, Thomas, 64
Heidelberg, 12, 14–16, 22, 25, 27
Herborn, 38
Herkimer, N.Y. *See* Burnetsfield, N.Y.
Hesse, 9, 16
Hesse-Darmstadt, 7, 15, 33, 38
Hesse-Kassel, 14
Hezel, Johann, 32
Hite, Anna, 138–39
Hite, Jost, 138–39, 145
Holy Roman Empire
  inheritance patterns in, 17–18
  literacy in, 18–19
  migration within, 12–14
  and religion, 13–16
  Rhenish principalities, 2–3, 9–10, 19
  and serfdom, 17–18
Hudson River valley, 137
  as site for naval stores project, 71, 73
  See also East Camp; West Camp
Huguenots, 14, 21, 42, 54, 59–60
Hunsrück, 38
Hunter, Robert
  appointed governor of New York, 72
  apprentices German children, 80
  arrival in New York, 79
  deals with German resistance, 94–95, 99–102, 105, 135
  establishes naval stores project, 83, 86, 88, 91–92
  and German migrants in Schoharie, 128–29, 131–33

and payment for naval stores project, 106, 108, 146
proposal for settling Germans migrants in New York, 72–73
suspends naval stores project, 111–14, 123
and troops for Canada expedition, 107
view of German migrants, 81, 93, 109
Hunter subsistence lists, 167–69
Hunterdon County, N.J., 145
Hunterstown, N.Y., 89

identity, British, 58–59
identity of German migrants, 2–4, 6, 9, 12, 55, 65–66, 83
as characterized in America, 146–47, 157
as characterized by British, 5, 8, 43, 53–56, 59–63, 66, 71
as characterized by Robert Hunter, 75, 81, 93, 105, 109
as hardworking, 43, 54, 60, 75
as lazy, 35, 93, 109
in New York, 137, 145, 155, 166
as opportunists, 35–36, 56, 76–77
as Palatines or poor Palatines, 1, 3–9, 12, 43–44, 53–56, 61–66, 74, 81, 146, 166
as portrayed by selves, 1, 3, 6, 57–59, 65–66, 81, 155
as Protestants, 3, 53, 59, 62, 66, 70, 83
as refugees, 1, 6, 53–55, 66
as victims of Catholic persecution, 1, 54–55, 59, 62
Immigration Day, 145
Indian kings. See Iroquois kings
Indians
German conceptions of, 117–20, 122
in promotional literature, 29, 117–18
See also specific tribes
inheritance patterns, 17, 21
Ireland, 67, 75, 170
Iroquois, 115–16, 119, 121, 128–29
alleged negotiations with German migrants, 129, 158

and Christianity, 154
control of Delawares, 152–53
and expedition against Canada, 107–8, 118
view of the Germans, 155
Iroquois kings, so called, 74, 116, 135–36, 200 n11

Jamaica, 68, 75
Jan, "a negro from Martinico," 148
Jews, 13–15
Johann Ernst, count of Nassau-Weilburg, 31, 38
Johann Wilhelm, Palatine elector, 15
Johnson, William, 154–55
Jones, Henry Z, 167–70

Kaiserslautern, 12
Kast, Anna, 144
Keith, William, 139
Kingston, N.Y., 138
Klein, Johann, 32
Kneskern, Johann Peter, 124, 144, 150, 195 n10
Kneskerndorf, N.Y., 124
Knittle, Walter, 4
Koblenz, 22
Kocherthal, Joshua, 25, 37, 83, 98–99, 145, 148–49, 168
and early Lutheran services in New York, 84–86
and German migration of 1708, 30, 55
See also Ausführlich und Umständlicher Bericht; "golden book"
Kocherthal, Sibylla, 38
Kraichgau, 27, 37
Kurpfalz. See Palatinate, the

labels for German migrants. See identity of German migrants
Lambsheim, 14
Lawyer, Johannes, 144
Leibeigene (serfs), 17–18, 23
Leibfreie (free subjects), 17–18
Leutbecker, Caspar, 151

listmasters, 51, 84, 114, 120, 124–25, 209 n10
  in the naval stores camps, 91, 99, 105, 195 n10
literacy, 18–19
Liverpool, 49
Livingston, Alida, 107–9, 194 n37
Livingston, Robert, 105, 126, 134
  and land for naval stores project, 88, 138
  opinion of German migrants, 146–47
  provisions naval stores project, 89–91, 107, 110–11
Livingston, Robert, Jr., 162
Logan, James, 153
London, 2, 4–5, 8, 57–58, 61
  arrival of German migrants, 39, 43–45, 50, 70–71, 75
  German community in, 40
  German migrants remaining in, 75
  and refugee camps, 47, 51, 53, 61–63, 67, 75
Lovelace, Robert, 72
Lutherans
  in Holy Roman Empire, 13, 15–16, 21, 31
  in London, 51, 60, 64
  missionary work among Indians, 154
  in New Jersey, 148
  in New York, 84–86, 148–50
  in Pennsylvania, 150–52
  and pietism, 16, 76, 149
  and slavery, 148–49, 164
  See also Boehme, Anton; Kocherthal, Joshua; Ruperti, George; Tribbeko, John

Mahicans, 115, 118, 153
Mainz, archbishopric of, 9, 14, 22
Manck, Jacob, 195 n10
Mannheim, 12–13, 22, 25
Marlborough, duke of, 39, 43
Matheus, Johann Martin, 20
Mennonites, 13–14, 21
Michel, Franz Louis, 68

migration
  from German southwest, 24–25
  to German southwest, 12–14
  See also German migration of 1708; German migration of 1709
Miller, Peter, 151–52
Millstone River, 138
Mittelberger, Gottlieb, 183 n2
Mittelstaedt-Kubaseck, Carla, 168
Mohawk River, 73, 116
Mohawk Valley settlements, 141–45, 147, 153, 164–65
  and Revolutionary War, 162–63
  See also Burnetsfield, N.Y.; Stone Arabia
Mohawks, 86, 88, 118, 141, 153, 158, 163
  and German migrants in Schoharie, 119–23, 125, 127–28
  and rum trade, 145
  in Schoharie Valley, 115–17
Montgomery, N.Y., 145
Moravians, 152, 158
Morris, Lewis, 84, 126
Muhlenberg, Henry Melchior, 152, 198 n56
Müller, Anna Maria, 83

Nassau, 9, 22, 38
Nassau-Dillenburg, 8, 23–24, 35, 38
Nassau-Idstein, 38
Nassau-Weilburg, 30–31, 33–34, 39
Native Americans. See Indians
naturalization, 41–43, 55
Naturalization Act of 1709, 2, 39, 42–43, 75
naval stores, 2, 72–73, 88, 103–4, 110
  defined, 103
naval stores camps, 80, 88–89, 97, 118.
  See also East Camp; West Camp
naval stores production, 103–4
naval stores project, 72–74, 79, 82–83, 86, 89–92, 103–6, 108–11
  comes to an end, 111–14
  German resistance to, 92–96, 98–102, 104, 106

Neuwied, 9, 13, 38, 97, 145
New Bern, 68
New Jersey, 81, 107, 113–14, 123, 137–38, 145, 148
New York, 2, 4–5, 107, 113, 137, 145, 155, 166
  German petition describing life in, 134–37
  land market, 125, 143–44
  plan to settle German immigrants in, 71–73
  See also Mohawk Valley settlements; naval stores camps, New York City; Schoharie Valley
New York City, 78–83, 89–90, 97, 114, 145, 148
New York colonial council, 78
Newtown, N.Y., 89
Nicholson, Francis, 136
Niederbieber, 38, 91
North Carolina, 67–68, 170. *See also* Carolina(s)
Nutten Island, 79, 84

Oberweisersdorf, N.Y., 124
Oneidas, 154, 159
Orange County, N.Y., 145
orphans, 80–81, 110
Ott, Peter, 32

Palatinate, the, 2–4, 8–9, 12–19, 74
  British views of, 45, 55
  defined, 175 n6
  as victim of the French, 54
  and the War of the Spanish Succession, 22
Palatine elector, 9, 15, 55
  Johann Wilhelm, 14–15, 93
  Karl Ludwig, 13
Palatines. *See* identity of German migrants
Palatines Catechism, The, 62
Pastorius, Daniel, 26, 29
Peace of Westphalia, 12, 15
Penn, William, 26, 39

Pennsylvania, 4, 138–39, 141, 146
  compared to Carolina, 26, 29
petitions of the German immigrants
  in London, 57–59, 65–66
  to migrate, 23–24
  concerning treatment in New York, 126, 131, 134–36
  See also Weilburg petitioners
Petri, Philips, 34
Pfalz. See Palatinate, the
Philadelphia, 4
pietism and pietists, 15–16, 18, 26, 76, 148–49
Pisquetomen, 158
pitch. *See* naval stores
poverty of the German migrants, 23–25, 61, 63
Presley, Elvis, 211 n19
promotional literature for British colonies, 25–27, 35, 117–18
  spread in an illiterate society, 34
  See also Ausführlich und Umständlicher Bericht
proprietors, Carolina, 27, 49, 51, 67–68
Protestants, 6, 40, 59, 70, 85
  compared with Catholics, 44, 54, 62, 85
  as desirable settlers in Britain and Ireland, 55, 67, 75
  See also identity of German migrants: as Protestants; *specific denominations*

Quainant, 120
Queen Anne's War, 107, 116. *See also* War of the Spanish Succession
Queensbury, N.Y., 89, 95–96

Raritan River (N.J.) settlements, 114, 138, 148
redemptioner system, 24
Reformed church members
  in Holy Roman Empire, 14–15, 21, 31
  in London, 51, 60, 64
  missionary work among Indians, 154

Tulpehocken, 139–41, 145, 151, 158
Tulpehocken Confusion, 151–52
Tuscaroras, 68

Vacating Act of 1699, 125
viticulture and vinedressers, 16–17, 20, 71
Vrooman, Adam, 127–28

Wagner, Margaretha, 7, 143
Wagner, Peter, 7, 143–44
Wallkill River valley, 138
Walrath, Gerhardt, 134
Walworth, 41, 45
War of the Palatine Succession (1688–97), 12–13, 15, 25
War of the Spanish Succession (1701–14), 2, 15, 22–23, 39, 107
Weijel, Jacob, 24
Weilburg, 38
Weilburg petitioners, 30–34
Weiser, Anna Magdalena, 8
Weiser, Anna Maria, 152
Weiser, Conrad, 133, 141, 144, 155–56, 201 n28
    and Indians, 120, 127–28, 153, 158, 163
    and religion, 150–52

Weiser, Johann Conrad, 8, 120, 128–29, 153–54, 195 n10, 201 n28
    as listmaster, 91, 125
    and petition to Board of Trade, 129, 134–36
Weiser, Samuel, 153
Weisersdorf, N.Y., 124, 141
Weiss, George Michael, 154
Wernig, John, 156
West Camp, 89, 97, 102, 145, 168
Westerwald, 9, 21, 33, 38, 145
Whigs, 41–42, 54, 60, 70, 75, 106
widows, 45, 80–82, 110, 167
Windecker, Hartmann, 125, 144, 195 n10
winter of 1708–09, 22–23
women, German, 18, 21, 51, 75, 104, 129–31, 164–65
Worms, 12
Wulfen, Godfrey, 105
Württemberg, 8–9, 12, 15–16, 18, 27, 39, 145

Yoland, Wilhelm, 183 n113

Zee, Magdalene, 129–30, 165
Zenger, Hannah, 81
Zenger, John Peter, 81, 204 n1
Zöller, Maria Catharina, 148